W9-AXX-811

PRAISE FOR HARRIET BROWN'S
PREVIOUS BOOKS

"A well-researched and cogent argument for more rational scientific approaches and humane cultural attitudes toward health, eating, and the concept of being overweight. Written in an approachable style and peppered with short first-person interview narratives. . . . A solid general overview of the scientific and cultural issues surrounding fatness and weight loss with an excellent starter bibliography."

—*Library Journal*

"Brown's conclusions . . . will likely shock most readers and make them rethink much of what they assume, what they think they know about weight and fat. . . . This book may be just what most of us need, so we can be kinder to ourselves and others and truly take care of the bodies we have. It's a revelation."

—*San Francisco Book Review*

"A must-read for anyone ready to start shaking this fat = bad, thin = good obsession. . . . Brown's book can help you love your body now."

—*Bustle*

"More than a health guide: it's an important consideration for any social issues shelf and blends science, history and health in an examination of changing precedents for body image."

—*Midwest Book Review*

"At turns harrowing and heartbreaking, *Body of Truth* is ultimately life-affirming and always, always brave and honest. A book every woman—no, every*one*—should read."

—*Ann Hood, author of*
The Obituary Writer *and* An Italian Wife

"An inspired and inspiring book about our cultural obsession with weight, our fetishization of thinness, and our demonization of fat. *Body of Truth* is a compelling read, one that will make you rethink your attitudes towards your body and your health—and, in the process, enable you to enjoy your life a bit more and count calories a bit less."

—*Daphne Merkin, novelist, cultural critic,*
and author of The Fame Lunches

"One of the most up to date, relevant, and honest accounts of one family's battle with the life threatening challenges of anorexia. Brown has masterfully woven science, history, and heart throughout this compelling and tender story."

—*Lynn S. Grefe, former chief executive officer,*
National Eating Disorders Association

"As a woman who once knew the grip of a life-controlling eating disorder, I held my breath reading Harriet Brown's story. As a mother of daughters, I wept for her. Then cheered."

—*Joyce Maynard, author of* Labor Day

"Harriet Brown is an intelligent, elegant writer and this book offers both solace and useful information for families struggling with eating disorders."

—*Audrey Niffenegger*

SHADOW DAUGHTER

ALSO BY HARRIET BROWN

Body of Truth
Brave Girl Eating

SHADOW DAUGHTER

A Memoir of Estrangement

Harriet Brown

DA CAPO PRESS

Da Capo Press
Hachette Book Group
1290 Avenue of the Americas, New York, NY 10104
www.dacapopress.com
@DaCapoPress

Printed in the United States of America

First Edition: November 2018

Published by Da Capo Press, an imprint of Perseus Books, LLC, a subsidiary of Hachette Book Group, Inc. The Da Capo Press name and logo is a trademark of the Hachette Book Group.

The Hachette Speakers Bureau provides a wide range of authors for speaking events. To find out more, go to www.hachettespeakersbureau.com or call (866) 376-6591.

The publisher is not responsible for websites (or their content) that are not owned by the publisher.

PRINT BOOK INTERIOR DESIGN BY JEFF WILLIAMS

Library of Congress Cataloging-in-Publication Data

Names: Brown, Harriet, 1958– author.
Title: Shadow daughter: a memoir of estrangement / by Harriet Brown.
Description: First edition. | New York, NY: Da Capo Press, 2018. |
Includes bibliographical references and index.
Identifiers: LCCN 2018014384| ISBN 9780738234533 (hardcover) | ISBN 9780738234540 (ebook)
Subjects: LCSH: Brown, Harriet, 1958– | Brown, Harriet, 1958—Family. |
Journalists—Family relationships—United States. | Mothers and daughters—United States. | LCGFT: Autobiographies.
Classification: LCC CT275.B7634 A3 2018 | DDC 306.874/3092 [B]—dc23
LC record available at https://lccn.loc.gov/2018014384

ISBNs: 978-0-7382-3453-3 (hardcover), 978-0-7382-3454-0 (ebook)

LSC-C

10 9 8 7 6 5 4 3 2

For my other mothers—
Esther, Vivian, Ellyn, and Lois

CONTENTS

A NOTE TO READERS

I've always wondered how memoirists manage to reproduce conversations from ten or twenty or thirty years earlier with such precision. How can they remember whole paragraphs of dialogue, not to mention those perfectly telling details? So if you're wondering how I have accurately reproduced conversations from ten, twenty, thirty years ago with such perfect recall, the answer is that I have kept a detailed journal since I was a teenager. Any scene I've reproduced here is accurate to the best of my knowledge and according to my journals. The other people involved in those interactions might have different memories and perspectives, of course. My mother's perspective would certainly differ from mine. This narrative, though, reflects my memories and perspectives and interpretations. I've been as fair as possible, and any factual errors are mine alone.

As a journalist I'm used to using people's full names and biographical details in an article or book. Given the intensely personal and sometimes excruciatingly sensitive nature of this subject, though, I've chosen to use first names only, and in some cases I've used pseudonyms and/or altered specifics to protect people's anonymity. Every quote is verbatim (I taped all interviews), and even when identifying details were changed I presented the emotional content of these narratives as accurately as I could.

PROLOGUE:
FIRST AND LAST

I did not attend my mother's funeral. I went instead to the island of Maui, five thousand miles away. On the day her mortal remains slid into a drawer in a mausoleum in southern Florida, I was hiking the Lahaina Pali Trail with my husband and daughters, following the five-mile-long path that hugs the cliffs over the Honoapiilani Highway, with views of the Pacific below and fields of lava and igneous rocks above.

Over the years I'd imagined her death a thousand times— imagined killing her myself, in fact—and in every one of those scenarios I saw myself weeping and devastated at her funeral. Even after years of estrangement I believed her death might miraculously heal something inside me. And I thought I still wanted to be healed, though it had been years since I'd cut off contact with her or thought about her daily, years since she'd appeared in my dreams.

I'd often joked that my mother would outlive me out of sheer spite. I made my husband promise he'd keep her away from my deathbed, just as I'd made him promise years earlier to keep her out of the delivery room. In a weak moment, disorganized with pain and panic, I thought I might succumb to the longing for a mother and let her in. And then, in a mash-up of the dramatic scenes we'd played out over the years, she would swoop into the room where I lay hooked up to tubes and machines, unable to speak but conscious, thereby giving her the opportunity to cry and kiss me and loudly and repeatedly proclaim her love and her overwhelming grief. She would make even my dying about her.

Much later I saw that was both the defiant joke of a child who can't imagine a parent's disappearance and a talisman against that very possibility.

As it turned out I was the one who stood at her hospital bedside, watching the mechanical rise and fall of her chest keep time with the ventilator's hiss. Her dyed blond hair slid across the pillow; her beautiful straight nose was bent to one side by the adhesive holding the tube in her mouth. Deep in septic shock, with her organs failing, she resembled a large doll, her skin swollen and smooth and rubbery. Liquid pearled along her arms and the backs of her hands, forced out through her skin as her kidneys failed and her cells wept. The shape of her hands, their curving thumbs slack now against the hospital sheet, was deeply familiar. I could picture those hands in motion, scrubbing a kitchen counter, bringing a cigarette to her red-slicked lips, slapping my face.

I'd flown to Florida from my home in upstate New York for my sister and father, to be there with them while whatever was happening to my mother played itself out. That's what I told myself, anyway. I loved my father despite his willingness to give me up because my mother said so. I loved my sister despite her closeness with our mother; she and I had worked hard over the years to stay connected, and we held a deep affection for each other that bridged the family schism.

A nurse glided through the glass doors, adjusting tubes and dials, checking vitals. She called my mother by name, asked her to open her eyes, and I backed away from the bed, my heart pounding. I did not want my mother to look at me. She couldn't speak, she was as close to death as a living person can get, but still I did not want to see what she thought of me, what she'd always thought of me, reflected in her deep-set blue eyes.

I put myself in the far corner, in the only bit of shadow in that too-bright hospital room, and listened to my sister talk and cry and sing, trying to coax our mother back from wherever she had been carried. I knew my mother was dying, though no one said the word. I knew she was helpless and vulnerable and still I felt afraid. My sister begged her for a sign, an acknowledgment that she was still fighting, even as I dreaded it. In life our mother had been quick to judge, to criticize, to punish with her words; what terrible pronouncement might she deliver, what barbed look might she send my way now that she had nothing else to lose? Even if I'd known for sure that she would say nothing I would still have backed into the shadowy corner where she couldn't see me. I would still have felt my stomach drop and my heart stutter.

I flew home the next morning. I wasn't there a few days later when my sister and father took her off life support and she died, or rather was finally allowed to be dead. By the time my sister sobbed her goodbyes I was thousands of miles away. My husband and I had planned a family trip to Hawaii long before my mother complained of a pain in her belly and asked my father to drive her to the emergency room, before the curtains opened and then closed on this particular act of our family tragedy. I thought about canceling our trip and flying back to Florida for the funeral, but the truth was I didn't want to be there, and no one else wanted me there either. I thought I should *want* to be at the funeral, to say goodbye on all sorts of levels to my mother, who had after all been such a defining force in my life. But I didn't.

I didn't want to sit through the service, dry-eyed, as my sister grieved and our father asked everyone in bewilderment how this could have happened. I didn't want to listen to the eulogies of praise and loss that would feel like they'd been written about someone else's mother. I didn't want to hear people talk about how happy-go-lucky and carefree and fun my mother was, the one who wasn't afraid to wear a silly costume or lead the conga line or play a practical joke. I'd been puzzling over that reflected version of her my whole life, a version I did not recognize and had never personally experienced. If I went to her funeral all the old feelings would wash over me and I would become once more, in my own eyes and everyone else's, the cold and withholding child who'd destroyed my mother's life. Whose story broke the family narrative. Whose chest held a stone instead of a heart.

So I went to Hawaii with my husband and two daughters and set out on the trail that morning. I felt little about my mother's death; after so many years of estrangement, maybe I was out of feelings.

Or maybe not. The Lahaina Pali Trail can be steep in spots, but that didn't explain why I couldn't catch my breath. And it didn't explain why great purple bruises, exotic blood flowers, bloomed suddenly on my legs from thighs to knees. I had to stop every five minutes, waving my husband and daughters ahead, to lean over and look out at the placid Maalaea Harbor as my heart raced way too fast. Crouching beside the dirt trail, I felt my tongue and lips go numb. I started to choke, though there was nothing in my mouth. A sentence popped into my head: *my mother was buried today.*

I sat hugging my knees in the dirt, which had once poured red-hot and molten from the mouth of a volcano, sluiced across rock and moss and fern and hardened into landscape. The sun threw my shadow across the trail, where it looked much larger than I felt. I was small again, small enough to be my mother's daughter, to feel the stomach-dropping mix of fear and longing and rage that had shaped my childhood. That had shaped the essence of *me*, the synapses and neurotransmitters, the habits and choices that had led me to this patch of volcanic dirt, this sense of being both erased and present. For so long I'd been that shadow daughter, the shape of me thrown without choice across a rocky trail, separate from the solid body of my family but still connected. A stiff unyielding thumb jutting out of a closed fist. I was used to feeling broken but this was different, this feeling of unwilling connection, as if the molecules of my body were coming together in a new way and there was nothing I could do about it. The only other time in my life I'd felt this was during labor, when a monstrous force pushed through me and my brain, with its thoughts and rationalizations and ideas, went dumb.

Slowly words swam up through the inner darkness. My mother was dead and I would never hear her say *You're a good person*. My mother was dead and I would never, now, get her blessing. I'd spent so much of my adult life walling off my feelings for her. Now that she was dead the walls were coming down. I felt a thunderbolt, a pain in my chest. This was not hearts and flowers love, not happy family love. This was brutal love, the kind that brings on a cold sweat and makes it hard to breathe. For the first time in my adult life I was feeling it for my mother.

I sat in the dirt for a long time, until the sweat cooled on my neck and my heartbeat slowed. Only when my mother was dead could I let myself feel love for her. It was an irony she would not have appreciated.

◇◇◇◇◇

MY EXPERIENCE OF family estrangement, like everyone's, is both simple and complicated. For nearly forty years my mother and I fought and reconciled and separated. I don't remember a time when we got along. My sister, three years younger, was the one who hid behind our mother's legs, who clung to her, who brought out her maternal instincts. I was the aloof child, the one who was always reading, the one who worried silently, who wrote poetry and could not sleep. From the start my mother did not seem to know what to do with me.

We looked good on paper: two parents and two daughters, a house in the suburbs, food and clothes and books, trips to the Jersey shore, dinner out once a week. No one whipped me or starved me, pimped me or burned me with cigarettes. I knew even then that lots of kids led much tougher lives than I did. I knew it in part because my mother explained it to me, then and much later, during some of our many attempts at reconciliation. "You have a pretty good life," she'd say, wagging a finger. "You have nothing to complain about." My words would evaporate and my brain would feel fuzzy. She was right, I believed. Not until much later would a thought swim up out of the blankness: if she was right, if I was loved and nurtured, why didn't I feel it?

As a child I did not have the words to explain or even describe what happened behind our closed doors. All I knew was that our family dysfunction was somehow my fault, the way I believed in my twenties I'd caused a particular traffic accident. It was dark, it was raining, I'd started through the green light when—this is how it seemed to me—my car leaped forward, crossed the yellow line, and with a sickening crack hit a car coming the other way.

I thought I'd lost control of my car without realizing it. The randomness of it made perfect sense to me. One minute I was confident, competent, in control, and the next I'd done the un-thinkable. I'd known forever that the evil inside me might leap out anytime and wreak havoc and now it had. And I would have gone on thinking the accident was my fault if not for a police officer standing at the corner. As I sat in the driver's seat, shaking and confused, he ran into the street and thrust his head through my open window.

"Did you get the license plate?" he yelled through the rain. I stared. What license plate?

He told me what had caused the accident: a third car, one with no headlights on, had run the red light, whacked the back of my car, and kept going. *That's* what made my car lurch forward and hit the other car. Not some essential destructiveness springing free from my soul. Not some random twist of the wheel I'd forgotten. The accident wasn't my fault, though I would never have known it without the officer's eyewitness account.

But in my parents' house there were no eyewitnesses, no observers to untangle what happened and how and why. There were just the four of us ricocheting off one another, bruising and being bruised in a drama with no beginning and no curtain. Imagine Clotho, one of the three Fates in Greek mythology, whose holy task was to spin the thread of life. Now imagine that instead of a spinning wheel she holds a can of Silly String and lets fly. Imagine the chaos that follows.

I imagine because I don't remember a lot about my childhood. Neither does my sister, actually. Maybe we share some neuro-lapse in our memory circuits, some synaptic kink that renders us forgetful. Maybe what happened drowned out the everyday, the uneventful. And of course memory is suspect anyway, infinitely malleable, subject to mental Photoshopping, vulnerable to erosion and decoration and revisions of all kinds. Maybe our lack of memories is a kind of memory in itself.

What I do know is that when I dropped out of high school to go to college at age sixteen it was in large part to escape my mother. I thought I was done trying to please her, but that was just the start of our long and painful dance of approach and avoidance, estrangement and rapprochement. After high school I never lived near my parents again. I spent thirteen years in New York City, ninety miles from their house in South Jersey. Then my husband, daughter, and I moved to the Midwest and my parents moved to Florida. By the time my mother died my family of four had moved back east to upstate New York, a different thousand miles away.

The geographical distance meant there were no casual encounters or chance meetings. For most of that time there was no internet, no social media, no way to lurk at the edges of one another's lives from a distance. Every contact had to be choreographed, scheduled, paid for, endured. When I lived in New York City a visit was less of a commitment. I could come down for a day or two and if things went wrong, as they usually did, I could thumb a ride to the bus station and take the next Greyhound to Port Authority. Later, when visiting required a plane trip or two-day drive, we saw each other mainly at funerals and weddings and bar mitzvahs, big family milestones.

My sister called our parents every Sunday, when the long-distance phone rates were lower, but my parents and I never developed a routine. At least half the time my mother and I were actively not speaking, and even when we were our communications were sporadic and often superficial.

For the rest of her life our relationship oscillated between moments of trying to connect and alternating periods of drama and silences. In my twenties and thirties hearing from my mother, even in a short uneventful phone call or email, sent me into a tailspin for weeks, triggering panic attacks and heart palpitations, obsessive ruminations and tears. Everyone who knew me during that time heard way too much about our relationship.

Being estranged from my mother was one of my defining characteristics, along with glasses, the gap between my front teeth, the long list of things I was afraid of (elevators, airplanes, confined spaces, heights, being alone, dying).

It defined me to the rest of my relatives, too. Estrangement always involves a wide circle of spectators. I was the selfish child, the stubborn teenager, the ungrateful and wounding daughter. My problems with my mother—and they were always *my* problems, not *hers* or *ours*—were the subject of countless conversations among generations of aunts and uncles. Many of those conversations happened in front of me. At a cousin's graduation party two great-aunts might whisper loudly *Doesn't she see what she's doing to her mother? How can she be so cold?* At a bat mitzvah, where I'd be seated across the room from my parents, I'd see the row of gray heads bent toward each other, the sideways looks. They didn't shun me, exactly, but I knew how they felt.

Our relationship was like an endless shaggy-dog story and I believed in the end that my mother and I would score some kind of reconciliation, some version of a happy ending, though the details of that ending remained hazy and unimaginable. That's a common belief among estranged families, maybe because of what researchers call the "non-voluntary" aspect of these relationships: you don't choose your parents, children, sisters and brothers, and so you can never un-choose them. I think of it more as immutable: whether we talked once a week or once every five years, she was still and always would be my mother. That's the kind of phrase people often use to suggest that despite superficial conflicts, there's something sacred and meaningful and worth preserving about the mother-daughter (or any parent-child) relationship. I mean it as a statement of plain fact: no matter how often or how much I wished for a different mother, she was mine. And maybe my mother felt the same way. Maybe she would have been a better parent to a different sort of child. Actually I know this is true because she was a better parent to my sister. Where I turned inward my sister roared her anger and hurt. What I held back my sister flung into the air. She was a better fit with our mother, who thrived on *Stürm und Drang,* high-decibel conflict and equally loud reconciliations.

I got along better with my father; we were both introverts with a tendency toward the philosophical. But he chose the path of appeasement, telling me frankly that my mother would leave him if he didn't take her side. So my mother and I talked occasionally, calls that ended with shouting, tears, and a phone slammed down. Later we emailed, coming face-to-face at an ever-diminishing number of family weddings and funerals, though I avoided some of those events and wasn't invited to others; estrangement happens to the whole extended family, not just the particular people involved.

I was that girl, and then that woman, the one with a screwed-up relationship with her mother. The one who couldn't stop talking about it. I wasted thousands of hours fighting with her and then processing those fights, trying to figure out what she was thinking, why she said this or that, how she could do whatever it was she was doing. I drove away friends and significant others with my chronic anxiety and perseveration. What I really wanted to understand was why, when my mother told me over and over how much she loved me, I didn't *feel* loved, at least not in any way I could recognize. I couldn't process the cognitive dissonance and so it had to be my fault and there had to be some way I could, and should, fix it.

Over the decades of our alienation I talked to and about my mother in rage, in sorrow, in grief, and in hurt. I loved her and I hated her and eventually I felt neither. I spoke to her in anger, out of a wish for revenge, from a desire to understand what was wrong between us, all the while believing I would never under-stand the problem or find a solution. Our relationship remained a mystery to me and I think to her as well. There were many versions of what happened between us; certainly there was her version and my own, and to say they were different is like saying a centipede is different from a mastodon. For a long time I could not figure out how to interpret what had happened and was happening between us. I still struggle with that.

A few years before my mother died, after an especially harrowing exchange, I realized that I was done. The constant tide of longing and rage and sorrow had receded, leaving an absence in the shape of nothing. When I stood at the back of her room in the ICU we hadn't communicated in three years. Breaking off contact with her wasn't the end of our relationship, of course, just as her death wasn't the end. But it did finish one long chapter of the story, the chapter where over and over I put aside our history and my feelings and tried to come up with a happy ending. Over the years our relationship often reminded me of the recurring *Peanuts* cartoon where Lucy promises to hold the football steady so Charlie Brown can kick it. Each time she promises and each time he believes her, running at the ball only to have Lucy yank it away at the last second, sending him flying through the air to land with a *whump* on his back. By the end of my mother's life I had finally walked away from the football. I'd broken the connection between us for good, closed the door, to use my mother's favorite metaphor, as in "The door between us will never be closed." She meant that as a promise, I know, but I heard it, especially in later years, as a threat.

Of course this is my particular perspective; my mother would certainly have a different one. As in all stories there is no single truth, no omniscient point of view. There's no such thing as objectivity because we see and touch and feel and tell everything through the filter of our perceptions and memories and experiences. My mother was complicated, contradictory, and inconsistent—in other words, she was human just like the rest of us. Flesh and blood. Capable of both tenderness and viciousness. A woman and not a monolith.

What I long for is the definitive story of my mother and me, or at least the one I can tell myself, the one I can live with. As Jonathan Gottschall illustrates in his book *The Storytelling Animal,* humans need stories as much as we need air and food and shelter. We use them to make order out of the chaos, to make sense of the mysteries that surround us. "Humans evolved to crave story," he writes. "Stories give us pleasure and instruction. They simulate worlds so we can live better in this one. They help bind us into communities and define us as cultures. Stories have been a great boon to our species."[1]

The stories we tell ourselves roll around the private tumblers of our minds like rocks being polished into gemstones. The stories we tell other people roll across time and space, gathering up whatever's in their path. Stories, it seems, are dynamic, not static. What we think determines our words, and the words we use shape what we think. There is always interpretation. There is always point of view. There are always details that don't fit, that contradict, that challenge.

We can know all this and still long for the real story, the one that will make sense of it all, that will peel away the layers within layers and tell the truth, the whole truth, nothing but the truth. It's in our nature to want the story, just as it's in our nature to not be able to tell it. For a long time I tried to suss out the "real story" of my relationship with my mother until finally I realized the only story I would ever know was the one I told myself. Instead of continually analyzing my feelings and observations against some idea of what I *should* be feeling and thinking, I came to trust what my body and heart were telling me. That was the real story—for me.

My mother is gone now and I will never know what she told herself about our failed relationship. About us. I know only my own story, which starts like this: my mother is dead and I have been missing her my whole life.

That's as good a place to begin as any.

Chapter One

THICKER THAN WATER

Why, just because we're related by blood, do I feel this sense of duty or responsibility to take this bad treatment?

—**MARION**, forty-two, estranged from a brother

You can't consider estrangement without thinking about what it means to be intimate. The word itself, *estrangement,* implies that the default position is closeness, that it requires muscle and nerve and will to resist the gravitational pull of that original connection. It incorporates a sense of the past, of a time when you weren't strangers at all but rather were close in some crucial way. It tells a story of change about a kind of relationship that is in a certain sense infinite, which will continue to exist in your mind whether you see the other person every day or never again.[1]

You can't be estranged from someone you've never cared about, but you can care deeply about someone you're estranged from. To be estranged is to be distant, physically or emotionally or both, to be moving away from the other, less a state of being than an action. And it implies choice, at least for one person. It requires a decision, conscious or not, to impose that distance. Families can drift apart out of indifference or circumstance, but estrangement grows out of strong feelings.

Those strong feelings are reinforced by our ideas of what family should and does mean. "Culturally we think families can't end, even when your lived experience might suggest otherwise," says Kristina Scharp, Ph.D., an assistant professor of communication studies at Utah State University. After all, we say, blood is thicker than water and families are forever. "In the media you see families having fights but because they're family they'll do anything for their brother who stabbed them, or other crazy things," says Scharp. The philosopher George Santayana reportedly once said, "Family is one of nature's masterpieces." But sometimes it's also one of nature's disasters.

The bond between parent and child has roots in our very cells.* It is our primary survival mechanism as a species, driving us forward biologically, socially, evolutionarily. No other relationship gets to the core of who we are in the same way, and we are both hardwired and acculturated to protect that connection. To break that bond is a profound and wide-reaching violation, and its consequences can last a lifetime.

Which helps explain why, no matter how toxic that parent-child connection becomes, most people want to and do find ways to maintain it. It survives the ambivalence and exhaustion parents feel when they give up so much sleep, money, time, and emotional energy for their children. It survives the necessary tearing away of teenagers trying to separate themselves from the

---

* This is literally true, since cells can actually migrate between a mother and fetus through the placenta. It's hard to imagine a deeper connection than that.

parents who have overseen their lives. These kinds of normal family conflicts tend to be transient, though when you're in the middle of them they can feel endless. But most families find ways to muddle through and resolve—or at least resolve to put aside— their differences. When they can't, they wind up somewhere on what Scharp calls the estrangement continuum. They might talk or email occasionally but never visit. They might interact superficially at large family gatherings. They might send birthday cards but never call or meet. Or they might refuse contact of any kind. Estrangements can be short or long, temporary or permanent, and they're rarely linear. They are a process rather than a fixed destination. By definition, says Scharp, they are always in flux. It's common to slide from one part of the spectrum to another as people reconcile and fall out and try again to find some way to manage the relationship, some level of relative peace.

The social, emotional, and financial ripples from family estrangements can reach through time and across generations. Breaking a parent-child link is one of our most primal taboos. "The power we give biology, and what that means and what that does, is astounding," says Scharp. That blood bond exists beyond reason, beyond experience, beyond the evidence of our own senses and feelings. No one has to tell us in so many words to hold it dear. We see and feel the supremacy of the genetically connected family in a thousand ways throughout childhood. By the time we're adults it literally goes without saying.

And we don't say it. We don't talk about the fact that for some people, staying connected with family is far more destructive than stepping away. That sometimes estrangement is the healthiest option. That despite what we see in advertising, online, in media, not all families are meant to be together. Scharp told me that when she first floated the idea of doing her Ph.D. dissertation on family estrangement, her committee tried to talk her out of it. "They said, 'You're never going to get anybody. Why are you doing this dissertation on a topic no one has studied?'" she remembers. But when she put out her research call she was deluged with people who'd been through family estrangements—and who wanted to talk about them, even *needed* to talk about them. That surprised her because other researchers have found that people who are estranged often lie or avoid social situations altogether to hide the fact that they're not in contact with a parent or sibling or grown child.[2] They're likely to feel shame and guilt and grief even if they're the ones who initiated the break. When someone we love dies we cover the mirrors, light a candle, wear black, tear our clothes, sit *shiva*. We choose the rituals that tell the world we're grieving, that speak for us and to us. But there are no rituals for estrangement, no rule book to tell us what to do with such a layered loss.

◇◇◇◇◇

I GREW UP knowing there was something wrong with me. I was cold and arrogant, unable to love and unlovable. I was broken in some fundamental way, not just different but dangerous, wrong, irremediable. I was lucky then that my mother loved me despite my essential ugliness, which was an affliction of the spirit and mind rather than a judgment of my physical appearance (though that too was subject to criticism). Other people might tell me I was smart or funny or kind but my mother knew me, the me I hid from everyone else. She saw me for who I really was: conceited, selfish, incapable of affection or caring. I was lucky to have a mother who put up with me but I was too self-centered to appreciate my luck.

One of the many proofs my mother offered of my moral inadequacy was a picture of my sister and me, ages three and six, taken with our family's Brownie camera. All my mother had to do was pull out the photo, its scalloped white edge stamped with the date—July 1964—and there was the evidence of my shame in black and white. In the photo my sister sits on a tricycle, her small face turned toward me, her smile tentative under crooked bangs. I stand beside her, one hand on her shoulder, scowling into the camera. *You were mean to your sister even then,* my mother would say. *All she wanted was your attention, and you were too selfish to give it to her.* It was true that my sister followed me around and that I often did not want to play baseball or cowboys or Barbies with her, that I preferred reading or drawing or my own projects. The summer I was ten, for instance, I covered the square gray keys of my grandfather's manual Adler typewriter with masking tape and taught myself to touch type, pounding away for hours. Then I composed, on the typewriter, a book about Amelia Earhart. That was the best summer of my childhood and I spent it far from my sister and the rest of my everyday life.

No one questioned my mother's narrative. Not my grand-parents, who seemed, against all reason, to love me despite my conspicuous flaws. Not my father, who never shouted or cursed, whose rare smile made my heart leap and whose hands patting my back were gentle. Not my sister, who heard all her life that I was an imperfect and unloving big sister. Certainly not me, at least not until years later, when it occurred to me that maybe on that day in July, six-year-old me had been squinting into the sun rather than scowling. That maybe my well-documented aloofness was shyness rather than disgust.

But it didn't matter; there was plenty of other evidence of my essential brokenness. When I stubbed my toe my mother told me it was God's punishment for talking back. When I brought home straight As she scolded me for thinking I was better than other people and told me there was more to life than being book-smart. When she found me reading in bed after lights out she punished me for being sneaky and deceitful. When I woke with nightmares she advised me to think about someone other than myself once in a while and I'd have better dreams. And I believed her. I believed that her wide blue eyes saw through the façade I presented to the rest of the world. I might pass for normal to my grandparents and teachers and the rest of the world but my mother knew the truth. She told me over and over that I couldn't fool her and it never occurred to me to wonder whether I was trying. She said she alone knew me for what I was, a monster incapable of loving anyone but myself, and I believed her.

And if I hadn't believed her, if I'd ever questioned the judgment she passed on me, the nightly dramas that punctuated our family life would have persuaded me she was right after all. They usually started at dinner, the four of us arranged around the kitchen table, my sister swinging her legs and fidgeting, our parents discussing the mysterious things grown-ups discussed— husbands divorcing wives, business deals gone bad, heart attacks and accidents and politics. I never figured out exactly what happened on those nights, only that my mother's voice rose and her wide smile faltered. Her face took on a look I'd come to dread, fury veiled in excessive politesse and then unveiled, pure rage and righteousness. My sister danced around the kitchen laughing or cursing and then the two of them whirled howling around the room and up the stairs in a *pas de deux* of ferocious misery. My father stayed at the table, forking up bites of hamburger or shepherd's pie, and I sat with him, eating and eating until the shouting died away.

And later, after I cleared the table and shut myself in my room, I sat on my bed, with its cross-stitched fairy-tale bedspread and lineup of stuffed cats, and waited for the shouting to subside, for the moment my mother flung herself through the door, her hair disheveled, mascara staining her cheeks as she threw her arms around my neck and sobbed *What did I do to deserve this?* She rocked me on the bed until her tears slowed and she took my face in her hands, insisting *All I ever wanted was for you to love me. Is that so much to ask?* My hands pressed against the fairy-tale bedspread, feeling for the raised lines of the stitches—Cinderella in rags, the Snow Queen launching splinters of ice. *Why don't you love me? What have I ever done to you that's so terrible?* Her hands on my cheeks shook. *Is it so much to ask, that a child loves her mother? You think you're better than everyone else?* Her face inches from mine, her eyes spilling over. Flecks of gold in her blue-green irises. *There's something wrong with a daughter who's incapable of basic human love.* Cinderella's carriage turned into a pumpkin; Snow White slept among thorns. My mother launched herself at me, her arms crushing my shoulders, her face buried in my chest, sobbing *I love you so much, I just want you to love me, I love you, I love you* until the engine of her grief and rage ran down. When she left I stood at the bathroom mirror and scrubbed at the mascara staining my shirt, wondering why I felt nothing, not impatience or sadness or longing and certainly not love. My mother was right; something was wrong with me. I could feel it and she could see it, even if no one else could.

Afterward I climbed into bed and stared at the shaft of light from the hallway that touched my bedroom wall. I held my eyes open, resisting the urge to close them, and waited for darkness to creep in from the edges of what I could see, for my vision to narrow to a single dot of light, flicker, go out. For one brief moment my eyes were wide and unseeing, until the burning got so bad I had to blink the world back. But it was enough, somehow, to break the spell, to let me drop finally into sleep.

◇◇◇◇◇

FAMILY DYSFUNCTION IS the stuff of myth and literature: Cain and Abel. Clytemnestra and Electra. Loki and all the other Norse gods. Basically every family in Shakespeare. *Who's Afraid of Virginia Woolf?* Dysfunction means conflict, and conflict makes for a compelling narrative. That is, no doubt, what Tolstoy was getting at in his much-quoted aphorism, "All happy families are alike; each unhappy family is unhappy in its own way." A story needs drama, action, something happening, or no one will keep reading. No conflict, no story. And what better place to look for that conflict than at home, with the people you're closest to? There's a reason most of the heroes in children's literature are orphans, or abandoned by terrible parents, or in some way, literal or emotional, cut off from the family tree.

When you actually talk to people who say their families were unhappy, though, it's the similarities that resonate, not the differences. In dozens of interviews with people who say they come from unhappy families I've been struck by how much their stories have in common. The details may be different but the overall narrative arc often feels familiar to anyone who's grown up in a particular kind of dark place. Deep, unresolvable conflicts, whether they're acknowledged or not, produce a predictable array of family troubles.

But it doesn't seem predictable when it's your family, and maybe that's what Tolstoy meant. Your own family's unhappiness *feels* so personal, so specific. My mother-in-law, Vivian, who was married to an alcoholic, used to drive around her Westchester, New York, neighborhood for hours at night, longing for the happy family life she imagined behind every lit window. She was idealizing those unseen families, of course, projecting her own fantasies outward into the world. It was the 1960s, the era of John Cheever and *Mad Men,* and at least half the marriages she glimpsed through those windows eventually dissolved in a toxic bath of booze and adultery. Even those that survived wrangled and sparred because that's what families do. It's impossible to live so close to other people and not bump up against one another's tender spots. All families fight. If they don't, that's another kind of problem.

My husband's family was warped by alcoholism and depression and forged around a strong social imperative to suppress feelings and suffer in silence. It was, like all families, imperfect by definition. But also like most families it never came apart, at least not for any length of time. My husband grew up knowing he was loved and that his parents believed in him, and he was able to sidestep or forgive the rest.

For most people, that's enough. Families have a powerful drive to stick together despite whatever problems and conflicts they encounter; "intergenerational solidarity," as sociologist Marc Szydlik describes it,[3] seems to be our default setting. Every one of my friends in high school fought with their parents. That's pretty normal developmentally; emotional problems between parents and children peak in late adolescence,[4] as teens are figuring out who they are apart from their families. But by the time we hit our late twenties and started having our own children, nearly everyone had found ways to mend what was broken and preserve some kind of relationship with those parents: The friend whose father abhorred his sexual orientation. The friend whose mother couldn't stop criticizing. Even the friend whose parents failed to protect her from abuse. Everyone worked through or around or past the difficulties. One friend forgave her abusive father; another went to therapy with her mother and forged a level of détente. Another focused on feeling compassion for her parents' limitations, which dispelled a lot of her anger and frustration.

The only person I knew who didn't heal the breach seemed to be me. For pretty much my entire adult life my parents and

I cycled through periods of silence, connection, and conflict. When I had children of my own the conflicts sharpened and the silences grew longer. The older I got the less willing I was to keep fighting with my mother, to keep going around and around in the same mutually destructive circles. And there never was another way for us to connect.

I thought I was the only one but it turns out most people have some experience of estrangement, whether it's their own or lies elsewhere in their family. It might be short-term or permanent, with a clear beginning or a long murky history. Some people think family estrangement is on the rise, a "silent epidemic."[5] They point to trends like blended families, divorce, addiction, and intolerance that cause or exacerbate family tensions. The most recent studies suggest somewhere between 5 and 10 percent of parents are estranged from at least one adult child.[6] Fathers are more likely to be alienated from adult children (27 percent) than are mothers (7 percent),[7] though in one recent survey more than half the participants said they were estranged from a mother.[8] Young men are more likely to distance themselves from parents than are young women.[9]

There's been little research on the phenomenon of family estrangement, and no authoritative statistics, maybe in part because estrangement is a rather fluid concept. One person's estrangement might be someone else's baseline, and people move in and out of estrangement, often over a lifetime. "No two people have the same experience or trajectory," says Lucy Blake, a social and developmental psychologist and lecturer at Edge Hill University in Ormskirk, England. That's for sure. In trying to organize the stories I've heard, I quickly realized how hard it would be. It's not just that the specifics of every relationship are different, but each person tells his or her story differently as well, and that too becomes part of the narrative. Not to mention the fact that few estrangements are fixed; for every person who hasn't seen or talked to his family in years there are ten more who go in and out of varying degrees of contact, whose feelings shift and mutate with every new relationship twist.

Kristina Scharp spent years trying to come up with a working definition of estrangement. The one she finally settled on is fairly academic: a communicative process of decreasing interdependence, where at least one family member voluntarily and intentionally distances themselves from another family member because of a negative relationship. The key idea here is that estrangement is a process, one described by distance and levels of dependence rather than feelings. In that sense, Scharp's concept differs from other definitions.

One of the best known of these came from Murray Bowen, a twentieth-century psychiatrist who saw families as deeply interconnected and interdependent systems, seething with tension and anxiety. In Bowen theory, each family member's feelings and behaviors affect the others' and can stabilize or disrupt the connections among the rest. Bowen saw "emotional cutoff," as he labeled estrangement, as a harmful effort to reduce or avoid unresolved emotional issues between family members. He believed estrangement actually created more conflicts than it fixed because those original unresolved issues would spill over into other family relationships, weakening the whole network.

Bowen's concept of emotional cutoff, which is still widely cited when people write about estrangement, focuses on the often unspoken psychological currents in a family. Other researchers see estrangement as more of a behavioral issue, meant to create boundaries and/or distance between family members. "'Estranged' sounds binary, like I'm either pregnant or I'm not pregnant," explains Scharp. But estrangement, in her view, exists on a continuum of both time and space; people are more or less estranged at any given moment. It's a cyclical process rather than a fixed state. Scharp believes most estrangements fall into two basic categories: continued estrangement, as in "We're never talking again," and "chaotic disassociation," where people bounce back and forth between connection and estrangement, fighting and reconciling. Within those categories, of course, there is an infinite number of shadings.[10]

Peg Streep, author of the book *Mean Mothers: Overcoming the Legacy of Hurt,* agrees that estrangement doesn't always look as we expect it to. "Most people are either in low-contact situations that are estrangements without the label, or controlled situations that aren't even labeled as low contact. They've either moved away or they set very strict parameters for visits," says Streep, who has interviewed thousands of women about estrangement. She says that full-on no-contact—what we tend to think of when we hear the word *estrangement*—is a rare last resort. That jibes with both my own experience and the stories I've heard from others. I've talked with people who haven't laid eyes on family members in twenty years, with people who see estranged relatives but interact only superficially, and with people who have experienced both, plus various states in between.

Lucy Blake believes estrangement may be more of an identity than a specific situation. "Some research might say if you haven't had contact with a family member for a year you're classified as estranged," she says. "But perhaps there are people who have very infrequent contact but they're happy with that level and they don't consider themselves estranged." My husband, for instance, talks to his brother maybe once or twice a year, and sees him less often. They haven't argued or fallen out and they don't consider themselves estranged. They're certainly not close, but that's been true their whole lives. "What do we *expect* our relationships to look like in adulthood, anyway?" asks Blake. "That's not something research has really delved into because they're more interested in what *is*."

Whether estrangement means no contact at all, occasional phone calls, or face-to-face conversations that never go beyond the superficial, the assumption is that it's a problem to be solved, an obstacle to be overcome so families can get on with the happy-ever-after process of reconciliation. As studies attest, it comes with many costs, not just for the parent and child (or siblings) at the heart of the conflict[11] but also for the entire circle of relatives. There are social costs, emotional costs, medical and financial costs to family estrangements. There are costs in inconvenience, in embarrassment, in loneliness and rage and grief. There are missed opportunities and lost time that can never be made up.

Among other primates, estrangement "extracts a substantial biological price," write evolutionary biologists Michael T. McGuire and Michael J. Raleigh.[12] They observed lower immune function, changes in brain activity and metabolism, and other physical declines in individual monkeys who had been ostracized by the larger social group. Black bears, rabbits, red foxes, and water voles that stayed in or close to their birth habitats—and their familial social groups—grew more quickly and lived longer than those who were more isolated.[13]

Of course, animals don't consciously decide to estrange themselves from their families; it's typically decided for them by the group as punishment for some transgression or as an act of protection for the greater good. Only for humans does personal choice play a role, at least for those contemplating estrangement, and most people choose to stay connected. For much of human history, our physical and emotional needs to be linked with other people were filled mainly through family, nuclear and extended—the parents, the clan, the in-group. Without them, humans wouldn't have survived or evolved as we have. I think of medieval England, where the survival of the house you belonged to, whether it was Lancaster or York or Tudor or any other, far outweighed your own happiness or survival. You could be married off for the good of the family, sent to war for the good of the family, sacrificed for the good of the family. Your place in the family, and your family's place in the world, was life and death. We still act like this is true. And maybe it is.

It's only in the last 150 years or so that the way we live has given some of us options for building a social foundation out of more than just our native tribe. We can now create alternatives to family, build virtual and real-life networks of friends, leave our hometowns and original identities behind. We move to the city, lose ourselves in the thrill of urban anonymity. We cross the globe and take up a completely different way of life. But family still matters. Still matters most, in many ways; the cellular, physiological, and psychological patterns established in the first dozen years of life overshadow everything that happens in the years that follow. And they are clearly meant to. Our earliest memories and experiences, though they're likely fragmented and nonlinear, though they swim randomly to the surface of our childhood soup, carry a power far beyond the everyday details of our childhood lives. Even when we don't consciously remember those early experiences they shape our interactions with the world in a million ways, starting with the very structure of the developing brain.

We're born with roughly eighty-five billion neurons, the nerve cells in the brain that become our physical and psychological infrastructure. (By comparison, a cat's brain contains about a billion neurons, a chimpanzee's about seven billion.) Each one of those neurons comes with about 2,500 synapses, potential bridges to other neurons. From birth to age two, the human brain goes through an explosive process known as synaptic blooming; those bridges multiply and proliferate until each neuron sports some fifteen thousand of them, the most the brain will ever contain and way too many to sustain long term.

By the time a child is ten years old, the synapses that are used least often have withered, while those that get the most use continue to flourish. If you grow up surrounded by English speakers, for example, you don't need to be able to interpret tones the way Mandarin or Bantu speakers do, so the neural wiring that supports it falls away. Synaptic pruning, as it's called, is an elegant and efficient mechanism. And scientists are just beginning to understand the power of this kind of patterning. In particular, they're coming to understand that the emotional sensitivity (or lack thereof) of a young child's primary caregiver shapes that child not just for a few years but throughout adulthood. One 2015 analysis found that "early maternal sensitivity," as measured by watching mothers interact with children at six months, two years, and three-and-a-half years old, correlated strongly with kids' academic and social success later in life.[14] The researchers wrote, "Sensitive care during the first several years of life plays an important role in shaping the child's mental representations of relationships, broad capabilities of emotional, attentional, and behavioral self-regulation, and neurobiological systems." A mother or father who genuinely supports and nurtures a very young child is investing in that child's ability to not just survive physically but thrive emotionally long after the parent is out of the picture.

And the reverse is also true. Research suggests[15] that toxic stresses in childhood—like a parent's abuse, neglect, illness, or depression—can disrupt the brain's delicate circuitry, raise levels of stress hormones like cortisol, and physically change the architecture of the growing brain.[16] Severe, ongoing stress in young children can enlarge the amygdalae, a pair of tiny almond-shaped structures deep in the brain involved in processing fear, anxiety, and emotional memory, and can also shrink the hippocampus, which helps mediate long-term memory and spatial navigation. Damage to these organs can set up a kind of feedback loop in the brain, making it hyperreactive to anxiety and fear[17] and leading to lifelong problems with learning, health, and behavior.

Swiss psychologist Alice Miller spent a lifetime exploring the subtle and not-so-subtle power dynamics between parents and children. Miller, a Holocaust survivor, rejected Freud's theory that children invented tales of abuse, especially sexual abuse, as a way of working through fantasies about their parents, and wrote a series of books looking at how the consequences of real parental abuse and neglect played out. In her 1985 book, *For Your Own Good: Hidden Cruelty in Child-Rearing and the Roots of Violence,* she wrote, "An enormous amount can be done to a child in the first two years: he or she can be molded, dominated, taught good habits, scolded, and punished—without any repercussions for the person raising the child and without the child taking revenge."

The experiences of those early years can ripple through a lifetime, triggering psychological distress and altering the very structure of the genes, even if the child has no conscious memory of them. Researchers in the field of epigenetics are finding links between early experiences and changes on the molecular level. One 2013 study[18] found that maltreatment in childhood was linked to a distinct pattern of changes to DNA methylation, a chemical process that affects the way the information coded onto genes is translated into actual physical characteristics. Researchers consistently saw these epigenetic markers in adults who had experienced childhood abuse. Long after those early events the cells in the body continue to bear witness, putting people at higher risk for depression, anxiety, PTSD, suicide, and a host of other health consequences.

So family matters—for better, for worse, for the rest of your life. That's a big part of why even one estrangement can disrupt

an entire family, rippling across continents and through generations. The costs are high because of what's at stake: survival of
the individual, survival of the genetic material, survival of the
species. Some common misconceptions about family estrangements are that those who initiate them don't care about family or don't want to be bothered or don't like being crossed. For
most people, though, nothing could be further from the truth.
Several years ago, Lucy Blake conducted a survey of about eight
hundred people who said they were estranged from family and
then published the findings in conjunction with Stand Alone, a
UK nonprofit with a mission to support estranged adults.[19] Most
people who responded had cut off family members completely;
a few described minimal contact. About half of them made the
break in their twenties to mid-thirties—a time of life, according
to developmental psychologist Erik Erikson, when people focus
on establishing and deepening intimate relationships. (Or, alter-
nately, grappling with the challenging nature of those relationships.) Eighty percent of the respondents said the estrangements
had led to positive changes. "It saved my life," wrote one participant. "Estrangement has been nothing but a blessing for me."
Another responded, "I feel like it has made me a stronger, more
independent person."

For those of us who feel this way estrangement is not a problem; it's a solution, a *response* to an otherwise unsolvable problem. It's an extreme response, no question about it, a last resort
people choose only after they've exhausted other possibilities.
But it's an effective one. For some people in some relationships
the physical and emotional costs of staying connected are far, far
higher than the social costs of estrangement. One of the most
poignant stories I've heard came from Bill, age thirty-five, a project manager in Buffalo, New York. Bill's father began physically
abusing him when he was five. By the time Bill was a teenager he

was in therapy for bipolar disorder. He thought about suicide a lot. After college, he moved to Japan to teach English, in part to escape the ongoing abuse, and decided to take a short break from communicating with his parents and sister. His father responded by writing Bill a letter—which Bill's mother and younger sister also signed—saying that Bill was a terrible person, one of the worst he'd ever known, who'd made up all the stories of abuse.

Bill thought maybe his sister had been coerced into signing, so he called her and asked. Did she really believe he was a terrible person who'd invented a history of abuse for attention? She said yes. Bill thought *I guess all you guys are done.* He cut off contact with his parents and sister, and then the rest of his extended family cut him off.

The first year or so of the estrangement was rough, but gradually Bill began to notice a shift in how he was feeling. For years he'd thought of himself as bipolar and suicidal, a depressed person by nature. He believed that was who he was, his identity. But the estrangement gave him the mental and physical space to work through the abuse he'd survived and discover the truth about himself. "I'm actually quite positive," he says with a laugh.

Bill believes his estrangement saved his life; if he'd stayed in touch, he might have followed through on killing himself. But it wasn't a decision made lightly, then or now. He compares it to amputating a gangrenous arm. "It's going to kill you, so you have to chop it off," he says. "It feels better. You're healthier. But you're missing an arm, an actual part of your body, and how you can interact with the world has been completely changed. No more family experiences. No more family. Even if they're bad, at least there's someone there."

Every single person I've interviewed who has estranged themselves from family members agonized over the decision. They say they did it to save their lives and the lives of their children.

They did it to preserve their sanity, their physical health, their marriages and livelihoods. They did it because they had tried everything else they could think of and none of it had worked. Because their relationships with family brought pain into their lives rather than joy and closeness. As Janey, a fifty-year-old Australian publishing executive, explained, "It's not like I bailed at the first drama, and it's not like I didn't leave the door open. But there comes a time when your health and your wellness and my family today is better off without my mother in our lives. Because she doesn't bring anything positive."

For Tracy, fifty-eight, a teacher in Ann Arbor, Michigan, estrangement wasn't just one decision but many, made over and over. She was estranged from her abusive father for decades, though she did see him a few times as he was dying. Usually when she makes a decision that feels right, she can put it behind her and not look back. But the break with her father and other family members never felt permanent in the same way. It was like a zombie that kept popping back up. Like a game of Whac-A-Mole, something she had to question every single day.

Whether they're still estranged or have reconciled or are somewhere in the ping-ponging process, none of the people I've talked to are sorry for their decisions. They might feel sorry they had to make those decisions in the first place, but I have yet to interview anyone who regrets their actual estrangement. Faced with a set of difficult choices they did what they felt they must. Natalie, a thirty-nine-year-old math professor at a New England university, hasn't seen or talked to one of her brothers in ten years. His history of mental-health issues makes it hard for him to hold down a job or maintain relationships. He'd floated in and out of the family for decades, disappearing for months and then popping up again to ask for money or a place to stay. When he reappeared, he was often mean to their parents and manipulative to

Natalie and their other two siblings. Natalie has given up trying to understand him, to figure out why he does what he does. "He just blows shit up wherever he goes," she says. "I can't tell where mental illness starts and where some people are just kind of jerks. I think he's kind of a jerk. *Plus* he's mentally ill."

For a while Natalie acted as a kind of liaison between her brother and her parents. She would have dinner with him and report back to them about what he was doing, where he was living, how he was feeling. She hated being in the middle. One Christmas he asked her to take a letter to their father instructing their mother not to contact him anymore. Another time he revealed to their mother via email that their sister had had an abortion in high school.

Eventually his emails and phone calls dwindled away. He came home for Christmas one year and then disappeared completely. Natalie's main feeling was relief. When their father was diagnosed with the illness that would kill him, Natalie asked if she should contact her brother. Her father said no, he deserved nothing, including information. And Natalie was fine with that. "He left us first," she says. "But then we decided to leave him too. It takes two to be estranged, you know?" She's still furious at the pain he caused the whole family. "Nobody has the right to come and firebomb my life," she says. "You don't get to do that to me." And she has zero regrets about the estrangement. If someone else told her the story of her family it might seem sad. But she's not sad about it. Not even a little bit.

Becca Bland, thirty-four, a journalist who founded the nonprofit Stand Alone, says she has no regrets, either. Bland, who grew up in Yorkshire, in the north of England, cut off contact with her parents at age twenty-five, after years of what she describes as psychological abuse and many efforts to get her mother to address it. Her problems with her mother destroyed her connections with others in the family as well. "There really wasn't a way to make the relationship work, and it took my grandma and my dad with it," she says. In 2012, as part of her struggle to come to terms with her situation, she wrote a piece for *The Guardian* about how tough it is to be estranged at Christmas and how hard it can be to explain that estrangement to other people when just about everyone else is focused on family togetherness. She was overwhelmed by the flood of mail and emails she received thanking her for breaking through the stigma around estrangement and writing openly about it. "It seemed that many people had been facing those choices of what to say to people and how to explain and feeling pretty miserable about themselves, as I had done," she says now.

Bland was especially moved by letters from young college students, who recounted practical and logistical problems in addition to the emotional traumas that had led to estrangement. Some students couldn't get loans for college because they couldn't prove they had no access to family support. Many felt too ashamed to talk about their estrangements with mental-health professionals, so they couldn't get the required documentation for government help. Students wrote to her saying they couldn't get into student accommodations without having family as a guarantor, or a huge security deposit. Some told her they faced a choice between staying in a dysfunctional family and homelessness, since those under twenty-one in the United Kingdom aren't eligible for their own housing benefits.

Bland created Stand Alone soon after her *Guardian* article ran, and in the last five years the nonprofit has worked with universities, legislators, and clinicians to tackle some of these issues. She's also looking at ways to measure "family capital"—the kinds of emotional, financial, and advisory resources available in families—so it might be used as a measure of disadvantage. "It would be quite powerful if people could be assessed on how much family capital they have around them and therefore how much support and help they might need," she says, citing issues like housing, child care, and elder care as areas where the lack of a supportive family can be problematic. "Family capital is not only something the young lack."

The stigmas associated with estrangement play a huge role in creating the kinds of problems Bland is addressing. They can also shape both the decision to estrange in the first place and the form that estrangement might take. Ongoing no-contact estrangement is relatively rare, in part because of the strong cultural proscriptions around breaking that bond. Many people who might want to cut off a relationship with a parent or grown child stop themselves because of the potential consequences—not so much the reality of making the break as the fear of the familial and cultural judgment that will come their way. And that judgment *does* come at anyone who makes that choice.

"Every time I introduce myself to someone they're like, 'Oh, how's your family?' And I either have to lie or tell them the whole story," says Bill, the project manager in Buffalo, New York, who's been estranged from his family for thirteen years. "Some people stop being friends with me as a result. Some people just don't become friends with me at all if I tell them that story."

That story includes a long history of physical and emotional abuse, including the day Bill's father tried to strangle him. *You're my son and I have the right to kill you,* he told eighteen-year-old Bill. That was the most extreme example but not the final one; Bill didn't break off contact with his family until five years later. He tends to avoid talking about the estrangement, in part because of the judgments of others. "I think even the best-intentioned people blame me after a little bit of time," he says now. "Even after I've told them these stories."

The kind of clean break Bill made with his family tends to happen only after years of what Kristina Scharp describes as chaotic disassociation, a term that perfectly captures the toxic conflation of misery and hope, longing and anger that characterizes estrangements. Bill was only twenty-three, though he'd endured years of abuse before that. It took me until the year I turned fifty to finally cut my mother off. In the years right after I graduated college and moved to New York City, we saw each other every few months, for Seders and Thanksgivings and the occasional weekend visit, which more often than not ended in arguments that led to frosty silences. After I moved to the Midwest our visits became more sporadic and often happened in the context of larger family events like weddings and bar mitzvahs. We fought by phone and, later, by email and text, and there were times when I took a break from the relationship, always thinking it would be temporary. Once or twice my mother did the same. We often went months without interacting even when we were officially in contact. As I birthed my daughters and went through therapy—grew up, really—my rage at and need for my mother settled into a kind of background angst that occasionally bloomed into desperation. Even a benign phone call could trigger weeks of anxiety and depression, longing and anger. In truth, I was calmer, happier, more functional when I didn't hear from her.

Most people who have chosen to break from their families agree. Tracy, the teacher from Ann Arbor, wants people to feel OK about choosing estrangement. "There really are cases where it's the better course," she says. "It's horrific, it's sad, it's tragic, *and* it's better than the alternative."

"For a lot of people estrangement is not a problem," acknowledges Becca Bland. "It's actually a healthier way."

Bill, the project manager, says he's now the happiest and healthiest he's ever been in his life. "I can trace that back directly to cutting my family off," he says.

That's been my experience, too. Despite my guilt and grief the break with my mother was a solution to a problem that had obsessed and distressed me my whole life. I would make the same choice again.

Chapter Two

THE ROOTS OF
ESTRANGEMENT

It's not like I purposely went out to stop contact with my brother. I just stopped making the effort. And that's when I realized I was the only one making the effort all along.

—RACHEL, thirty-nine

Everyone who is estranged has a personal litany, an often rambling and circular account of how they became disconnected from a mother, a father, sisters and brothers, aunts and uncles and cousins and stepfamilies.

Sometimes these narratives give accounts of final interactions before they, or their families, walked away. Sometimes they're origin stories that go back to the beginning of the problem, trying to trace how it started. Usually they're both. "People don't become estranged like one thing happens once and I'm never talking to you again," says Kristina Scharp. Estrangements are more like filo dough, layer on top of layer until it's impossible to name a single cause. It takes time to break a family apart, time and a pattern of emotional crises, fractals of conflict and avoidance that might look different up close but that with enough distance reveal the same shape over and over. And it's always evolving. The cultural default is togetherness; it takes continuous effort to not just disconnect from family but to stay disconnected.

While all estrangements test the boundaries of blood and custom, none do it as starkly as those between parents and children. Maybe that's why I read estrangement stories compulsively. I am looking, I think, for reassurance that my situation was just as bad as other people's, that all the times I cut off contact with my mother were justified, reasonable responses to an unreasonable situation. But even as I write this I know this is a pointless exercise. There's no one alive who can pronounce judgment on my story, no one who can definitively say that what I did was OK. Comparing myself to others is, as always, unhelpful. The guilt and rage and grief and shame I've carried for so many years are still mine to carry. They cannot be fully healed by other people's stories.

What I am really looking for, I think, is for someone to tell me I'm not evil for choosing estrangement. Mostly I know there's no dishonor in taking care of yourself. I even *feel* it sometimes. But then something will happen—say my aunt calls, the one I'm close with, whom I've confided in over the years, and she tells me she has never felt sorrier for anyone than my mother, who really is clueless, who has no idea how even to think about her problems let alone figure out how to handle them. My mother, she says, is way out of touch with emotional reality. As she speaks I feel both elated—I'm not crazy! My aunt sees what I see!—and guilty, both for the choice I'm making and for my pleasure in hearing my aunt's assessment.

The real power in hearing other people's stories comes from knowing I'm not alone. That while no one else's story will unfold exactly like mine, there are clear patterns of events, interactions, behaviors in families that become estranged. Abuse, divorce, mental illness, neglect, miscommunication, generational traumas—the play and players may change but the set and staging seem eerily familiar.

Family estrangement is framed as a problem by experts like Joshua Coleman, a psychologist who has written about it extensively. For most of us, though, the real problem is the unresolvable conflict between parents and grown children, among siblings, or in the wider circle of extended family. Estrangement is a last resort, a way to live with an unbearable conflict. It's pretty much never a choice made quickly or easily, and those who make it believe—and often have good reason to believe—that the costs of staying connected are higher than the costs of going it alone. It's not an ideal solution. But for some of us it's the only one we can live with.

◇◇◇◇◇

MY EARLIEST MEMORIES of my mother are mixed up with a recurring dream that appeared in early childhood, after an ear infection, and plagued me until long after college. In the dream I'm small, three or four, and I'm floating near the ceiling of an auditorium in the South Jersey synagogue my family attended. From the vantage of the high ceiling I look down and see a crowd of people dressed in beads and furs and suits. The women wear their hair piled high or arranged in flips that I know from watching my mother are sprayed into place. Everyone is drinking and smoking and talking, and I should be hearing the clink of glasses and the buzz of a hundred cocktail-party conversations. But the

grownups far below me are silent, a room full of strangely ani-
mated dolls, and I am suddenly afraid.

I float lower and lower, straining to hear something, anything, until I'm hovering over a group that includes my parents,
my mother blowing smoke from her lipsticked mouth, my father
darkly handsome by her side, his boyish grin lighting up his face.
Still I hear nothing, and now I'm not just afraid; I'm terrified
because not only can't I hear them—they can't see or hear me.
I drop down until I'm floating directly in front of my mother,
so close to her open mouth I'm practically on top of her, but
she doesn't see me. Her blue eyes look right through me as she
throws back her head in sudden laughter. The dread I've been
fighting blooms inside me. I will never hear the laughter and the
talk, never be part of the party as others are. I open my mouth
and scream but nothing comes out. I am erased, voiceless, cut off
from the rest of the world forever.

It's not exactly an image of parental reassurance. I wish I
could remember something of how I felt about my mother as a
baby, when I must have taken some comfort from her presence.
We are physical creatures first and at the core, and over the years
my mother's body became the locus of my rage and sorrow and
of what the Portuguese call *saudade,* a melancholy longing for a
permanently absent beloved. Friends would describe how a hug
or a phone call from their mother calmed them and I wondered
what they were talking about. In almost every photograph of my
mother and me, my mouth is guarded, my eyes narrowed and sus-
picious—more proof, I thought, that something was wrong with
me. There are one or two black-and-white Brownie photographs
of her holding me as an infant, smiling at me, bottle-feeding me.
She was twenty-three when I was born and she still looked like
a teenager in her sleeveless blouses and pedal pushers, her hair

curled and her lipstick dark against her pale skin. I wish I could remember feeling safe in the circle of her arms.

One of the few stories she told about me as a young child took place in the hospital when I was four. I'd gone in to have my tonsils removed, which at that time meant an overnight stay in a ward full of other children. The way my mother told it I was the only child on the whole ward who wouldn't let her mother sleep next to her in the hospital bed. *I had to sleep in a chair by your bed,* she said. I still don't know if it was true. And it didn't occur to me then to wonder why a mother would tell a story that painted her four-year-old as selfish, cold, and ungenerous. Whenever she brought it up I would feel a strange deadness creep over me, as if I were an ice sculpture rather than a girl, which seemed to prove my mother's triumphant point: even at age four there was something wrong with me.

Much later I wondered what had to have happened for a four-year-old to not want her mother in the hospital.

Over the years, whenever my mother asked what the problem was between us, why I was so hostile or angry or hurt, a fuzzy blankness would overcome my brain and I would go mute. Once or twice I managed to explain that her explosions and lashing out and need to always be right were part of it. I said that when she criticized my weight, my bookishness, my need for time alone, it was as if she wanted to change the very traits and talents that made me myself. What I never said was that I did not trust her, that I couldn't remember *ever* trusting her. It would have been just one more sign of my deep inadequacy. But it was true.

◇◇◇◇◇

So why do some families become estranged in the first place, and stay that way for years or decades or forever, while others maintain their connection, however rough or tenuous? What makes some people choose a path that breaks some of the most deeply held social conventions, that can make their lives painful in nearly every sphere, that can trigger years of guilt and shame?

When you ask people how their estrangements started, you usually get a rambling account that starts in one place, doubles back a dozen times, and winds up somewhere else altogether. That account will almost certainly be miles apart from the one told by whoever's on the other end of the estrangement. So when researchers ask people about the causes of their estrangement, the answers depend on who's doing the talking: the person who walked away or the one who was left behind. Nearly all the research looks at estrangements between parents and adult children rather than, say, among siblings or extended family (though those are often involved as well). In these relationships it's the parents who tend to be the ones left behind, and they[1] tend to blame outside factors like divorce or their children's partners for their difficulties. For instance, a parent in one study reported,

> [Our son] has been dating a girl for two years and this is when all the trouble began. He has had a complete personality change and he is now engaged to her. We, as parents, don't like her and neither do his friends. We think she brings out the worst in him. He was so nice and considerate before this girl and he is completely different.[2]

Conflict with a child's partner is a fairly common theme, though there's usually more to the story. Another common theme is fallout from the parents' divorce, as this comment from a different study illustrates: "[My wife had] done an excellent job of poisoning those children. Basically she turned them against me."[3] Another parent explained, "After my divorce from his father he seemed to start to hate me as his father did after our divorce."[4]

The parents in these studies, and those who join online support forums, seem to blame factors outside themselves for their relationship problems. Significant numbers of them say they have no idea what caused the estrangement. They say their relationships with their children were good—or at least good enough—until some major event took place or someone outside the family stepped in. The books written by and for estranged parents tend to reinforce this perspective. For instance, in *Done with the Crying: Help and Healing for Mothers of Estranged Adult Children*, life coach Sheri McGregor writes,

> Contrary to what so many who haven't experienced estrangement from adult children believe, only a few mothers mentioned a big disagreement or incident that led to their rejections. Many described loving relationships that suddenly soured for no logical reason. . . . Even when a reason is given it makes no sense.

McGregor goes on to describe a mother named Sondra, whose twenty-eight-year-old son apparently stopped taking her calls out of the blue. When he finally did talk to her, writes McGregor,

> he lit into her with an abusive verbal barrage. Shocked, Sondra nearly hit the floor. Though confused, she apologized. He hung up. Later, she called again, but he wouldn't speak to her. She left messages: "What did I do? Why are you angry with me?" Her son sent ranting emails and cursed her, but he never explained.[5]

I believe Sondra. That is, I believe she's telling the truth about what she experienced. I also believe her son would have quite a different take on the situation. Likewise the child of this estranged parent, who commented on an online article about Mother's Day:

> Unfortunately a growing number of adult children continue to decide they want no contact with their parent(s) and they have no intention of mending things. Most of the time the reason is unknown. . . . There are thousands of good parents who put forth their best efforts for decades to raise great children only to be rejected by them in the long run. The pain is unsurmountable.

As a parent myself I can't read this without feeling empathy for this grieving mother. I can easily believe she put forth her best effort. That doesn't make her a good parent, though, and it doesn't mean her best effort was good enough. It also doesn't mean her child would agree. I've read many comments from estranged parents that suggest that because their intentions were good, because they covered the basics of food, clothes, and shelter for their children, their relationships were good ones. Or at least there were no problems that could justify estrangement.

The following comment was left on a Facebook page aimed at unhappily estranged parents. It illuminates some of the most common feelings and complaints I've seen online:

> She now barely speaks to her dad and me not at all. We took trips together, just her and I. We got up at 4 a.m. on Black Friday for shopping trips. We were best friends. I find myself crying for no reason except that I miss her and it truly feels as if she died. Normally I am everyone's rock but when

I am alone I am nobody. I feel so helpless and unimportant. It breaks my heart that she seems to hate the one person who loves her and will always love her no matter what.

I have no idea what actually happened between this mother and daughter; maybe it's something like what she describes. I feel compassion for her and pity for her pain. But I also see some big red flags in her description. Kristina Scharp explains that adults who are estranged from their parents aren't confused at all; they tend to know exactly why they initiated the break. That's been my experience too, both as an estranged daughter and in interviewing people for this book. I don't believe this grown daughter just "drifted away." *Something* had to go wrong between being best friends and no longer speaking. Probably many somethings. Maybe this mother genuinely thinks she was supportive but the daughter didn't experience her that way. Maybe the daughter actually hated those Black Friday trips.

And maybe it's my own history with my mother that makes the last sentence of this post so chilling: *It breaks my heart that she seems to hate the one person who loves her and will always love her no matter what.* This suggests that this mother is the only one who loves her daughter, that no one else can or will, that in the great competition of life only her love matters. And maybe therein lies the real problem between them. So many of the anguished, bitter, hostile, grieving pleas I've read or heard from parents suggest a black-and-white vision of both the past and present. This one, for instance, was left by an estranged parent on an online story about estrangement and Mother's Day that quoted McGregor:

As others have said, these adult children have their own agenda, a different, unrecognizable version of events and absolutely no conscience or compassion. I have been through hell. If only this subject could come out of darkness and into light, it wouldn't change anything for us but at least we may be better able to support each other through this unexpected and undeserved maltreatment.

In defending themselves against the stigma of involuntary estrangement, parents often insist that they were good, nurturing, loving parents and their children are ungrateful or confused or messed-up or heartless. It's an either/or perspective, a zero-sum game. Someone must be right and someone, therefore, must be wrong.

But that's not how relationships work, especially between parents and children. Three siblings might be fine with their parents when they grow up while the fourth insists on distance. That doesn't mean there's something wrong with the fourth child. No two children grow up with the same parents, or with the same needs and perceptions. My sister and I, for instance, share some memories of our mother but hold very different feelings about those memories. My sister felt seen and loved despite our mother's unpleasant explosions; I did not. And maybe my mother did see my sister in a way she never saw me. She was a better parent to my sister; I don't know why and it doesn't really matter. It also doesn't make my sister right and me wrong, or vice versa.

You can do your best as a parent and your child might still feel hurt, wronged, betrayed, or abused. Though that phrase, *do your best,* feels suspect to me; you can pretty much always find a way to do better as a parent. Either way, merely reiterating your good intentions and parenting accomplishments isn't enough. Another forum parent wrote, "I was a loving, engaged, fair, stable single parent. I worked really hard and she never went without anything she needed, ever. I have nothing to apologize for! She was lucky to have me as her mother." I understand her defensiveness; I also know it doesn't come anywhere near the heart of the issues with her daughter. There's a lot of terrain to cover between the extremes of shoddy parenting on one hand and stellar parenting on the other.

In his popular book *When Parents Hurt: Compassionate Strategies When You and Your Grown Child Don't Get Along*, psychologist Joshua Coleman opens a chapter on adult children with these words:

> It's every parent's worst nightmare. The child whom you put everything into moves away, won't return your calls, ignores your e-mails, and rejects your attempts to be close. He has his reasons, of course—your lousy parenting, your treatment of the other parent, your selfishness, your inattention, your cruelty, the divorce—whatever; he has decided to execute the nuclear option, which is to completely cut off contact.[6]

I was feeling empathy right up until the word *whatever*, which suggests that the reasons put forth by this adult child are meaningless distractions from the real issue—his decision to "execute the nuclear option." The implication is that none of those reasons could possibly be important enough to justify such a decision. And the way it's worded signifies disbelief, as if no "lousy parenting" or "cruelty" could warrant such a response.

A few pages later, Coleman lists "parental mistakes" as one of the reasons adult children cut off contact with parents: "Parents who were verbally, physically, or sexually abusive, drug or alcohol addicted, neglectful or overly critical may have left emotional scars on the child, making that child reluctant or unwilling to give the parent another chance."[7] These are some pretty damn big "mistakes." In parenting my daughters I've made plenty of mistakes and no doubt will make plenty more. I've been late to pick them up; I've been cranky and preoccupied. Those are mistakes and I take responsibility for them. But abuse is not a mistake, especially a pattern of abuse. Many of us who grew up with abusive parents have tried to address the issue through talking, behavior modification, mediation, meditation. The problem isn't that we're unwilling to give our parents a second chance; most of us have given them hundreds of chances. The problem is that unless something changes, that fifth or fiftieth chance is just another excuse for the same kind of treatment. It's Charlie Brown flat on his back after Lucy pulls away the football again. For many of us the only way to make it stop is to walk away.

In Kristina Scharp's studies, adult children say they are estranged because of things their parents not only did in the past but continue to do. They list parental abuse, neglect, and toxic behavior as the driving forces behind their decisions.[8] Their comments suggest that they don't walk away from their parents because of one or two incidents but because the relationship as a whole causes them great pain. As one adult child explained, "I needed to cut off my mother. She is mentally ill and is dangerous. I need to protect myself and allow myself to one day have a healthy family of my own."[9] I could have written those words myself. Another commented, "My father is an extremely self-centered person, who seems incapable of any kind of real relationship. He uses people until they are no longer useful, then discards them. Finally . . . my sister and I decided we'd had enough."[10]

To dig deeper into these reasons, Scharp asked fifty-two adult children to tell the stories of their estrangements, and then she coded their responses into half a dozen categories: parental maltreatment, parental indifference, long-term expectations, close relationships, internal process, and external events. Humans, however, are messy creatures; how we feel and what we do rarely fit neatly into one category or another, something Scharp's study acknowledges. The categories overlap in important ways. For instance, one participant, June, wrote that she'd realized her mother had never been a good parent and never would be, and that's why she decided to cut ties. Scharp cites this as an example of the internal process category, which makes sense. But June's backstory reveals that her stepfather had abused her, sexually and otherwise, and her mother neither believed nor supported her. So parental abuse and neglect were also part of the picture and certainly led to June's realization and processing of the relationship.

In fact, every single one of the fifty-two participants described abuse and/or neglect from parents. It's a theme that comes up again and again in what little research exists on estrangement. In a 2017 study of twenty-five adult children in Australia, participants reported three main reasons for estranging from parents: abuse, poor parenting, and betrayal.[11] A Texas Christian University study of 352 adult children uncovered two main reasons for estrangement: parents' toxic behavior and feeling unsupported and unaccepted.[12]

Scharp didn't interview her subjects' parents, so she doesn't know their side of the stories. But the research suggests it would be quite different. A group of twenty-five estranged parents in a 2015 Australian study gave three reasons for their children's decisions: differences in values and behaviors, a child's choice of someone else over a parent, and a child's punishment of a parent for a perceived wrongdoing.[13] The Texas Christian University study interviewed 546 parents and found they mainly attributed their estrangements to their children's "objectionable" relationships and sense of entitlement.[14]

This discrepancy is consistent with what you find in many of the online forums for estranged parents, which have names like "Living with a Broken Heart," "Estranged Parents and Adult

Children: A Silent Epidemic," and "The Bill of Rights for Parents of Adult Children." Posts on these forums often comprise litanies ranging from the heartbreaking to the vindictive. *He did this to me. It's not fair. I don't get to see my grandchildren. My son is an alcoholic who can't face the truth. I don't like my daughter's boyfriend so she cut me off.*

The parents who post in these forums mostly say they don't know why their children have cut them off; if they do have an inkling, they dismiss their children's reasons out of hand. They write movingly about grandchildren they've never met, gifts returned unopened, pleas for explanations. Many talk about the estrangement as if it happened in an instant, as if one minute they were a loving family and the next their child shut the door in their face, leaving them bewildered and abandoned.

Elizabeth Vagnoni, a former advertising executive who has become something of an unofficial spokeswoman for estranged parents, runs one such forum. She speaks openly about her own estrangement from her two grown sons, which she says was triggered when they looked through her private emails and misinterpreted something she'd written to a friend. Vagnoni says many of the women who post on her site become severely depressed when their children cut them off. Their marriages come apart; their friendships fall away. They post about contemplating suicide and substance abuse, anything to escape the pain of losing their child and the shame of being estranged.

Vagnoni, sixty-three, has experienced estrangement from both sides; for a while she was estranged from her mother but now talks to her on the phone every day. "Trust me, I get it," she says with a laugh. "My mother is toxic. People I know ask 'Why does she have to speak to people the way she does?' She literally has a barbed tongue."

A therapist once told her, "You've got two choices. You can either decide in your mind that your mother's dead, and good luck with that, or you can figure out how to deal with her." By "good luck with that" the therapist meant that it's not so easy to permanently sever ties with a parent. "You can cut off your friends and never see them again, but your parents are people who did something for you somewhere along the line," explains Vagnoni. "They are part of your DNA and part of who you are, and clearly they don't just go away. No matter how hard you try to make them go away, they're in your head somewhere."

This is true, of course, for reasons of biology and sociology and culture and genetics and theology. We are bound to our parents with a matrix of connections as dense and persistent and multi-layered as a rhizome, the creeping roots of plants like lily of the valley, which send out runners and shoots that infiltrate the soil. You can't kill a plant like this by pulling it up (and I've tried) because each root connects to ten more, twenty more, a hundred more. Vagnoni's rather circular argument seems to be that since you can never completely cut a parent out of your life, you should find a way to tolerate or accept that parent because . . . it's your parent.

And a lot of people do that. They put up with physical and emotional abuse, they accept unwanted criticism, they struggle with debilitating anxiety and depression, they swallow their own thoughts and feelings, all to maintain the parent-child connection. Until they just can't do it anymore. Until they have what Kristina Scharp calls a "last-straw" moment, an experience that may not be qualitatively different from anything that came before it but that comes at just the right (or wrong) moment, when the feelings and events of years shift in an instant, like the colored glass in a kaleidoscope falling into a different pattern with the tiniest adjustment.

That's what happened to Jill, sixty-five, a retired schoolteacher near Philadelphia who hasn't spoken to her elderly mother in more than a year. But the roots of their estrangement go back decades. Jill remembers chafing under her mother's constant criticisms: *Why are you wearing your hair like that? I don't like that dress. How dare you do that?* Their phone calls after Jill left home often consisted of her mother trash-talking Jill's father and grandparents and brother. She would hold the phone away from her ear and say *Uh-huh* every so often, and hang up feeling aggravated. But she tolerated the calls and the comments because she felt some level of obligation—after all, it was her mother—and because she wanted to be able to see her adored father.

The family situation was complicated by the fact that Jill's younger brother, Sam, has severe chronic depression and needs a lot of support and care. For a while, before Sam was able to go on disability, Jill's husband put him on the payroll of his small business so he could get health coverage. Then the business shifted and Jill's husband couldn't cover her brother anymore. That, too, became a source of conflict with her mother, who accused Jill of abandoning her brother. After every visit Jill would walk out in tears. Her father once told her that if things had been different when he was younger, he would have divorced her mother.

So Jill balanced her teaching job with the needs of both her parents and her own husband and two children. It wasn't easy on any level, especially after her grown son committed suicide. A few months after that, at a restaurant with her parents, a random comment triggered her grief and she began to cry. Her mother said *You know, you're not the only one to have bad things happen to you,* and launched into a story about *her* father's death years before. After that, Jill stuck to superficial small talk with her mother, refusing to engage with her emotionally. She considered it a partial estrangement; she didn't want to make a total break because her parents had no one else to drive them to medical appointments or shopping or out for a meal. And she didn't want to lose the connection with her father.

The last time she spoke to her mother was two years ago, during her father's last illness. For a while, when he was in the hospital, Jill saw a lot of the whole family. She would pick up her mother and her brother, take them to the hospital, take care of the paperwork and insurance and medical tasks, and drive them home again at the end of the day. That went on until the afternoon Jill called the hospital to get an update on her father's condition and was told they weren't allowed to give her any information; only her mother and brother were on the list for updates. Jill called her mother and asked what was happening. Her mother said, *What do you expect? You haven't really talked to us in five years.*

"I said, 'Can you repeat that? I'm not sure I heard you correctly,'" Jill says now. Her mother said it again. *What do you expect?* So Jill said, *OK then, find someone else to drive you to and from the hospital.* She hasn't spoken to her mother since.

These days, Jill's mother lives in a small apartment in a senior complex. She is alone, since she doesn't speak to her own brother, and Sam has been too depressed to drive or visit. Sometimes Jill catches herself thinking that it's a shame her mother is all alone. Then she remembers everything and she gets over it. Her only regret is that she waited so long to cut her mother out of her life, that she tortured herself for so many years, holding on to a relationship that did nothing but hurt her. She did it for her father's sake, and for her own. Now she thinks it wasn't worth it.

Not long ago one of the guys in Jill's morning Starbucks group commented that he didn't understand how she could be estranged from her own mother because life is short. She said, *That's right, and I'm going to be as happy as I can, and being away from my mother is the only way to do that.* She's determined now to put her own health and well-being first, especially since losing her son. "Some people go through this and feel horrible guilt," she says. "I don't feel a drop of guilt. Estrangement can be something that helps you live a better life."

⬦⬦⬦⬦⬦

LIKE KRISTINA SCHARP'S study participants, many of the people I interviewed for this book attributed their estrangements to abuse and/or neglect of one kind or another. Even more of them cited toxic or narcissistic behavior on the part of a parent, sibling, or other family member. The distinctions between them may be semantic. Whether you call a parent's behavior abusive or toxic, it amounts to pretty much the same thing.

Jo, a forty-three-year-old writer in New York City, describes both her mother and father as narcissists, and is now estranged from both of them. As the only child of two only children who divorced when she was nine, she's felt pressured by both of them to maintain their connections despite the distress it's caused her.

She describes her father as a "Trump-esque dictator with undiagnosed narcissistic personality disorder" and says from the time she was a small child she knew he wasn't like other parents. He told her often to shut up. She was never allowed to disagree with him; if she did, he would force her to stand in one spot and repeat *You are the father, I am the daughter, everything you say is right, everything I say is wrong.* He told her she was his property. In elementary school if she didn't tidy her room to his satisfaction she'd come home to find her clothes, her toys, her books all gone, thrown down the apartment building's incinerator chute. Almost worse, he joked about it for years after she'd moved out, saying *I'll come over and help you clean up, ha ha ha.* When she was in college he showed up unannounced at her dorm room for an "inspection," threatening to stop his contribution to her tuition if it wasn't up to his standards. For twenty-some years Jo tried to create as much distance as possible from her father without cutting him off entirely. She tried to placate him while taking care of herself because she finds him scary when he's mad. But that was an exercise in frustration.

Take their annual Thanksgiving dinner, for instance, put on each year by a cousin. Jo characterizes this as the single worst day of the year for her, which leaves her debilitatingly depressed both beforehand and for weeks afterward. Part of the problem is that she has to see both of her parents at the same time. Part of it is that she has to see them, in all their dysfunctional glory, in the context of a "normal" family, one where people love one another and behave decently on the whole. For ages Jo tried to screw up the courage to skip the dinner and figure out a way to do it without pissing off her parents. When she turned forty a few years ago she decided it was time; she just couldn't face another year of it. She told her father she was going to be on the West Coast for work (true) and had been invited to the home of an old friend whose kids were her godchildren (also true). She was fed up enough to be somewhat forthright about it, telling him *I don't have any brothers or sisters, I'm never going to have nieces and nephews, these kids mean a lot to me and I'm going to celebrate the holiday with them for once.*

He seemed OK with it, but after she got home from the trip her mother called to say that her father was really angry and had decided to boycott Jo. She said, *He's not going to your apartment, he's not going to return your calls, and when you realize what it's like to not have your father in your life you're going to realize he's the best father in the world and you're going to want to spend every weekend hanging out with him. Oh, but don't tell him I told you about this boycott because you're not supposed to know.*

At first Jo was furious, at her father for being a jerk and at her mother for getting in the middle of things. Then she realized his boycott was exactly what she'd always wanted. "For the majority of my adult life I'd been saying leave me alone, I don't want to talk to you, stop calling me and making racist jokes, stop showing up at my door and barreling through my boundaries and telling me I'm an ingrate," she says. Now he was doing just that, and she hadn't had to be the one to cut him off. She told her boyfriend, "Long live the boycott!"

The situation with her mother has been both more complicated and harder to navigate. One of Jo's earliest memories is of sitting with her mother, patting her hand as she cried, saying *Mommy, what's wrong, how can I fix it?* She describes her mother as needy and overbearing, narcissistic in a different way from her father. The older and sicker her mother has become, the more she's insisted that Jo take care of her, emotionally as well as physically. At one point she told her daughter *I can't do anything for myself, I need you to run my life.* Jo pushed back, saying *I can't run your life! You're an adult! I'm not your mother!*

Eventually Jo told her that unless her mother started taking the medications the doctor had prescribed for her Parkinson's, started taking even a *little* responsibility for herself, Jo wouldn't see her or take her out. Her mother refused. Now Jo sends her mother birthday and Mother's Day cards but keeps her distance. "A parent should care about their kid's needs and should prioritize their kid's needs at least as much as their own," she says. "She's unable to see me as a person who has any kind of needs separate from existing to fix her and help her and make sure she's OK." This kind of role reversal is known as parentification, and it's common among narcissistic parents, especially those who are enmeshed with grown children.

For those who aren't enmeshed, estrangement sometimes comes more easily. Lynn, fifty-seven, an art historian in Milwaukee, was estranged from her father for more than a decade. Her mother had died when she was ten, and he remarried and became very religious. He more or less kicked her out of the house when she was a senior in high school, and they really didn't speak for twelve years. He developed Alzheimer's soon after they reconnected, so they never had much of a relationship again.

Lynn is very clear about the fact that she never liked or loved her father. He was, she says, a damaged person who had never recovered from a terrible childhood. "And of course damaged people raise damaged children," she adds with a wry laugh. "I think I was estranged from him from day one."

She's matter-of-fact about the distance between them and says it causes her little pain. And that makes sense in a way. It's often the children who were most connected who wind up being estranged. Children who are overly emotionally involved with parents—like Jo—may struggle to differentiate themselves as young adults. "With the parent super involved the uglier it is and the uglier it becomes because that's the only way the child can get away," says Elizabeth Vagnoni. "Whereas the parent who lets the kid go off and be themselves, there's less to get upset about because the parent's not that involved with you anyway."

I'm not sure letting kids be themselves constitutes lack of attachment, and I think there's some middle ground between enmeshment and neglect. Still, Vagnoni's got a point. If you were never close in the first place, maybe you're less vulnerable than someone who's been riding that merry-go-round for years. Maybe you've got a lot less to lose.

Chapter Three

MEAN MOTHERS
(AND FATHERS)

I realized by the time I was ten that this was a person
I did not like. Even though he was my father he was
just very cruel and hurtful and made me feel awful
and unsafe and insecure.

—**TRACY**, fifty-eight

P eg Streep has spent years researching and writing about
parents she calls "mean mothers," mothers (and fathers)
whose children find them nasty, overly critical, hurtful,
and abusive. Unless you've grown up with a parent like that yourself it's hard to believe the stories told by people like Sharon, a
forty-seven-year-old therapist from Columbus, Ohio. Sharon was
close with her mother growing up despite the fact, she says, that
her mother was "mean." She couldn't understand why she felt
such admiration for her mother—hero worship, really—but still
felt terrible every time they interacted. And for good reason: her
mother often told Sharon she was a piece of shit. She made dire

predictions about Sharon's marriage ("It will fall apart! Your husband will get bored with you! You'll get bored with him!"). She once called her daughter and said, *I need to tell you something and I just need to tell you and I don't want to argue with you about it, but I think you're ruining your children's lives, there I've said it and I don't want to talk about it anymore.*

In graduate school Sharon began to try to get a little distance from her mother. Her sister was and still is quite enmeshed with their mother, but Sharon was starting to see that she needed boundaries, the kind of reasonable ground rules observed by most mothers and grown daughters. Her mother didn't react well, and after a few years of conflict and rapprochement things came to a head one afternoon. Her mother had been babysitting Sharon's then-eight-year-old daughter, and when Sharon came to pick her up, in the middle of a conversation, her mother yelled *You have a cold black heart!* It wasn't the first time she'd said something like that, but it felt different to Sharon. "My daughter was sitting on the couch listening to this," she remembers. "I said, 'You know what? You're wrong about that. My friends like me. My friends think I'm a lovely person.' And she said, 'Oh, I know all about you and your *friends.*' And that's when I realized, she's crazy. This is not something you would say to your child." That was three years ago, and they haven't talked since.

Streep has heard thousands of stories about mothers like Sharon's and mine, and lived her own with her mother, who told Streep's first boyfriend that despite her daughter's pretty outside she was "rotten inside." Streep spent twenty years breaking with her mother and reconciling, trying to make the relationship work. Her decision to finally end things was the result of an internal process rather than triggered by something her mother did. She was thirty-eight when she learned she was pregnant with a daughter. "Five minutes after I got the news from the gynecologist I called my mother and said 'Goodbye, it's over, I'm pregnant, I never want to see you again,'" she remembers. "There was no way this woman's poison was going to wash over this kid. None. Zero."

She did see her mother once more, when her extended family pressured her to let her mother visit the baby. Her mother came to the hospital, saw the baby, and left. That was that. Years later, when Streep's mother was dying, her therapist and others urged her to visit, to get "closure." In a piece for *Psychology Today* she explained why she didn't break down and do what they'd suggested:

> I was wise enough to realize that they hadn't walked my path, and their vision of closure was based on novels and Hollywood movies in which a-ha! moments flourish and mothers always love. In real life, I would ask the question I always wanted answered—"Why didn't you love me?"—and she would refuse to answer, as always, but this time her silence would stretch out into eternity.

I remember the terror I felt standing in my mother's ICU room, hearing the nurse encourage her to open her eyes. I remember backing away to stand behind my sister, so if she did open her eyes she wouldn't see me. Like Streep, I knew my mother didn't love me in the way I longed to be loved. After a lifetime of dealing with that reality I didn't want to come face-to-face with it. Since her death I've thought through all the possibilities of that moment. What if she *had* opened her eyes? What if she'd looked at me with the kind of love I'd once longed for? Would it have changed anything? I don't think so. By then there was no scrap of trust for my mother left in me. No look or words could possibly have outweighed the years and years of actions. Yet I stood there, cowering behind my sister, as if she could still hurt me and, therefore, still bless me.

◇◇◇◇◇

THE KIND OF essential meanness Streep describes can affect more than one parent; it can run through a family like fat marbling a steak. In some families patterns of estrangement as well as abuse and neglect seem to be handed down from generation to generation. Sharon's mother, for instance, hasn't spoken to one of her own brothers in decades; and for a while was on the outs with all three of her sisters and their mother. Jill's mother doesn't speak to her own brother. One Stand Alone participant told researchers, "As a mum myself I worry constantly that 'karma' will bring the same situation to me with my children. I think the stigma is that if you don't honor your parents you can't be a good parent yourself." I know exactly how she feels. One of my mother's favorite threats was "Someday you'll have a daughter who will do to you what you've done to me."

I planned to never have children, though. I was terrified that I would inadvertently do to them what my mother had done to me, and afraid, too, that my mother's ill wish would come true. Then my grandmother died and the need to have a child bloomed in me like a magnolia flower, no warning or softening greenery, just a flower opened suddenly on a dark branch. I was pregnant two weeks later and the next nine months stretched endless and full of worries. What if the child I carried found me selfish and cold and unworthy of love just as my mother had? What if I didn't love it enough or in the right way? What if my child filled me with rage as I seemed to do with my mother? What if my mother's curse came true?

Night after night my husband listened to me cry and told me the same things over and over. *I know you. You're not the person your mother thinks you are. You are a good person and you will love this child.* I did not believe him. I also didn't *not* believe him. In the infinitesimal space between his words and my mother's I could hold myself still. I could take one breath, then another, and get through the limbo between what I had been and what I might become. I could imagine myself into a scene unlike any from my own childhood.

But for some people such fears are realistic. About a third of the people I interviewed for this book mentioned that their parents were also, and separately, estranged from other relatives. They pointed out patterns going back two or three generations— grandparents who didn't speak to siblings, parent-child breaches, whole branches of families cut off from one another. Jennifer, fifty-six, a hospice-care physician in Allentown, Pennsylvania, says she and her brother are the only siblings on both sides of their large extended family who have never had an estrangement. Her father was estranged from his mother for more than thirty years. Her mother didn't speak to her own sister. "Cutting people out of their lives seems to be a reasonable coping strategy in my family, or at least an acceptable one," she says.

If estrangement is passed down genetically, it makes sense that it would run in families. If it's learned behavior, it also makes sense that you'd find it across family trees. If you watch your parents freeze out their parents, their brothers and sisters and cousins, maybe you're more likely to do that too. If, like Jennifer, you grow up in a house where everyone avoids conflict by walking away, that becomes one of your coping mechanisms as well. Whether estrangement is driven by nature, nurture, or some combination of the two, it makes sense that it would be both contagious and heritable.

Andi, a thirty-five-year-old physical therapist in New York City, has been completely estranged from her parents for five years. Unlike many of the people I interviewed for this book, she remembers feeling very connected to her parents and three siblings while she was growing up. They went to ballgames and for ice cream and spent whole weekends hanging out together. Her parents showed up for her dance recitals and sports meets and Girl Scout events. She grew up being told that her family was very close, that they loved spending time together, that they really loved each other, and she felt it. She believed it despite the fact that her father had crossed some boundaries sexually and her mother was prone to hitting her—not abuse-level hitting, more smacking and slapping, but still.

The more independent she got, though, the shakier those family bonds became. When she and her girlfriend moved to New York City, about six hours away from where she'd grown up, she saw less and less of her family. By the time she was planning her wedding in 2012, she'd begun to realize that maybe her parents weren't actually as unconditionally loving as she'd thought. "I realized, Oh my god, these people don't even know who I am, they don't prioritize me, they can't see what's important to me. I just represent an object, their property," says Andi now.

A conflict involving one of her sisters a year later triggered the final crisis. "My parents called me and left thirteen scathing voicemails telling me what a total shit I was and how they'd done everything for me and sacrificed their lives for me and that I was this crazy narcissist," she recalls. She hasn't spoken to any of them since. The hardest thing, she says, has been giving up the illusion of unconditional love she once had. She misses the idea of the loving and supportive family she thought she had, or maybe once had. But she doesn't miss her actual family.

⬦⬦⬦⬦⬦

SOMETIMES WHAT PEG STREEP calls *meanness* comes from substance abuse or mental-health issues. Howie, a thirty-four-year-old nurse in the New York City area, has been estranged on and off from his father, who has been hospitalized a few times with paranoid schizophrenia. Howie's parents divorced when he was eight, and he wasn't allowed to see his father for several years. His father, he recalls, was prone to "odd behavior" and paranoia because of his illness. When Howie was eleven, a therapist helped him reconnect with his father, and for a while they had a good relationship. Even as a child Howie was able to realize that his father was a whole different person when he was on medication.

A few years ago, though, his father developed dementia, which retriggered some of the paranoia and difficult behaviors Howie remembered from childhood. These days his father, now in a nursing home, oscillates between thinking Howie's out to get him and thinking he's the best thing that ever happened to him. Howie limits his visits with his father but doesn't want to cut him off completely. "My dad is a great person, and he's still my dad, and I love him," he says. "But when he gets abusive it's very hard to go see him."

Eric, a forty-seven-year-old CFO in Los Angeles, has been fully estranged from his younger sister for seventeen years, though their connection had long been difficult. He says there was always a certain amount of conflict and drama in the house when they were growing up, and that his sister was often angry at him for what he considered small offenses, like doodling on a Post-it note she'd written to herself. As adults, their relationship has been tumultuous. One year his sister, an observant Catholic, would be furious because Eric's then-girlfriend, now his wife, was staying over. The next year she'd call all the time and cry about a bad break-up. "We never knew who we were going to get," says Eric. "The angry sister or the not-angry sister? The crazy sister or the benign sister?"

He still doesn't entirely understand the incident that provoked their estrangement. It involved about a thousand dollars' worth of maternity clothes, which Eric and his wife bought and which was shared between them and Eric's sister. His sister's second pregnancy produced a baby with a genetic defect, and when the baby died a week after being born she was understandably devastated. Then Eric's wife got pregnant again, and after several months he asked as tactfully as possible if he could come pick up the clothes because his wife needed them. "And she says, 'You were never supportive of me when my baby was dying, and I am particularly offended that you do not believe my son has gone where I believe he has gone,'" says Eric, who converted to Judaism when he got married. "Which was sort of laying down the religious gauntlet."

He told his sister he was sorry but he wasn't going to say the baby was in heaven because he didn't believe in heaven, and they would have to agree to disagree. That was the last time she spoke to him. Later, when she gave birth to a healthy baby, Eric and his wife sent a set of monogrammed towels as a gift. His sister returned them with a note telling him to never contact her again.

Eric minds the estrangement more for his aging parents' sake than for his own. He wonders if he should be doing more to try to fix the situation. But he doesn't want his sister to lash out at him once more, and he definitely doesn't want to put his wife through that again. "The fact that the relationship with her was so fraught and so unpleasant for so long means that I mourn it in theory more than I mourn it in practicality," he says. "But there's an ambivalence there, an always sort of wondering whether I could be doing something else."

The vast majority of mental health–related estrangements seem to center around a family member who's considered a narcissist. I say "considered" because there is rarely an official diagnosis made. And they can't all be pathological narcissists, because only about 1 percent of the population is clinically narcissistic.[1] According to psychologist Craig Malkin, author of *Rethinking Narcissism: The Secret to Recognizing and Coping with Narcissists*, most of us fall somewhere on the narcissism spectrum, and in fact some level of narcissism is both healthy and necessary.

But many of the stories I've read suggest that there might be more narcissists out there than psychologists think. There are huge online communities for people who believe their parents are narcissists, including an active subcategory on Reddit called "Raised by Narcissists" with thousands of posts and comments. One forum user recently asked people to describe how and when they realized one or both of their parents were narcissists, and got a number of replies, including this one:

> I always knew something was wrong with the NM [acronym for narcissistic mother]. As a kid I could only describe it as being mean, crazy, or unpredictable. As a teenager and adult I just internalized all her BS and that every problem was my fault because I was by default always a wrong, unworthy, horrible person. I tried to avoid contact with her while still trying to be in contact with my dad. That seemed to just drag out the problems. It wasn't until six years ago when I ended up back in regular contact with her and dealing with family members again that I realized what a massively toxic mess all of this was. Then I started doing more research and realized what she was. Lots of things now make sense.

People who post on the Reddit site refer to going NC (no contact), LC and VLC (low contact/very low contact), and SC (structured contact). They call themselves and other family members ACoNs (adult children of narcissists), GCs (golden children), and SGs (scapegoats).* They discuss strategies for dealing with narcissistic family members, including techniques like gray rocking, an evocative term that describes the process of sidestepping emotional provocations and drama by sticking to boring superficial commentaries on, say, laundry or weather.

Another popular site, Down the Rabbit Hole, takes an analytical look at online forums for estranged parents and concludes that many of the parents who post on those forums express classic narcissistic/abusive beliefs. The site's creator, who goes by the name Issendai, deconstructs some all-too-familiar examples of the kinds of comments and behaviors discussed on these forums:

> When faced with evidence of their children's true feelings about unwanted contact, parents minimize ("What have we been doing to him? Nothing but telling him we love him!"), deny ("She's saying that because her abusive husband ordered her to"), demand explanations ("Why should she be afraid of me? I'm a weak little old woman who wouldn't hurt a fly!"), assert that they are still doing the right thing ("How can this estrangement end if we don't talk about it?"), and dismiss their children's emotions. . . . The common attitude is that estranged adult children shouldn't feel the way they do, so their nonconforming emotions can be ignored. Even when estranged parents get direct, unvarnished information about how they affect their children, they refuse to believe anything that goes against their idea of how the relationship should be.

---

* Many narcissistic families include one or more "golden children" who can do no wrong and at least one "scapegoat" who's typically blamed for every problem.

Rachel, a thirty-nine-year-old journalist from Cincinnati, Ohio, describes her mother as an "ignoring narcissist" (as distinct from an "engulfing narcissist"), someone who wants to be there for the big days in her life but who never shows up otherwise. Rachel has used gray rocking to create an estrangement that's more emotional than physical, to keep her mother at a distance without actively fighting. The two were never close, and were formally estranged for a year or so when Rachel was in her twenties. But their alienation intensified a couple of years ago after Rachel invited her mother-in-law to a ceremony honoring her but did not ask her mother. "She'd never expressed any interest in this award, barely called me, and I didn't want her to take credit again for one of my successes," she explains. Her mother saw pictures on Facebook of Rachel and her mother-in-law at the event and went ballistic, defriending her daughter and calling her to say *Why do you hate me so much? Why do you have so much hatred?*

Rachel now sees her mother only at parties and events her sister organizes for her niece. For her sister's sake she's learned to ooze niceness while keeping her mother at bay. If her mother asks how her new job is going, for example, Rachel says *Oh, it's great, thanks!* She offers no details, no follow-up, no invitation to go deeper. That way both of them can attend her sister's events without any public conflicts. It works for Rachel.

I didn't know the term *gray rocking* during the years I was struggling with my mother, but I tried something like it from time to time. It usually worked for a little while, but after a few phone conversations where I refused to get angry or upset or engage with her emotionally, my mother would up the ante until I inevitably gave her what she seemed to want: a fight. It took me a long time to learn how to not engage with her, and the only way I could do it was to more or less give up on her. As long as I actively wanted something from my mother—an acknowledgment, a specific conversation, an apology, a believable declaration—I could not stop myself from falling into the well of her rage and bitterness. I could not stop myself from rising to her bait, lashing back at her with angry words, slamming the phone down in frustration.

One of the few times I was able to hold back was the weekend of my grandfather's funeral. I'd been close to my grandfather all through his long life; he was the adult who taught me to ride a bike, drive a car, balance a checkbook. His death at ninety-eight was sad but not surprising. I knew my mother would be grieving too; she'd barely known her own father, and her father-in-law had been good to her. And I knew that because she was upset she was much more likely to blow up. So I'd been careful all weekend, avoided coming face-to-face with her, avoiding even the slightest eye contact. I'd perfected the trick of arranging my mouth into a smile and turning in her direction without actually looking at her.

But now, on the morning after the funeral, in a New Jersey hotel full of family and strangers, my mother stalked into the dining room where my husband, daughters, and I sat eating toast and drinking coffee. She came around to our table and stood behind my chair. Beside me my older daughter, age twelve, threw me a worried look. She'd seen my mother's rages before.

"You know where I am," my mother announced in a penetrating voice, her hands on either side of my chair, holding it in place. I put down my fork and waited. A number of heads went up around the dining room. My sister, who was walking by the room, paused in the doorway. *Uh-oh.* Our mother was in full performance mode.

She stood there for a long thirty seconds without speaking, holding her audience, and then, raising her voice a notch, said, "I've reached out to you many times, every way I know how. Now it's up to you."

Ten years earlier I would have been standing nose to nose with her, shouting back. Now I sat unmoving in my chair, thinking *It will be over soon*. My daughter's hand snaked under the table and touched mine. I knew the rhythm and pacing of my mother's outbursts; I knew she would make one more dramatic gesture and stalk off and we'd be done. For today.

Sure enough, my mother bent over. She grabbed my chin in her hand, pulled it roughly toward her, and planted a lipsticked kiss on my cheek. "Have a nice life," she pronounced. It was a curse, not a blessing, and we both knew it. Sweat started down my spine as she released me and walked slowly, majestically out of the room. My daughter's stricken face turned to follow her. I let out my breath, lifted my mug, took a swallow. Mostly I felt relieved; it could have been a lot worse.

Much later I heard the rest of the story: how my mild-mannered husband followed her out of the dining room and into the lobby and confronted her as the front-desk staff watched. How he told her that he was sick of listening to her go on this way, that he'd been watching her do this to me for the last eighteen years and he'd had enough. She needed to stop, he said. She needed to keep her poison to herself. How my mother turned on him, shouting. How that afternoon, after we'd left, my mother reported the scene to my father, leaving out her kiss and her curse, her last dramatic flourish. When my sister tried to interject with what she'd seen and heard, our mother's retort was *Yes, but you didn't hear what she said back to me!*

I was standing right there, my sister told her. *I didn't hear her say anything.*

No one ever hears what she says back!

I had answered her back—my mother called it "being fresh"— many times over the years, but not this time. Not in front of my twelve- and eight-year-olds and a roomful of strangers.

I tell this story not to prove that my mother was a narcissist; I don't know if she was, though I suspect so. While I used to feel that I needed to know exactly what was wrong with her, what was wrong between us, I don't any more. The way she acted and the things she said seemed normal to me as a child, before I'd seen how other families behaved, but I knew by the time I was twelve that what happened at our house was not like what happened in other houses. We may have looked reasonably ordinary from the outside, but inside was another story.

That dysfunctional discrepancy between the shiny surface and the seething interior is another common theme among estranged families, especially those where narcissism—or suspected narcissism—plays a role. "The fact that your family can appear fine, and you're fine on paper, but it's really, really awful—it's like you're being gaslit," says Tracy, the teacher from Ann Arbor, Michigan. As an adult she was estranged from her father for many years, though the roots of their problems went back to her childhood. He beat her two brothers so badly there were a few times they couldn't go to school. With Tracy he was emotionally abusive. He always knew the exact wrong thing to say. "It's like every bad voice you've ever had in your head—the self-loathing, self-deprecating voice all of us have," she says. "He was that voice, only he wasn't in my head."

He didn't save his cruelty for the family alone. Tracy remembers one incident from childhood when her father said something so insulting to a waitress that the manager came and kicked the whole family out of the restaurant. Acquaintances compared him to Tony Soprano and Donald Trump. Tracy thinks he was a narcissist, though he never saw a therapist and never got a diagnosis. He had a gift for making other people miserable while he remained untouched. More than a few of his close relatives wound up in therapy because of him.

Still, Tracy maintained the relationship with her father until her mid-thirties, when her mother died. Ironically he was the one who cut things off, at least at first. During one of her father's first solo visits he fought with Tracy's husband and stormed out early. Later he told Tracy he would come visit only when her husband was out of town. She said no; she knew she needed a buffer, her husband's presence, between her and her father. Her father said, *Well then we're done*, and that was that. A few times in the months after, he tried to re-enter her life. But Tracy had found a huge sense of relief and even liberation from the estrangement. She thought about Ann Landers's famous question to women considering divorce—*Are you better off with him or without him?*—and applied it to her relationship with her father. The answer was clear.

◇◇◇◇◇

ELIZABETH VAGNONI ALSO believes narcissism is to blame for many of the family estrangements she's heard about, including her own. But she sees it not so much as a problem affecting individuals as a generational failing, a level of immaturity on the part of Gen-Xers and millennials. A few years ago she did a non-scientific survey of the several thousand visitors to her website and found that most of the families represented there were upper-middle-class, earning $100,000 a year or more, and well educated. From this she inferred that these families had provided their children with lots of material things, as she had for her sons. She told me a long story about giving her then-sixteen-year-old an old Ford Maverick to drive, and how livid he was at not getting a convertible like the other kids in their suburb. "I did well but not that well," she says. "This may be why they don't ever speak to me again."

Vagnoni is joking, sort of. Or maybe not. She hears from a lot of estranged parents who say their children don't appreciate or respect the material things they've been given. She told me:

As a parent I can stand to look at myself in the mirror and know I did everything from a position of love. I put myself in financial positions to do everything I could to make sure those boys had everything they wanted, everything they deserved. . . . I see a lot of people find the same frustration. There appears to be a lack of respect or lack of appreciation for those things.

Vagnoni is making two distinct points here: 1) that the financial support she's given her sons demonstrates her love for them; and 2) that her sons, and other adult children, take that support for granted, fail to appreciate it, and disrespect it when they initiate an estrangement.

I'm sympathetic, to a point; I can imagine how galling and hurtful and upsetting it is to be rejected by a child for whom you've sacrificed plenty of money and time. But the problem with looking at estrangement through this lens is that it sets up the parent-child relationship as transactional: *I will support and love you as long as you do what I want and be who I want you to be.* It creates a conditional relationship, which is problematic on many levels and is a common precursor of later estrangement.

In reality, parents make a commitment to support and love a child long before they know anything about that child. To quote every kid ever, they didn't ask to be born; that was a choice determined by parents. To make the financial argument is to suggest that whatever investment of time and money a parent makes in a child demands a direct return in the form of gratitude, affection, respect, and time. There's nothing wrong with a parent hoping for these things; don't we all? But that's different from believing that love is a quid pro quo for the privilege of being raised, that children owe their parents a relationship in exchange for the food, shelter, and other expenses a parent has incurred.

In this culture, as in many others, money tends to stand in for other things that are important to us—love, attention, approval, power, entitlement. Conversations about money are rarely only about dollars and cents. They are fraught with some of the most powerful emotions we feel toward one another, but they use a different vocabulary, one that may be easier for some people than the language of feelings. So it's not surprising that money comes up often in estrangement narratives.

"We've put an awful lot of emphasis on our children and how they feel and are they happy," says Vagnoni. "Everybody is so politically correct or everybody is so afraid of making their children unhappy that they are in effect creating this walk-on-eggshells [situation] because the second our children get upset then it's bad." Her argument—a common one among estranged parents—seems to be that kids today are spoiled. They don't respect their parents or appreciate what their parents give them. And also, parents give them too many things, which makes them even more spoiled and selfish. As one parent wrote on a forum, "I bought into the whole 'Self Esteem' nonsense and over did it [sic] with making them feel good about themselves, believe me they do, so much so that they think they are too good for us!" I can understand the hurt and frustration behind this comment. But I also have a *lot* of empathy for this person's children. What parent would begrudge a child self-esteem? Maybe a parent who doesn't know the difference between self-esteem and arrogance. Or one whose relationship is based on that child's lack of self-esteem.

Estranged parents often complain that their children don't respect them as much as they should. Vagnoni cites the work of Ron Taffel, a clinical psychologist whose most recent book is *Childhood Unbound: The Powerful New Parenting Approach that Gives Our Children the Authority, Love, and Listening They Need to Thrive.* According to Vagnoni, Taffel describes a culture shift where children now rely less on their parents for approval than they do on peers. "With the beginning of Facebook suddenly you've got 1200 friends who will tell you how great you look rather than having your parents have to talk to you about what you did or what you look like," says Vagnoni. "They find outside forces to get approval. Therefore what the parents think becomes less important."

I don't know. I remember feeling exactly the same way as a teenager in the 1970s, way before social media or the internet or email or cell phones. Teens are *supposed* to look to friends and peers for validation and acceptance and approval. The way they do it now may be different than it was a generation ago, but it's the same basic phenomenon. And it doesn't mean they no longer need their parents' support and input. On the contrary.

Vagnoni says many of the estranged parents she hears from have made the mistake of being too close to their children, that they've tried to be friends rather than parents, and she believes one result is that they never gave their children a chance to mature into full adults. "The reconciliations we've had on our website are typically an adult child who had some sort of trauma of their own with regard to their children, had some sort of wakeup in terms of maturity and understanding being a parent, and they then were able to forge some sort of relationship with their parent," she explains. "Maybe it's not as close, but it's not like 'You need to be banished to hell and never be seen or heard from again.' And it usually comes when the adult child grows up."

A slightly different tack on the spoiled-children argument, which I've seen in online forums, is the "Honor thy father and mother no matter what" argument, and it's reflected in this comment from an estranged parent:

Things have changed so much in the past 30 years. It used to be that we grew up with very strict/abusive parents, who required we work inside the house and outside the house and contribute money to the family needs. We always loved our parents no matter how much we got abused/ slapped/ beaten/grounded. We kept in touch with our parents after we became adults.

In other words, we dealt with it and they should have to too. They don't deserve better than we got. They should be grateful for anything we give them. And they don't have the right to question us, because we're the parents.

A wishful-thinking version of this theme is highlighted by this post: "Underneath the separation, sometimes I see a sort of fear of being too attached to us. (What will happen when Mom is gone, when I love her so much? Maybe I should separate myself now!)" Maybe such thinking explains this meme, which often pops up on forums for estranged parents:

My promise to my children as long as I live. I am your Parent first, your friend second. I will stalk you, flip out on you, lecture you, drive you insane, be your worst nightmare and hunt you down like a bloodhound when needed because I LOVE YOU. When you understand that I will know you are a responsible adult. You will NEVER find someone who loves, prays, cares, and worries about you more that [*sic*] I do!! If you don't hate me once in your life I am not doing my job properly.

This rant sounds more like threats from an abuser than promises to a beloved and vulnerable child. It equates love with stalking and requires the child to be always and permanently available and vulnerable to the parent. It suggests that the child is somehow unlovable, since no one else in the world can or will ever love her as much as the parent does. It makes the hairs on the back of my neck stand up in both fear and recognition. I can imagine my mother saying these words and meaning them. Clearly many other parents say them and mean them, too.

All of which leads me to wonder: don't parents *want* better lives for their children than they had themselves? As hard as I try, I frankly can't imagine where the "things have changed" parent was coming from. This argument gets to the central question not just in estrangements but in any relationship, especially in families: what do we owe one another? If I as a parent expect lifelong fealty and unquestioning devotion from my children, and that's not how they see it—yeah, we're going to run into conflicts.

Another forum commenter laid out her expectations in this post:

Parents owe their children a roof over their head, food on the table and clothes on their back for the simple reason it was the parents who chose to bring them into the world. They also owe the children schooling on proper behavior and what to expect when they enter the REAL world as adults. After that and when the children are adults they are owed NOTHING and in fact it is the children who then become responsible TO the parents. By that I mean they must never behave in a way which either embarrasses or in any way shows disrespect towards the parent(s). Children who have parents which have done what is expected and whose children nonetheless are ungrateful, nasty, demanding and otherwise a huge pain in the ass should be summarily and permanently rejected.

I have a feeling this attitude wasn't very effective. Just a hunch.

A common post on estranged-parent forums might go something like this: *I wasn't a perfect parent but I did the best I could. I made some mistakes but I'm not bad. I'm not a bad person.* And I get it. People on both sides of an estrangement want reassurance that they're not "bad," that they're lovable and worthy of respect. That they're good people. So maybe parents like Vagnoni, who believe their children estranged themselves casually, on a whim, from spite or laziness, are acting in self-defense. Maybe they're protecting themselves from the possibility that something in their own behavior has contributed to the problem. Maybe that would be way too threatening. So if a child can't be bothered to keep up a relationship with a parent, that's the child's problem, not the parent's. If someone else cuts them off it can't be a judgment on anything they've done or on who they are.

"People have gotten permission that it's OK to never ever speak to your parents again," says Vagnoni. "You don't respond, you don't have to write them back, you don't have to do anything." I think what she's expressing is a variation on the "Honor thy mother and father" theme, which frames filial connection as a responsibility, as the default position, where anything less than that violates the social contract. She's right, actually, because more of us *are* questioning that social contract now. And maybe that's progress, a step forward, a liberation for anyone who's ever felt bruised or diminished by family obligations.

Kate, a thirty-eight-year-old artist in Philadelphia, has been officially estranged from her parents for several years, though their relationship was always difficult. She grew up feeling like she was at war with her father, and her mother usually deferred to her husband. When her father found her blog, where Kate had described—anonymously, without naming him—how he had forced her to diet starting when she was seven years old, and how much that had hurt her both physically and emotionally, he insisted that it was a lie and demanded she take it down. She told him he had made her feel so bad about her weight as a kid that she'd legitimately wanted to kill herself; his response was that she was a liar and she had to take down the post. She refused, and that was the last time she spoke to either of her parents. "People are sort of baffled by it," she says now. "It's not like I'm a teenager and I slammed the door. My best friend thought my mother would try to make it right with me, but I knew that wasn't going to happen. They've never even *tried* to make contact with me again."

Like most people in her position, Kate says the estrangement has both pros and cons. She feels stronger and healthier without her parents and sister in her life. She gets how people might find this threatening; what if *their* child gets mad and never talks to them again? But the way she sees it, sharing DNA doesn't obligate people to put up with one another. "We earn our relationships by the way we treat each other every day," she says.

On the downside, it's hard and sometimes socially awkward to be disconnected from every single person in your family of origin. Having to tell new acquaintances that she doesn't speak to her family makes Kate feel as if she's outside the human tribe somehow. Even before the estrangement she never liked holidays, which tended to bring out the worst in her family, and she finds it both ironic and a little heartbreaking that days like Christmas and Mother's Day now bring on waves of grief. They force her to give up on the fantasy that her family will ever be like other "normal" families.

One thing Kate is very clear about is that so-called casual estrangements are rare, if they exist at all. Even when estrangement makes your life better, it's still an incredibly difficult decision. She says adult children don't choose it just because they didn't get a candy bar one day when they were twelve, or new clothes, or a car; assuming that people walk away from parents for such venal or superficial reasons underestimates how painful estrangement can be. "Everyone I have talked to who has gone no-contact with their parents, there are *severe* problems there," she says. "It's not something people do lightly."

What little research there is on the subject suggests that Kate is right, that adult children (because that's mostly who's doing the estranging) don't just walk away from their families of origin on a whim. The people I've interviewed and read about have spent years, even decades on the estrangement merry-go-round. They've tried to repair or at least tolerate their family bonds over and over and over, and they've often blamed themselves when things don't work out. They've put themselves and their adult families through drama and trauma, and in the end they decided—right or wrong, true or false—that estrangement was the only way to save their own well-being, marriage, sanity. The only way *for them.*

I respect those decisions, just as I respect the hurt and anger of those on the receiving end. I don't remember how many times my husband advised me to just ignore my mother's words, to let them wash over me and evaporate. They were just words, he said; they couldn't hurt me unless I let them in. It was excellent advice. I just never found a way to achieve that state of Zen-like detachment.

◇◇◇◇◇

I DON'T KNOW if my mother ever joined one of those forums for grieving parents, though my guess is that she did. And if so, I imagine that she, like many other parents, poured her heart out, described the depression and grief she felt over our fractured relationship. I imagine her writing that she didn't know why we were estranged, that she hadn't done anything so terrible, that I'd been fed and clothed and loved, even pampered, and that my coldness to her now was an enduring wound, a terrible mystery. That she'd tried and tried over the years, had begged me to open my heart. That she didn't understand, when she loved me so much, why I refused to love her back, why I was so willfully cold and selfish and withholding.

Whether she wrote about it online or not, I'm sure she genuinely believed all of these things. I'm sure she believed that on the spectrum of parenting she and my father had done an excellent job, and that any mistakes they'd made were negligible, certainly no reason for my walking away. I wondered that myself sometimes. One of my interview subjects told me his parents were crappy parents 90 percent of the time and good parents the other 10 percent. He wondered how that all shook out. Does the 10 percent of good parenting count for more than the 90 percent of bad parenting? What if the percentages were 75 percent crappy and 25 percent good? What if it was 50/50? In other words, at what point do the crappy parts outweigh the good ones, or vice versa? I think of Elizabeth Vagnoni, who seems to feel that in most cases, certainly in her case, the good eclipses the bad. That the only justification for cutting off close family members is "serious" physical and/or sexual abuse. But who gets to say what's serious and what isn't? Whose perspective counts in this emotional equation and whose does not?

I think everyone who estranges from one or both parents wonders about this. I know I still do. Like the parents I've encountered online, my mother believed that despite whatever parenting "mistakes" she'd made, I still owed her a relationship. No matter what she said or wrote or did I was required to not just hear it but be grateful for it. In the years after I left home her communications with me took on a predictable pattern. After a period when we were in contact, with varying results, she would write me an "honest" letter in which she would "lay it on the line" or "set me straight," telling me some "hard truths" in the hope of inspiring "an aha moment." Those truths generally consisted of her insights into my personality and behavior, insights only she was brave enough and perceptive enough to offer because, as she often told me, *The relationship between a mother and daughter is very special* and because *Everyone else is afraid to confront you but I'm not.*

After getting one of these confrontational letters I'd be stunned into anxious, self-loathing silence. I'd stop sleeping. I'd eat too much. I'd cry all the time. I learned early not to respond, that nothing I said or wrote made things better. After a week or so, my mother would follow up her letter grenade with a cheerful note or email professing her love, punctuated with exclamation marks, hearts, and underlines. When I once again failed to respond she would send another angry letter, which would now reference my failure to write back and my "withholding nature," and the cycle would begin again.

This back and forth was actually a recognizable stage in a familiar pattern. As children my sister and I came to understand the reliable sine curve of our mother's moods: the buildup of pressure, the dangerous explosion, the cooling off, the inevitable rise toward distress once again. We learned to diagnose her emotional state from subtle telltales—a certain sidelong look, an impatient clearing of her throat, the barest note of friction in her voice—and to predict with near-perfect accuracy the very moment she would erupt, scorching us with her incandescent rage. And once she did, the scene could go on for hours.

As an adult I felt my mother's wrath more often on the page than in person because I rarely put myself into the room with her. We exchanged a flurry of letters around the time my older daughter turned one. Having a child, especially a daughter, was wonderfully clarifying. My daughter was not going to endure the same anxiety and despair and rage I did if I could help it, and she wasn't going to be exposed to my mother's explosions and criticisms. I spent weeks writing and rewriting a long letter in which I tried to articulate some of the issues in our relationship. I was careful to use "I" statements, describing my own feelings of depression and anxiety after our bruising encounters rather than accusing my mother. I explained that while I loved her, our interactions caused me a lot of pain, and that I thought setting some boundaries would help us begin to repair our relationship so that, in time, we could go on to something better and more meaningful. I wrote,

> I won't stand still and be screamed at, yelled at, cried at, or otherwise emotionally vented at in the future. If we're on the phone I will hang up. If we're together I will leave until things have cooled down and a calmer discussion is possible. You've accused me, over the years, of being the kind of person who walks away from confrontation. That has been my instinct with you, and it's been a good one. Those emotional outbursts not only do not resolve anything, they are very damaging. If we can't talk calmly about something, I would rather not talk.

I knew hearing this would be hard for my mother, who thought the only measure of love that counted was drama, who believed in what one of my therapists once called the heightened currency of emotion. To her, the tears and rage and grief reflected the depth and authenticity of her feelings, and only by provoking the same from me could she feel reassured. I told her again that I loved her and that I hoped she could both hear my honest feelings and share hers with me. I wrote that I wanted us to find a vocabulary of mutual respect. I was thirty-two years old when I wrote this letter, conscious of the fact that I hadn't always been tactful or kind to my mother in the past. I wanted to do better. I wanted us to do better.

The letter she sent me in response was not the letter I was hoping for. It ended with these lines:

> I certainly do not have the emotional stamina at this time to put up with your adolescent nonsense. I do not want to hear from you unless it is to hear your apology—it is very long overdue. The stories that you tell yourself and others are just stories. I have tried to work things out with love, but you turn it all into garbage. Your attitude toward me stinks! So, my daughter, you have been bullying people for years—I feel very sorry for you.

This time there was no cheerful follow-up note, and I was glad to be spared the usual cognitive dissonance.

I am amazed, now, looking back through our correspondence, at how many times this cycle repeated between us, how many bitter and ultimately ineffective letters and emails flew back and forth. And, also, how many times I tried and failed to explain what I saw as the root of our difficulties. In a letter sent four years later, after another round of dramatic messages, I wrote to my mother:

> What's wrong between us has little to do with the past and everything to do with the present, with the shape and content and tone of our interactions right now, in the present.

There isn't some mystery "thing" that I'm refusing to tell you about that's causing problems; it's the way we interact now, as adults. . . . If I don't call you when you think I should or send a card when you want me to, that has to be OK. And it's also OK for you to tell me you're disappointed or angry or upset. But it can't be a kind of condition of the relationship. I need time to sort out my emotional reactions. I don't want to feel like I'm always racing to meet some kind of reaction deadline you set.

Over the following decade there were other volleys of equally bitter letters and emails, but we saw each other in person only once a year or so, usually at large family gatherings.

Sometime in my late forties, in a phone call when I was having a rare hopeful moment about our tangled connection, she asked me for the thousandth time what the source of our estrangement was and I reminded her of an interaction that still haunts me, which took place on the night before my grandmother's funeral. The family had gathered at my parents' house to sit *shiva*, the ritual week of mourning in the Jewish tradition. The morning I heard the news of my grandmother's death I'd taken the first bus from New York City, desperate to cry with other people who'd loved her, to hug my grandfather. My grandmother's death was the first real loss I'd experienced. She'd been the lynchpin of the family and her absence felt surreal and unnatural.

Through the long afternoon the family ate and laughed and mourned. We told every story about my grandmother we could think of: How she could knit any sweater without a pattern. How she could beat anyone at double solitaire and canasta and bridge. The look she gave you if you were part of the family, a look glowing with love and belief in you. The way she would switch seamlessly into Yiddish when she was annoyed with my grandfather. How she used to cook extra chicken wings for me, my favorites, and so for the longest time I thought chickens came with four wings, not two.

After dinner, when the odd mania of the day was beginning to wear off, I went down to the basement to look for old photographs, which my sister and I would use to make a photo board for the funeral. The very first picture I found—an impossibly young version of my grandmother holding infant me—sent me to my knees on the concrete floor. When my mother appeared at the top of the basement stairs, I thought she'd come to comfort me. She sat down next to me, put her arm around my shaking shoulders, and whispered, "Your grandmother's not here to hold your hand anymore." Then she got up and went back upstairs, closing the basement door behind her.

Later, after most of the aunts and uncles and cousins had gone home for the night, she had a truly memorable blow-up. My sister and I sat on the screened back porch, exhausted. Our mother, having repeatedly refused our help with cleanup, stormed around the house, banging plates and silverware in the kitchen, shooing us out of the way when we tried to pitch in. I knew what was coming and my sister did too, and it wasn't long until our mother threw open the screen door to the porch and pointed at me. "Everyone else gets your affection!" she shouted. "All I ever get is your tears and grief. I never get your smiles and hugs and laughter!"

My sister and I looked at each other. We both knew anything I said would make things worse, so my sister tried. "Mom, this isn't the time," she began, but there was no stopping an eruption in process.

"She took you away from me," my mother yelled. "It was always your grandmother this and your grandmother that. I was never enough for you! Well, now she's dead, and you're going to *have* to deal with me."

I felt myself lift right out of my body and float up toward the ceiling, hovering over the brown pleather couch where my sister and I sat. "Mom, come on," I heard my sister say. "We both loved our grandmother. She paid attention to us. What's wrong with that?"

"Your sister got plenty of attention at home. Don't give me that," hissed my mother. I felt only a vague curiosity about the ceiling. It was a wonderfully calming shade of white, softened with layers of dust; how come I'd never floated up here before? I would have to remember this.

Years later on the phone I didn't tell my mother that part, just the words seared into my otherwise leaky memory, sealed into writing in my journal. She claimed none of it had ever happened, that I wasn't even at the house that night. *I would never have said such a thing,* my mother insisted. If I didn't have the written record in front of me I would have believed her, no question; she seemed so sure. But I'd written it all down right after it happened. Was I delusional? Was she telling a bald-faced lie, or did she really believe her version of history?

I didn't bring any of this up, though, because by the time my mother and I had this phone conversation the story had passed, like so many others, into the realm of legend. There was no way to bridge the gap between our versions of reality, let alone between us. Every word I spoke entered the air lock between us and emerged on the other side vacuumed of meaning. *Why are you so stuck on the past? On a few things that happened a long time ago?* she'd say. Or *That's not what happened at all.* She was the tragically misunderstood heroine, rejected and bewildered, offering up her tender heart in innocence. I was the witch who took that heart, sat down at the table, and devoured its quivering chambers raw.

And if that's what my mother believed—my mother, the person who was supposed to love me best in the world—how could I possibly be right? When I woke up in the middle of the night crying, my husband told me, "You are a loving and lovable person and your mother is wrong." But I couldn't make myself believe it. It was like faith in a deity; you either believed or not. You couldn't will yourself to feel something you didn't. And anyway, as soon as I tried to think about my relationship with her my brain filled with static, like a computer caught in the endless loop of a logic error. The more my mother insisted on her version of our narrative, the more I questioned not just my feelings but also my memories of some of the most important things that had happened to me. If I felt one way and my mother felt another I always believed my feelings were wrong, mistaken, misguided. If we remembered a situation or event or conversation differently, I assumed she was right.

And if, that day on the phone with my mother, when I tried again to explain how I felt and what I wanted to change between us—if I *had* somehow conjured just the right alchemical combination of words, and if she'd understood, and if somehow she'd changed into the mother I longed for—I wonder how my life now might be different. Even as I write these words I know how ridiculous they sound. If, if, if. Things unrolled the way they did between us not because of some accidents of time and place and logistics but because of who we were on a deep and fundamental level.

We were, in psychological parlance, a bad fit, a mismatched mother-daughter pair. She seemed to resent what she saw as my emotional strength, my confidence in my thoughts and opinions.

She seemed to want me to be needier. Maybe she would have done better with a daughter who was more like her: pretty, popular, practical-minded, not bookish or introverted. She *did* do better with my sister, who as a toddler and child showed her need for love and attention and interaction in ways I never could.

Psychologists talk about state and trait; states are essentially moods, emotions that come and go and change over time. Traits are more or less permanent parts of personality, though they can evolve. Shyness, for example, is a trait, while anger and depression are considered states. Personality traits emerge at birth and stay relatively stable over a lifetime. They're innate rather than learned, and therein lies the problem for some families. My mother, who was extroverted and sociable, couldn't connect with a daughter who was introverted and philosophical. And vice versa.

The writer Andrew Solomon spent years investigating what happens when parents and children don't fit together well. In his book *Far From the Tree: Parents, Children, and the Search for Identity*, he writes about how families can either shatter or coalesce when faced with serious differences between parents and offspring. He describes children with "horizontal identities," who differ in some meaningful way from their parents; for instance, children who are deaf but whose parents can hear, or children with schizophrenia, autism, dwarfism, or musical genius, or gay kids born to straight parents. Children with "vertical identities," on the other hand, share one or more important characteristics with parents: an athletic child whose parents are also athletic, for example. "Vertical identities are usually respected; horizontal identities are often treated as flaws," writes Solomon.

The families he describes might all have qualified as unhappy at times, especially when their kids' differences were first revealed.

But nearly all of them, even the mothers whose children were born of rape, found ways to love their "different" children and integrate them into the family narrative.

I've often wondered what my mother felt when she looked at me, what echo or loss or trauma or frustration she saw in my face. She grew up poor, the youngest of three children raised by a single mother. Her mother had divorced her father, a brilliant man who gambled compulsively, who spoke eight languages but was unable to keep a job. My mother had had to go to work right after high school and she'd worked nonstop ever since. Maybe her constant critiques (*You know what your problem is? You don't watch enough TV*), which seemed absurd and inexplicable to me, were designed to cover her own longing for a life beyond wife, mother, secretary.

Parents do feel ambivalent about children; they are our legacy, our life's work, our joy and our travail. When we look at a spiky, hygiene-challenged adolescent we can't help seeing the sweet-smelling baby who once loved us best. The child, the teen, the young adult is a walking palimpsest to her parents, evoking a past she herself can never remember. Children are also conflicted, of course. Even at the moment they scream "I hate you!" at their parents they hold a number of clear and undeniable feelings toward them: Love. Need. The longing for approval. The wish to stay small and helpless and protected. No wonder one of the most striking qualities of even ordinary parent-child relationships is ambivalence.[2]

So, yes, in a way I can understand what my mother might have been feeling—might have been, because we never discussed it. But that changed nothing. Over time our estrangement deepened rather than healed, a wound that never scarred, though for years I continued to believe that if only I could find exactly the right combination of words in exactly the right order my mother would turn into the loving parent I had once wanted. It occurs to me now that maybe this is why I write. In some way everything I create, including this book—especially this book— is meant for her.

Chapter Four

THE MYTH OF THE
WORST-CASE SCENARIO

*My parents and siblings were used to teasing and
verbally abusing me and I couldn't articulate as a
kid that it was more than regular sibling teasing. It
was full-blown verbal abuse and name-calling. They
didn't see anything wrong. They just saw the crazy
ugly sister who my mother was desperately trying to
help. That's what I saw myself as too.*

—**MARY**, thirty-four

In this culture family bonds are considered so powerful, so
defining, so non-voluntary that we believe it must take extraordinary levels of dysfunction and pain before we can
even begin to think about breaking them. We don't choose our
families, and the bar for un-choosing them is vertiginously high.
Many people spend years in a back-and-forth dance of estrangement and reconciliation before stepping away for good because

they feel they haven't earned the right to walk away. They haven't suffered enough to justify estrangement.

One of the participants in the Stand Alone survey articulated the issue well:

> If I had been seriously physically or sexually abused by my family, I feel people would be more accepting of the estrangement. But emotional abuse and neglect is more ambiguous. I feel that in the opinion of others, this is not a valid reason to cut contact with parents.

For years I was reluctant to think of what my mother did as abuse because it didn't match the afterschool-special definition. It certainly didn't seem bad enough to justify my rage and coldness toward her. Humans are social creatures, and social comparison is a key part of the way we create our identities. It's a survival skill, though it doesn't always serve us well. When I tried to match my family to the stereotype of an abusive family—broken bones, cigarette burns, sexual abuse, imprisonment, starvation—there was literally no comparison. None of those things ever took place at my house; therefore I had no reason to walk away.

But a lot can happen between a mythical worst-case scenario on one hand and a happy family on the other (or a happy-enough family). For instance, the stereotype doesn't speak to emotional abuse, which is harder to define and recognize than physical abuse is, especially in the parent-child relationship, where the built-in power imbalance makes it easy for parents to cross the line. The scars it leaves are invisible to everyone but the child. And some of what we now consider emotional abuse and neglect might have been called good-enough parenting a generation ago. Few parents these days would leave an infant alone in a room for twelve hours or keep a toddler in a playpen all afternoon or let six-year-olds roam the neighborhood unsupervised. But in middle-class South Jersey (and many other places) in the 1960s and '70s, these were the parenting norms.

People who are the targets of emotional abuse often have trouble explaining exactly why it upsets them, in part because one common response from abusers is "I was only joking!"—a response designed to make the other person mistrust her own feelings. So maybe one way to think about identifying emotional abuse is in terms of how it feels to the person on the receiving end. That definition makes sense to me because it relies not on specific measures of cruelty (which are impossible to quantify anyway) but on validating someone's lived experience.

My mother was an expert at this kind of emotionally abusive gaslighting, and she didn't do it only to me. When my sister was a young adult, living at home between college semesters, she worked for a time at a Dunkin' Donuts. She developed a ritual of coming home after a late shift and eating a bowl of ice cream while she watched TV. One night my sister opened the freezer, took out what looked like a new gallon of ice cream, and lifted its lid. Inside the box, instead of ice cream, she found tightly packed garbage, along with a note that said *Gotcha!* Our mother insisted it was just a prank. But thirty-five years later, my sister still remembered the shame she felt that night.

This type of gaslighting can make you doubt memories as well as feelings. The night I graduated college, for instance, six of us drove to a fancy French restaurant to celebrate—my grandparents, parents, sister, and me. As we sat at the table I was thinking of how, in less than a week, I would borrow my grandfather's beat-up maroon Malibu and deliver myself to a Salvation Army women's residence in Greenwich Village to start my adult life. I was thinking about the eighty-mile drive into the city (I was a nervous and inexperienced driver), about hauling my typewriter, books, and clothes up five narrow flights of stairs to the tiny room I would inhabit, about the job I would start (at an ad agency, because that was the only one I could get, though I still hoped for something more meaningful).

Across the table my mother said my name and I blinked. She wasn't talking to me but about me, to the table at large. "I found birth control pills in her purse when she was fourteen!" she was telling my grandparents. "I mean really." She delivered her words lightly, not looking at me.

I sat at the table in a kind of shock. My mother's words beat their way down my spine, tiny hammers on bone. *She was fourteen! Fourteen!* My brain spun and fizzed. Was that what had happened? The way I remembered it, my favorite Saturday night activity at fourteen was playing double solitaire with my grandmother. I barely had breasts, had never been on a date, and had little interest in boys. I could have sworn I was sixteen the winter I lost my virginity with my boyfriend, on the fake leather backseat of his father's car in the empty synagogue parking lot. And it was midsummer, a few months later, when I came home and found my purse spilled open on the living room floor, my mother on the couch, bare legs curled under her, eyes swollen, surrounded by a blizzard of crumpled tissues. I had dropped out of high school and was heading to college in a few weeks, as terrified to go as I was sure I had to leave. When my mother saw me she burst into tears and pointed toward the telltale dial-shaped packet on the floor.

"How could you?" she wailed.

"We went to Planned Parenthood and got them," I said. "We were being responsible."

"You lied to me!"

"I never lied. Would you rather I got pregnant?"

"How could you do this to me?"

"This isn't about you," I said. "Anyway, you went through my purse! You had no right!"

"I had every right," said my mother. "Everything in this house belongs to me."

I knew what my mother wanted: for me to fall to my knees and apologize, not just for the birth control pills but for leaving home and for not being able to fill the hole inside her and for the thousands of other transgressions I'd committed over the years. She wanted me to apologize for who I was, which was not who she wanted me to be. She wanted me to stay home, go to secretarial school instead of college, give up writing, marry a high-earning Jewish boy, live close. She wanted me to deny myself before I even knew exactly who I was. If she thought I regretted wanting a different life she would pull me into her lap and rock me, weep herself hoarse. She would forgive me.

But I didn't regret it. I didn't want her forgiveness and I was immune to her tears, having been inoculated regularly through-out my childhood. In that moment in the living room, standing before my furious weeping mother, I felt no remorse, just the cer-tainty that if I stayed I would die. I turned and left as she shouted at me to come back. I kept going.

Four years later, at the restaurant table, my mother leaned back in her chair, all four feet eleven inches of her. Her hair was done, her nails polished; her hands, always prettier and better tended than mine, sparkled with the opal and diamond rings my father had given her. She seemed utterly serene. She seemed *right.* I wondered if I could have gotten my own history wrong. I'd studied psychology; I knew how easily memories could be manip-ulated, deliberately or not, changed by the very process of calling them back from wherever they'd receded to. My own memories were fuzzy, dislocated in time, riddled with holes, like letters from a battlefield, full of blank spots where someone had censored the details. Maybe my mother was right. She was, after all, as she reminded me often, the mother, the authority, the boss. Maybe on that summer night I *had* been fourteen, precocious in a way that wasn't a virtue.

The thought came first as a relief. I *wanted* to reconcile our dissonant versions. I wanted to believe I was wrong so my mother could be right. On a practical level, my life—hell, everyone's lives—would be much easier if I didn't challenge her. Challenges led to explosions, as I well knew. On an emotional level I couldn't understand why she would tell this story if it wasn't true. Or rather I didn't want to understand, didn't want to think about why a mother would tell a lie like this about her daughter. Was she proud of me for being sexually precocious? Envious? Vengeful? Worried?

But I couldn't *not* see the inconsistencies in my mother's story. In her timeline, I'd lost my virginity during my freshman year of high school, only a month after we moved to the town where she lived now. But I knew that my boyfriend and I had spent nearly a year together before deciding to have sex. And I knew I hadn't met him until we moved. It was simply not possible that I was fourteen when I began having sex. I was sure of it. All I had to do was lean across the table and say so. Set the record straight. Speak truth to the power that radiated from my mother like ultraviolet light, invisible but dangerous.

If I'd been sitting across from, say, Richard Nixon or Queen Elizabeth, I would have had no trouble speaking up. But at that dinner, which was supposed to celebrate my accomplishments and my future, I couldn't challenge my mother any more than I could self-induce a seizure. Whether she really believed her daughter had been a sexually precocious fourteen-year-old or she was knowingly changing the story, her disregard for me was made abundantly clear. To speak now would be to draw attention to the fact that my mother was my adversary. In any case, the damage was done. The table went silent. My grandmother's smile faded. I sat mute, shame staining my face, fists in my lap. The only person who looked happy was my mother, whose lips curved in a smile, whose foot tap-tapped under the table, whose lipstick left a glowing kiss-shaped stain on the glass in front of her.

Even though I know what my mother was doing (though I still don't know why), her gaslighting haunts me. My first instinct always has been to discount my own observations, to assume I'm misremembering. To distrust my memories and dishonor my feelings. To gaslight myself, in a way. I can't think of a more potent example of emotional abuse than this: to teach a child that she cannot trust herself. While children can certainly hurt parents in all kinds of ways, this isn't one of them. Our parents' lessons, on the other hand—whether of violence or tenderness, respect or betrayal—tend to stay with us for the rest of our lives. Which is why, writing about this so many years later, I get a familiar fuzzy, confused feeling in my head and feel the irresistible urge to lie down.

So maybe it's impossible to judge from the outside whether someone is being emotionally abused. Mikaela, forty, of Portland, Oregon, was at lunch in a restaurant with her brothers and step-mother when her father started yelling at her. It's tempting to read an account like this and think, *Big deal—her father yelled at her. So what?* And yes, if every parent who yelled at a grown child was then cut off, every family might wind up estranged. The fact that they don't tells you something about what it takes to break apart a family. The fact that they don't speaks for itself.

Mikaela was three years old the first time she remembers trying to intervene between her parents, asking her father to please stop hitting her mother. Around the same time, she told him she didn't want to play the "bathroom game" anymore, the one where they were both naked in the bathroom hugging. As she got older the household dysfunction and violence escalated. Her father never visibly bruised her or broke a bone, but he would pin her to the wall or hold her down on a couch and scream into her face. The last time he did that she was fifteen, and she promised him if he ever touched her again she'd call Child Protective Services. The emotional abuse continued, though, as she struggled through her twenties. Her father would belittle her in public, try to manipulate her with money, assert his power over her. Mikaela avoided him when she could but still occasionally saw him in group settings. She wanted to hold on to a sense of family as much as she could.

So the yelling might not have looked like a big deal, and it certainly wasn't new. But this time Mikaela's reaction was different. "I had this moment where I kind of zoomed out, kind of came out of my body, and I saw this happening from above," she says. "I looked at myself and realized I had a choice about whether I was going to take this. And I was like, Holy shit!" She stood up, said, "It's nice to see you, Dad," and left the restaurant. That afternoon, as she walked and walked, she realized that if she was ever going to feel OK in herself, if she was ever going to feel like a whole person, she had to sever their connection.

For Mikaela, every interaction with her father left her feeling beaten down, demeaned, and diminished, whether he intended that or not, whether his behavior "looked" like abuse or not, whether her reactions were considered inappropriate or not. That day at the restaurant, when she pushed back her chair and walked out, was the beginning of a process of healing for her. She hasn't spoken with her father since that afternoon, though she sent him a message when her mother died. She says she has no intention of reconnecting with him but not because she's angry; in fact, she says, choking up, she loves her father and feels empathy for him, despite his past abuse and despite the fact that she recently learned he'd been playing the same "bathroom game" with her niece. She has traumatic memories of him but she also has good ones. He taught her how to track animals. He taught her to love raptors and other birds; she never sees a red-tailed hawk without thinking of him. He gave her her first copy of the Communist Manifesto, which helped guide her on the path toward becoming a socialist. All of those things are still important to her, both for their own sake and because they came from him.

Mikaela's ability to hold such opposite feelings about her father at once—to feel both the pain of his abuse and her love for him—seems remarkable to me. I wish I could feel that way about my mother.

◇◇◇◇◇

WHETHER IT'S LABELED abuse or not, the kinds of family behaviors Mikaela and I and so many others experienced often go back a long way. The generational nature of child abuse has been well documented, especially sexual and physical abuse. Mikaela says her grandfather, her father's father, made her dad look like father of the year. "We're talking about multigenerational trauma here," she says. Child Protective Services around the United States find that about one percent of the children in the country are neglected or abused[1]—the so-called worst-case scenarios. That number, of course, captures only a fraction of the children who grow up with the kind of emotional or physical stress that can send shock waves through a life. And it doesn't account for the significant number of children who thrive as adults despite early traumas.[2] Researchers are beginning to study how for some people in some situations, early stress can actually promote resilience.[3]

Stress, of course, is different from abuse, and abuse can take many forms, from broken bones to broken spirits. There's no benchmark for what constitutes enough abuse or neglect to cause damage, and to some extent it's individual. The kind of trauma that infects one person's life in an ongoing way may be a bad but distant memory for another. We're only just beginning to understand why. For instance, a 2010 study looked at a group of Romanian children who spent their early years in horrifying institutional orphanages and were later adopted by English and American families. Their stunted bodies and pitifully blank expressions made news in the 1990s, and many developed profound emotional and psychological problems as kids and teens. Some of them, though, seemed to overcome those early deficiencies and go on to thrive, including a group with a specific genetic modification in the serotonin transporter gene, known as 5HTT.[4] When it comes to trauma, genetics matters, maybe as much as environment does.

We don't know how many children experience that degree of stress and abuse early on, or how many of them break off relationships with the families that damaged them. But that number is almost certainly low. Children who have been abused or neglected often defend the parents who hurt them; it's less painful, ultimately, than letting themselves know, *really* know and feel and take in a parent's flaws, a parent's rejection. They blame themselves rather than their parents so they can keep hoping that someday those parents will come through, will give them what they want and need. They hold on to the possibility of their parents' love because the alternative is so crushing. As one anonymous writer put it, "The act of separation from even the most abusive parent can feel like an amputation without anesthesia."[5]

The more indifferent or neglectful or abusive or just not especially warm parents are, the more children tend to cling to them, like the infant rhesus monkeys in psychologist Harry Harlow's infamous attachment experiments. Harlow removed the baby monkeys from their mothers and gave them, instead, inanimate mother-surrogates. In the 1950s, *Life* magazine ran a haunting series of photos of the baby monkeys clutching surreal-looking constructions of wood, wire, and cloth topped with creepily expressionless "faces."

One of the points of Harlow's decades-long experiments was to pinpoint the source of the attachment between babies and mother figures. Some experts thought it was food—that babies bond with mothers because they're the source of nourishment. So each monkey in the study got two "mothers," one made from wire with a rudimentary "face" and a system for delivering milk, the other made of wood covered with cloth and a more developed "face" (though still looking like the poster for a horror movie). Harlow and others theorized that the babies would prefer the wire figures because they offered food. But that's not what happened. The infant monkeys literally wrapped themselves around the softer figures, clinging to the cloth-covered wood. This demonstrated, according to Harlow, that the mother-baby attachment was based largely on the need for touch, even if the "mother" did not—could not—hug and comfort the baby in return. "The baby, human or monkey, if it is to survive, must clutch at more than a straw," wrote Harlow.[6]

The monkeys who got cloth mothers, it turned out, were the lucky ones. Harlow also used infant rhesus monkeys to study the effects of isolation, letting them bond with their real mothers for several months and then putting them into what he called the "pit of despair"—solitary confinement—for up to ten weeks. He explained that he was trying to re-create and explore the experience of depression on socialization and mother-child attachment. Unsurprisingly, the monkeys who emerged were profoundly and permanently damaged by their isolation, like some of the Romanian children who went on to develop social, emotional, cognitive, and physical problems that persisted long after adoption.

Clearly there are levels of early trauma, abuse, and neglect. The childhood experiences of the Romanian orphans, or Rwandan children during the genocide, or kids in foster care whose parents burned them or beat them or starved them or inflicted any one of a thousand psychological and physical tortures, are magnitudes of order more traumatic than what most of us experience.

Still, without loving and attached parents, or parent figures, we are all stunted and misshapen in ways that may never be reversible. And with parents who are sometimes cloth, a soft body to hang on to, and sometimes nothing more than wire and a scary face? That's when things get complicated. Behavioral psychologist B. F. Skinner was famous for unpacking the way positive and negative reinforcement shapes our actions and relationships. One of his most disturbing findings was that intermittent reinforcement lasts longer and is much more powerful than positive reinforcement. So, for instance, pigeons who are rewarded every time they peck will stop pecking quickly when the rewards dry up. But birds who are sometimes rewarded and sometimes not will keep pecking for hours, like people playing slot machines or cell-phone games, trying to elicit that elusive and therefore coveted payoff. There's nothing more powerful, behaviorally speaking, than occasionally getting what you want. There's always the hope, tiny though it may be, that the stars will align and you'll find it again.

So what is it, exactly, that I wanted, that Peg Streep and Sharon wanted, that all children want, really? In her best-known book, *The Drama of the Gifted Child: The Search for the True Self*, psychoanalyst Alice Miller describes it like this:

Every child has a legitimate need to be noticed, understood, taken seriously, and respected by his mother.* In the first weeks and months of life he needs to have the mother at his disposal, must be able to avail himself of her and be mirrored by her . . . provided that the mother is really looking at the unique, small, helpless being and not projecting her own expectations, fears, and plans for the child. In that case, the child would find not himself in his mother's face, but rather the mother's own projections. This child would remain without a mirror, and for the rest of his life would be seeking this mirror in vain.[7]

Miller is describing a child's primal need to be seen and understood. Even a young child can feel the difference between a parent who genuinely sees her for who she is and a parent who says and does all the right things but is blind to her essential self. Articulating that difference, though, can be nearly impossible, especially for a child or teenager.

And maybe when that doesn't happen, when we aren't seen in that way, that's a different kind of worst-case scenario. Alyssa, a twenty-eight-year-old marketer in Princeton, New Jersey, visited her dad every few weeks after her parents divorced. It was clear to her even at age seven that her father was disconnected from her in some fundamental way. He would feed her dinner and then spend the rest of the evening online, checking his eBay business. For years she tried to forge a more meaningful bond, sending him letters and emails telling him how she felt and what she hoped for. His response, time after time, was nothing.

---

* Miller uses the word *mother*, but in context it's clear she's referring to any primary caregiver.

As a young adult, Alyssa experienced chaotic disassociation, going through periods of total estrangement from her father and periods of trying to create some sort of limited relationship. Over time she came to realize that it's not that he hates or dislikes her; he just really hasn't been able to see her, in a way. "He wasn't a horrible person," she says. "He was acting based on what he knew and how he was raised. Nobody showed him love while he was growing up and that ended up being something, as a result, he made me feel too." She feels lucky that her mother, who pretty much raised her alone, was able to see her, know her, respond to her in a deeper way.

This isn't to say that parents must do everything perfectly for children to grow up feeling loved. You can make plenty of mistakes as a parent (as we all do) and still maintain a good relationship—if you can separate your own needs and wishes from your child's. That kind of love, which we call unconditional love, differs from empathy, compassion, and other forms of attachment. Researchers at the University of Montreal showed caregivers from a L'Arche community, which houses people with intellectual disabilities, images of people with such disabilities, and asked them to generate feelings of unconditional love. Using a functional magnetic resonance imaging (fMRI) scanner, they saw a distinct neural network light up. That network overlapped with patterns linked to romantic love and maternal love as well as with parts of the brain's reward system, suggesting, as they wrote, that "the rewarding nature of unconditional love facilitates the creation of strong emotional links between humans."[8]

Those links are an essential part of what it means to be human. We are all born needy and afraid, and it is through human connection and communion that we learn to walk in the world and to love ourselves and others. The simple act of looking into a baby's eyes, matching her expressions and sounds and gestures, passing back and forth between you an invisible current of delight and understanding—it's that process that gives us both the foundation we need to become fully alive and the ability to love and be loved.[9]

Parents who aren't able to do this, for whatever reason, raise children who feel their love is conditional. "Parents can say things and do things with respect to their children in which the implicit message is 'I will love you if you do and be what I want you to do and be, and I will not love you if you don't do what I want you to do and be what I want you to be,'" explains Dr. Edward L. Deci, a professor of psychology at the University of Rochester who has researched the subject. "It's a matter of loving them on the basis of their essentially carrying out the desires of their parents, and not loving them if they don't."

Conditional love must be earned by a child's doing things the way we want them done or performing up to our standards, according to Alfie Kohn, author of *Unconditional Parenting: Moving from Rewards and Punishments to Love and Reason* and other books about parents and children. He quotes a parenting expert who writes, "If I wish to take my child for a ride or even if I wish to hug and kiss her, I must first be certain that she has earned it."[10] This kind of conditional love is seen as a privilege, an economic transaction of sorts where good behavior is traded for the parent's love and approval. I can't even begin to understand the reasoning behind this parenting philosophy, but I do know it's ineffective. Kids know the difference between unconditional love and these kinds of transactions, even if they can't articulate it.

Unconditional love, on the other hand, doesn't hinge on how well children behave or how successful they are. It's given because of who a child is, not what she does. And, says Kohn, perception is a crucial part of the equation. "What counts is not just that we *believe* we love them unconditionally, but that *they feel* loved in that way," he writes.[11] Which makes sense, because love, like so many human emotions, can be defined only by the person experiencing it. What's love to you might not feel like love to me, and vice versa.

As Alice Miller notes, "The mother often loves her child passionately, but not in the way he needs to be loved."[12] As adults we come to understand that of course parents are human and of course they have their own problems, their likes and dislikes, struggles and longings. Your parents' unconditional love for you doesn't give you a free pass to act like an asshole or treat them like crap. But it does reassure you that you're loved for who you are rather than for what you do. That foundation makes it possible for us to grow and thrive and change.

Some people believe unconditional love is possible only between a parent and a young child, that the love between adults—even when one happens to be the parent of the other—is necessarily boundaried. I was once hounded at a party by a man who was intent on proving that I couldn't possibly love my grown daughters unconditionally. "What if they murdered someone?" he asked. "What if they tortured and *then* murdered someone? What if they took pleasure in that person's suffering and death?" These are, of course, unanswerable questions in the abstract, and I think they're part of a different conversation. In the real world, it's easier to identify conditional love than argue about what's unconditional.

Diane, forty-nine, works in the nonprofit world near Portland, Oregon. She's been estranged from her mother for fifteen years and says she had no idea what unconditional love meant until she became a parent herself. "Everything had a string attached," she remembers. "*Everything.* Nothing was done out of kindness. If we went to a store and she talked me into buying a shirt, she'd go home and add it to my bill. There was this running tab of owing my mom money my entire life."

Claire, forty-one, a stay-at-home mom in England, says her relationship with her mother has always been challenging. About ten years ago they fell out over the fact that Claire wanted to attend her stepsister's wedding, which her mother and stepfather weren't invited to. Claire wanted to go because she wanted more of a relationship with her stepsister. "I wanted to build bridges," she says. "I didn't want to have to toe a line for other people. I wanted to do the thing that felt right for me as an individual." Her mother told her she had to choose: go to the wedding or be part of the family. She couldn't do both. When Claire went to the wedding, her mother insisted on an apology, which Claire didn't feel inclined or required to offer. One of the most disturbing parts of their interaction for Claire was realizing that her mother would withhold love to get Claire to do something or as a punishment for something she'd already done. It opened her eyes to something she'd never quite articulated to herself before: her mother's supposedly unconditional love—that most celebrated and fundamental of emotions—actually wasn't. It could be predicated on what she did rather than who she was, and might be withdrawn whenever her mother was displeased with her. It was a devastating realization, and it changed their relationship permanently.

I think my mother truly believed she loved me unconditionally. She certainly expressed that many times. One of her favorite sayings was "The door is always open," and I think by that she meant she was always open to the possibility of reconciliation. What she didn't say, but what I heard loud and clear, was the unspoken half of that sentence: "The door is always open for you to approach me." It was my job to apologize, to bend to her will, to broach a reconciliation, and so the responsibility for our ongoing difficulties was mine. That perception was bolstered through the years by other interactions, most memorably a conversation I observed between my older daughter, who was then age seventeen, and my mother during a rare family get-together. "I know we don't know each other well because of extenuating circumstances," my mother said. "I'm really a very nice person, and I'd like you to get to know me better." My daughter murmured something and walked away, upset, feeling a burden had been dropped on her that had nothing to do with who she was. She was right.

Still, for the longest time I believed my mother's words rather than her actions. Over and over and over she told me how much she loved me and I thought it must be true because all parents love their children unconditionally, don't they? I thought the fact that I didn't *feel* loved, accepted for who I was, seen in that deep and fundamental way, meant that there was something wrong with my perceptions—something wrong with me, really. Any perceived lapses in my mother's love must be my fault, must come from my own basic brokenness, my unlovability.

That began to change when I became a parent myself. When my older daughter was still not sleeping through the night at nine months I asked my mother what kind of baby I'd been. Was I colicky, fretful, peaceful? Did I sleep through the night? "I don't know," my mother answered. "I put you in your crib and closed the door, and twelve hours later I opened it. I don't know what you did in between." I know this kind of hands-off parenting was common in the 1950s and '60s, and maybe my mother was advised by family and friends and experts to treat her children like this. But this story explains a lot to me. It tells me that my fears of being abandoned, my night terrors, my existential loneliness even as a young child did not come exclusively from within me. My feelings were grounded in experience, in a child's understanding of her environment. It occurred to me that though my mother insisted that she loved me unconditionally, her actual behavior didn't bear that out.

Another example: I brought that same daughter to visit my parents when she was not quite three months old. She was severely colicky, and only being held in a specific position kept her comfortable. My mother begged me to leave the baby with her and go take a nap, to let her take the role of doting grandmother, and eventually I agreed. I wanted to give her that pleasure. And I wanted my daughter to have the kind of grandmother I'd had. My mother had been so young, only twenty-three, when I was born; she was older now, more mature. Maybe she would be the kind of loving grandmother I wanted for my daughter. I put my daughter into her arms and climbed the stairs.

Almost immediately I heard my daughter start to howl, panicky cries that raised the hair along my arms. I lay on my childhood bed and waited for her cries to slow, to hear my mother singing to her, talking to her, comforting her. All I heard was the sound of my daughter sobbing. When I couldn't take it anymore I leaped off the bed, ran downstairs, and saw my daughter lying alone on her back in the middle of the living room floor, her face contorted and tear-stained, while my mother puttered in the kitchen, humming to herself. I snatched up my daughter. "I told you she needed to be held," I cried.

My mother turned to me, a wooden spoon in one hand, and laughed. She *laughed*. "This little girl's got to learn she can't get everything she wants," she said. I turned without a word and carried the baby upstairs, where she cried for a long time before finally falling into sleep. I didn't want to leave her alone and go down for dinner, so my sister offered to bring me a plate of food. But our mother said no, if I didn't come down to the table I could just go hungry. I left the next morning and never stayed at my parents' house again.

My mother's behavior didn't surprise me; I'd been experiencing scenes like this forever. But like Peg Streep, I could not, would not expose my daughter to my mother's blithe punishments. What had been just the way it was in our family, or my fault, suddenly felt like abuse when it was directed at my child. I could understand something of why my mother did what she did: her mother, who wasn't the warmest person in the world, raised three children alone during the Great Depression and World War II. My grandmother worked long hours to make ends meet and had neither the time nor the inclination to pay attention to my mother's feelings.

I got it then and I still get it now. I grew up knowing that my mother's love was always conditional and that I was always failing the test. I was determined that my daughters would not go through the same thing.

◇◇◇◇◇

SOMETIMES ESTRANGEMENT DOES happen in those worst-case-scenario families, the ones with documented abuses of one kind or another. But interestingly, the grown children from those families who do estrange themselves often say it wasn't the abuse itself that led to their decision to separate; it was how the family did (or more likely didn't) deal with the abuse and its aftermath. For Andrea, fifty, a registered nurse in Madison, Wisconsin, breaking off contact with her mother was a necessary component of healing from an objectively terrible childhood of neglect and abuse. The abuse came from her father, a violent alcoholic who spent time in jail. The neglect came from her mother, who failed to protect Andrea and her five siblings from their father and who left Andrea, the youngest, alone for days at a time when she traveled for her job.

In her twenties, Andrea started trying to come to terms with what had happened to her in childhood. But no one else in the family, not her brothers and sisters or her mother, would talk about it. Her mother refused even to acknowledge that the abuse had happened, that her father had been physically violent. More than twenty years ago, Andrea wrote to her mother asking her to go to therapy so they could talk about what had happened. She said that was the only way she could see going forward with their relationship. Her mother responded with the most painful kind of rejection a child can face: nothing at all. No letter, no email, no answer. Her silence was devastating, but it did make the situation absolutely clear. And once Andrea got over the sting of it she realized her life was better without her mother in it, without the dissonance of trying to pretend things were OK when they really, really weren't.

She hasn't seen her mother since, though for many years they lived only two miles apart. In the early days of their estrangement Andrea felt constantly anxious. "I felt scared of my secret, that I didn't have contact with my family, that people would think it was about me or something I did," she says. "Because we're taught to endure so much for the sake of family."

Indeed, we're taught to put up with all sorts of behavior from family that we wouldn't be expected to endure from other people. Andi, the physical therapist from New York City, says if her mother wasn't her mother, if they'd met at work, she would never have invited her mother into her life. "If anyone else had done to me what my parents had done to me I would not accept it," she says. "No one would accept it. They would be like, 'Oh my god, that's terrible, call the police.' But because it's your parents you're supposed to allow them. Because she's my mother I'm supposed to be making an exception, and that's really unfair."

No wonder many people find estrangement liberating. Victoria, a forty-four-year-old academic in Tucson, Arizona, is totally estranged from her parents, brother, and sister. She grew up in a white-picket-fence family: her father was the Sunday school superintendent, her mother was on the church council, and when Victoria was a child they seemed fabulously happy to the rest of the world. No one outside the fence saw that Victoria's father was sexually abusing her. Victoria is sure her mother knew. But no one ever talked about it, including Victoria.

She developed anorexia as a teen and was in and out of treatment for most of her adult life, even as she earned a Ph.D. and began a teaching career. Eventually she realized that if she didn't address the sexual abuse she would never recover. So six years ago she wrote her mother a letter laying out the details of what she remembered. Victoria thought her mother would be open to hearing it; after all, she'd found things her mother had written suggesting she knew about the abuse and had considered leaving her father. But she was wrong. In the one therapy session she and her parents went to together, it became painfully clear that neither parent would ever admit the abuse had happened, let alone deal with its fallout.

Victoria hoped she could salvage some kind of relationship with her mother while cutting off contact with her father, but her mother said, *We're a team, we're partners in everything we do, I'm not going to have a relationship with you alone.* So Victoria severed her connection with the whole family. It was the only way she could maintain her sanity and her health.

The relief was sharp and immediate. It was as if she'd been under a cloak of silence all those years that now had been lifted. "The freedom that goes along with speaking is something I completely underestimated," she says. She'd known for a long time that something was holding her back, keeping her sick and afraid, but she had no idea how deeply constrained she'd been. For the first time she could talk about the abuse and her feelings about it. She could let herself feel the things she needed to feel to recover, to go forward with her life instead of tracing the same closed loop over and over.

She still worries about being sucked back in. She's anxious, for example, about what will happen when her grandmother dies. If she goes to the funeral she'll have to face the whole family. If she doesn't go, if she doesn't pay her respects, maybe she'll burn in hell the way the church and her parents used to warn. She knows these worries are regressive and irrational. And she also knows they're a sign of just how important it is for her to stay estranged, to protect her hard-won freedom.

Ben, a sixty-two-year-old social worker in Columbus, Ohio, has cut off his relationship with his parents twice. The first time he was twenty-five and had just quit drinking, and found to his surprise that he suddenly couldn't tolerate being around his family. "At the time I didn't know what that was about," he says. "I just knew I didn't want to drink anymore but couldn't do that and still be around them." In therapy he began to process some of the physical and emotional abuse of his childhood, remembering bits and pieces of the past he'd tried to drown in a bottle. Eventually he decided to reconnect with his four sisters, which also meant re-establishing some sort of relationship with his parents. It wasn't a close relationship, but then they'd never exactly been his go-to people in a pinch. He tolerated his parents for the sake of family harmony.

Then, a few years ago, one sister fell down a flight of stairs and was badly injured. She was in a coma for weeks before she died, and during that time Ben's parents wouldn't let him, his other sisters, or her husband or children visit her. For Ben, that was egregious. "They seemed to think we were obligated to put up with this abusive behavior they were dishing out, and my two sisters and I were like, we're adults and we don't have to put up with that anymore," he says. None of the siblings have had any contact with their parents since then.

Ben is in a unique position because he sees estrangement from a therapist's perspective, too. He's had clients who have chosen to cut off the connection with their parents, and he believes there's always a good reason. "It's never because [the adult children] are bad people," he says. "And I have worked with the kind of people I would categorize as being bad people. But when that bond is broken it's always because of something fairly serious." Fairly serious to them, anyway, even if the rest of the world doesn't call it abuse or consider it grounds for estrangement.

Chapter Five

THE LAST STRAW

*There was a single event that made us estranged and
there were a million things that came before that.*

—AMY, forty-eight, estranged from her mother

The summer after my older daughter turned eighteen was
one of the worst seasons of my life. The very worst had
been four years earlier, when she was diagnosed with anorexia nervosa and we spent more than a year battling that terrifying disease.* She got better then, though not completely. But this
year, after we moved to a new state and I started a new career,
she had a major relapse. Because our daughter was eighteen we
couldn't force her into treatment, and we spent several months
navigating a lot of drama and heartbreak. Underneath my encouraging words I believed my daughter might die. I felt helpless in
the face of her illness.

---

* I wrote about that process in *Brave Girl Eating: A Family's Struggle with
Anorexia* (William Morrow, 2010).

Through that summer I wasn't exactly estranged from my mother, but we weren't in much contact either. I didn't have the energy or time to take care of her feelings or deal with her barbed comments, so I more or less ignored the relationship. I did talk often with my sister, though, who apparently kept our parents informed, and at some point my mother, surprisingly, began emailing me to offer sympathy and support. "You can turn to your parents, you know," she wrote, and though nothing in me believed her anymore I still felt the old tug of longing. What would it be like to have parents to fall back on, to cry with, to turn to in a crisis? I had no idea.

My mother kept emailing, every day or two for a week. She said she would do anything I asked, anything to help. *Maybe she's changed,* I thought. *Maybe something's different.* I remembered when my husband and I were planning our wedding, a lively but informal potluck dance party, and how my mother begged us to let her plan a different kind of wedding. *Please let me do this for you*, she'd said at the time, and though we knew it would mean we didn't have the wedding we wanted, though we knew there would be conflicts, we said yes because it seemed so meaningful to my mother. I thought we might get closer in the process. I was wrong; the planning process was a disaster filled with fighting and drama, and the reception was filled with my parents' friends rather than ours. But I remembered so clearly what I hoped for then. I was surprised to find myself still hoping for it, even just a little, and I wanted to honor that hope one more time.

So I wrote my mother back, thanked her for her concern, and asked if she could help me come up with some new recipes; my daughter needed low-volume but high-calorie meals and I was, I told her, out of inspiration. I didn't really need them; I'd become an expert on high-calorie meal planning. So if my mother didn't come through with the recipes, no big deal. If she did it would be lagniappe, an unexpected bonus. I was curious to see which mother would emerge. Would it be the unreliable mother who dropped out of sight? The mean one who took every chance to attack me? Or would it be the mother she said she was, loving and supportive?

I didn't have to wait long to find out. Less than an hour later I got an email from my mother with the subject line "Something I've been wanting to tell you." My stomach flipped with a familiar dread; she'd often prefaced criticism by saying she had an obligation to offer it. The actual email began, "There's something I've been wanting to say and it wouldn't be fair of me to hold back anymore." She wrote that she found it telling that my career involved writing about food and body image and eating disorders, that this was "very negative work," that it was "all about loving your body" and yet, as she put it, "Your own daughter clearly does not love her body. Think about that." She suggested that just as I had "rebelled" against her thirty years earlier, maybe my daughter was now rebelling against me by having a relapse. She wrote that she was sure many people had noticed this connection but probably no one else had been brave enough to mention it to me because, as she put it, "I will tell you my dear that you are a formidable woman. People are afraid to confront you. You should count your blessings that I'm willing to put myself on the line to talk to you about this."

There was more, much more, but the screen in front of me swam out of focus and I couldn't read it. Even if my mother genuinely believed that I was to blame for my daughter's illness, why choose this moment to tell me so? If she loved her granddaughter and wanted the best for her, why would she do something designed to break me down in the middle of this fight for her life?

My mother was of course entitled to her opinions about me and everything else. But how could she possibly think this was the time and way to share them?

As I sat in front of the computer, reading the email again, I felt suddenly dizzy, as if the room had tilted. I thought I heard the crack of something breaking and wondered if I was having a stroke. Blood rushed to my head and then away. My body seemed to rise and fall. And then it was over and I was done with my mother. I felt no regret or confusion, no rage or longing or resentment or anything, really. A great clarity settled over me. I knew our connection was broken in a way that couldn't be healed because I no longer wanted it to be healed.

And it never was. In the last few years of my mother's life, which of course neither of us knew were the last few years, she tried several more times to rekindle our relationship. She offered to visit the city where I lived, to see the therapist of my choice every day for a week. In the past I would have jumped at the chance to say all the things I'd been trying to say to my mother for years in front of a therapist. But now I said no thank you and felt no guilt. That night I sat cross-legged in bed in the dark, my husband asleep beside me, and considered her offer the way you'd poke at a sore tooth, waiting for the burst of pain that meant you'd touched the raw nerve. I imagined us in my therapist's office together—my mother's inevitable tears, the stone in my chest. I imagined my mother turning to me, her arms wide. No matter how I visualized the scene and its outcome I felt nothing. No pain, no joy, no fear—nothing. It was as if someone had finally, thankfully numbed the part of my brain where our relationship had festered for so long.

Did that make me a bad daughter, a bad person? I considered that too and found that the label had lost much of its sting. I was done with my mother. I knew she would never miraculously become the mother I'd always wanted, knew it now in my bones and blood and brain, and I no longer wanted her to. I didn't long for my mother, though I still longed to be mothered. When I was sick or tired or bowed down with despair I would still want a mother to lift me up, make me soup, tell me it would be all right. My own mother had never done that, not that I could remember, and now no one ever would. In that moment I accepted what was and began to give up on what I wished would be.

That moment of clarity, and everything that came afterward, was what Kristina Scharp labels a "last-straw" experience. She'd been wondering about the persistent narrative of estrangements: that they happen suddenly, randomly, on a whim or out of displeasure. In a study called, tellingly, "It Was the Straw that Broke the Camel's Back," she described interviews with fifty-two adult children (most of them women) who were estranged from their parents. She asked her subjects to describe what happened to cause their estrangements. Was there an incident or event that triggered the final break? Or did it come about in another way?

The study results challenged the idea that adult children flounce away from their families out of pique. Pretty much everyone described a "last-straw" incident, an interaction or conflict that led directly to the estrangement. But such incidents rarely if ever told the whole story. They were the catalysts and triggers, the bridges that went up in flames, but the true causes of estrangements nearly always went back a long, long time. As Scharp wrote, "What precedes parent-child estrangement is a complex process that often includes multiple attributions, internal decisions, and *external events that unfold over the course of years,*" she wrote (emphasis mine). "Because there's so much pressure for parents and grown children to find ways to get along it takes the momentum of many interactions over a long time to create a final break."[1]

In other words, there's always a backstory and it's always a long one.

On the surface these "last-straw" incidents can seem petty, minor, even contrived. For Amy, a forty-eight-year-old mom in Houston, Texas, the last straw involved an email she meant to forward to her husband eight years ago but sent to her mother instead (Freudian slip?), which included a snarky comment about something her mother had done. Her mother wrote back asking *Why do you even maintain a relationship with me if that's how you feel?* Amy's response was *Fine, I don't want to be in this relationship anymore, please write me out of your will, don't call me anymore, leave me alone.* They've been estranged ever since.

But of course there's much more to the story, which goes back to when Amy was about twelve and her mother's boyfriend, who lived with them, started touching her in ways that made her uncomfortable. She'd be standing at the sink doing the dishes and he'd walk by and slap her on the ass, right in front of her mother. When Amy protested, her mother would tell her to knock it off, that she was tired of hearing her daughter yell at her boyfriend all the time.

Amy got pregnant with her own boyfriend at fifteen, hiding the pregnancy until it was too late for an abortion. Her mother forced through an adoption, against the wishes of both Amy and the father. "It wasn't ever a conversation of what's best for you and what's best for this child and what does this child's father want," Amy says now. "It was this is a stray puppy we need to get rid of so I don't have to deal with it. And she would tell you that today. That's exactly how she felt about it. She didn't even try to candy coat it that adoption was best for the child. It was, get rid of this thing."

Six months after her son was born and given away, Amy was sexually assaulted by her mother's boyfriend, the same one who'd slapped her ass a few years earlier. She was a senior in high school by then, and in her subsequent slide into depression she started getting into trouble. One night she came home from a visit to her father's house to find that her mother, in a rage, had pulled all the clothes out of her closet, upended all her drawers, and thrown everything into a pile in the middle of her bedroom. Amy packed a bag and left, living with her father through the rest of high school. She told her mother's boyfriend she wouldn't speak to either of them again until he came clean to her mother about what he'd done. When the three of them saw a therapist together, her mother and boyfriend sat on one side of the L-shaped couch and Amy sat on the other, the physical space between them mirroring the emotional divide. That was the first and last therapy session they shared.

Her mother eventually married her boyfriend, and for a while they all put up a façade of connection. Years later, when Amy brought her own daughter to visit her mother and stepfather, she tried to talk to her mother about how wrenching it had been and still was to spend time with the man who had assaulted her. Her mother insisted he would never hurt Amy's daughter. Amy told her that, true or not, that wasn't the point; the point was her mother's forcing Amy to keep seeing her molester, to accept him as part of the family, to stay quiet, to not rock the family boat. The point was her mother's refusal to discuss what had happened, because every time Amy would cry and her mother would say, *We'll talk about this when you're not so upset.* Her mother owed her some kind of explanation, Amy told her. Her mother said, in exasperation, *What do you want me to do, leave him?* Amy replied that that wasn't for her to say. "I don't need her to slit her wrists in remorse," she says now. "I just want some kind of honest discourse. I want her to *want* to leave him. I want her to choose me and her granddaughter instead. And I want to not have to tell her that."

So, yeah, it's true that a single email might not have been enough to estrange Amy from her mother forever. But everything else that happened? It's a lot. And, more important, it wasn't just events that had happened in the past, that were over and done, though in the case of sexual abuse that would easily be enough. It was her mother's inability, or refusal, to process what had happened with her daughter, to address Amy's hurt in a meaningful way, that caused the rupture.

"I look at my daughter now and I see how much I love her and what I would do to protect her," says Amy. "And I think, wow, my mom really screwed up. And that's on her, not on me. It's such a relief to not have to be in that relationship anymore."

Even extreme triggering incidents are rarely the sole cause of an estrangement. One of Scharp's subjects, Janey, cut off her mother during a divorce case, when her mother—her own mother—wrote to her ex-husband offering to lie and say Janey was a bad parent so he'd get full custody of their son. That's a significant betrayal. But Janey's description of a pattern of emotional abuse going back many years made it clear that it was the last in a long line of such betrayals, not the first. So it carried even more weight than it otherwise might have and became the catalyst for their final break.

When an estranged parent like Elizabeth Vagnoni says "Please tell me, what did I do that was so horrible that my sons would not ever speak to me again?" she's looking for an event that's so blatantly terrible, so unquestionably taboo, that it needs no explanation. In Vagnoni's case, the catalyst was a venting email she'd written about her sons and sent to someone else. She says it was no big deal, nothing every parent in the world hadn't thought at some point, and she might well be right. But as Scharp's research and my own experience suggests, there's almost always a long history of offenses—perceived or real—behind an estrangement, especially parent-child estrangements. Grown children who initiate an estrangement with a parent believe, rightly or not, that they have very good reasons. They make their decisions based not just on one incident but in the wake of years of troubling interactions.

When I asked the people I interviewed to tell me what caused their estrangements, I never heard about just one incident. Pretty much everyone poured forth a saga of miscommunication, alienation, betrayals, and grief. A number of those stories spilled out over several painful hours. One of those long and winding tales came from Mark, a thirty-two-year-old criminal defense lawyer who lives in a small town in northeast England. He's been estranged from his parents, grandmother, sister, brother-in-law, and two nephews for several years, and while he's still hopeful that they might reconcile he's begun to doubt it will happen. Unlike many of the people I've interviewed, Mark has no complaints about his childhood. He was close to his parents and wanted their good opinion; he worked hard in school so they'd be proud of him and says he always enjoyed being part of the family.

Mark says there was no precipitating event, no single incident, that caused the estrangement. It was more of a snowball-type situation that started small and quickly rolled out of control. The trouble seemed to revolve around his engagement and later marriage to a woman I'll call Janice. Mark says he never quite felt comfortable taking Janice to his parents' house; he couldn't put his finger on the problem, but he knew it had something to do with his mother. Still, things went along pleasantly enough from his perspective until a misunderstanding with his sister sparked open combat with his mother. She told her son she was upset about his fiancée; she said everything was Janice's way or the highway, and this bothered her. Mark said, *This is between my sister and me, please don't get involved.* His mother responded with a list of grievances about Janice: she was bossy and controlling, she was a gold-digger out for Mark's money, and Mark had to put his foot down and stand up for himself now or it would be too late. Mark was shocked and then distressed by his mother's revelations, which were less about a specific incident than about his lifestyle and the dynamic she saw in his relationship with Janice.

The situation continued to deteriorate during the couple's wedding planning. Mark tried to maintain his usual relationship with his parents, but their conversations were now filled with awkward silences and unspoken criticisms. As the plans progressed, Mark says, he was still trying to repair the rift. "I'd send a text, and I'd be quite careful about how I worded it, and I'd think, Right, that's the text that's gonna do it," he says. "You've explained it all very well. You haven't been aggressive or overly critical. You've said all the right things. You've walked them into a corner where they can just be reasonable and fair and decent, full of good faith. But it never worked."

By then, he says, all he wanted was for his parents—his mother, really—to be civil to Janice. "I didn't want them to change, I didn't want them to say sorry, I didn't expect them to be best buddies," he remembers. "And I was very lucky that Janice was actually amenable to patching things up with them, because believe me, many girlfriends would have thought, Bloody hell, you and your family are a bunch of nutters, sod this, I'm off."

And he missed his family. He'd always cared what they thought of him, and the fact that now they saw him as a patronizing, nasty, disrespectful son who got a girlfriend and blew them off astonished him. He missed the easy relationship they'd had before, the comfortable pattern of visits and dinners and television. He spent months arranging a meeting for the four of them, a night to talk things through and find a way to move forward. His father and Janice both spoke, offering their thoughts and feelings in a non-accusatory way. His mother sat with her arms crossed, a

scowl on her face. Then Janice, trying to be straightforward, said
something along the lines of *Look, you don't like me and I don't like
you, but that doesn't mean we can't get along.* "A reasonable mother
who wanted to sort things out would have said, 'Well I'm sorry you
feel that way, it's not that I dislike you, I need to get to know you
better, and I hope in time you can come to like me,'" Mark recalls.
Instead his mother stormed out, leaving Janice in tears.

That was three years ago, and since then, says Mark, his contact with his family has been sporadic and painful. "I could very
easily reconcile with my family, but it would be a complete betrayal of my wife, and it would flush my marriage down the toilet,"
he says. He's calm throughout this long recital, though clearly distressed. At one point he says, in the same reasonable tone, "You
don't know what I'm telling you is true. There are two sides to
every story. For all you know it could be all my fault." It's true,
and it's certainly something I think of not just when I talk to other
people but when I ponder my own estrangement. I'm aware that
every story I tell myself and others would be, and often was, told
quite differently by my mother. Who's to say I'm right and she's
wrong, or vice versa?

Mark has clearly thought about this too. "I could be exactly
what they say I am," he acknowledges. "And the only answer to
that is that I don't think they would say that. I don't honestly
think my mother would say, 'Oh you're only hearing one side of
the story, mind, Mark could be the innocent party.'"

I try the same thought experiment, imagining my mother saying something like *This is just my point of view, but Harriet sees
things differently.* It feels about as believable as the tooth fairy. I
don't remember my mother ever even hinting at the idea that her
opinion wasn't the only one. I'm not sure my mother was capable
of acknowledging other points of view, and Mark feels the same
way about his mother. "I can't force my parents to accept the

woman I love, who I've chosen to spend my life with," Mark says, and he's right. He can't. None of us can.

While these "last-straw" experiences can be superficial or deep, minor misfires or major betrayals, it seems to me the reason they take on so much power and meaning in estrangement narratives is that they signify something much bigger than one particular conflict. Caitlin, a thirty-year-old journalist in Rhode Island, was close to her father when she was young, but ever since he had an affair and divorced her mother they've had an on-again off-again relationship. They go months without speaking, and when they do connect it's pretty superficial. "If your own parent can do this to you," says Caitlin, "*everyone* else is fair game." She's talking about losing trust. Friends, acquaintances, boyfriends— anyone can betray you.

Maybe that trust has already been eroded by years of incremental losses; maybe there's not much left of it. But the dissolving of the last shred of trust between a parent and child, sister and brother, aunt and niece, is still powerful. And when it's gone, no one, not another parent or aunt or uncle, not the king's own horses and men, can re-create it. It becomes a kind of death, far more final than any one act or incident. It's the death of possibility and of hope, the death of the faith one person holds in another. Without that trust there is no center, no connection. No relationship.

◇◇◇◇◇

FROM HER INTERVIEWS, Scharp outlined a number of themes common to people who'd estranged themselves from family, including one she calls internal realizations. "Some participants came to a realization that a parent would never perform their parental role as the participant would like, and thus would no longer be a part of their life,"[2] she wrote. "Other participants also discussed a realization that their lives are better without their parent(s)." These realizations are of course connected; one inevitably leads to the other. Once you let go of the hope that a parent will behave as you want her to, you're free to move forward without her. Or at least without her in a day-to-day way.

For Kerry, forty-eight, a dietitian in Australia, the last-straw incident seemed minor enough. She'd gone back to college in her thirties and was taking a night class, and her diabetic cat needed an injection and feeding while she was gone. She asked her three younger brothers, her mother, and other extended family members if anyone could pitch in. No one would. Nobody would pick her up from the train station at eleven o'clock at night, either, so she had to wait even longer for a bus and then walk ten minutes in the dark to get home.

Was that one disappointment worth what some people call the nuclear option of total estrangement? In and of itself, maybe not. But like many such incidents it didn't happen against a backdrop of a happy and devoted family. Kerry describes a childhood filled with emotional abuse. She and her three brothers were all born within five years of one another. Their parents were divorced, and their mother would lose her temper unpredictably. Kerry was "parentified," meaning she played the role of a parent to her own mother, responsible for taking care of things so her mother wouldn't explode. She didn't go to college right after high school because by then she thought she was a failure; she believed her mother and aunt when they told her she was stupid. When she eventually worked up the courage to start taking college classes, she found she was quite good at them. That was the start of a major shift in her perspective about herself and her family.

So her family's refusal to step up when she needed help wasn't a simple disappointment, a blip in the big picture. It was a

major eye-opener. Kerry realized she'd had high-functioning anxiety for most of her life, and her family—especially her mother
and her mother's sister—had made it worse. "It was like my
auntie got pleasure in me not succeeding," she says. "When I
went to uni it was like 'Kerry's going to get her shit together and
actually be something.' She was undermining me all the time."
So Kerry wrote them a letter saying she was tired of making everything OK for everyone else, that she'd struggled her whole life
without their help or empathy and now she was done. She told
them their relationship was over. She told them to fuck off even
as some part of her hoped her letter would be a wake-up call,
making her family realize what they'd done and show her the love
and care and respect she'd never had. Deep down she knew that
wasn't going to happen. She knew she had to break off with them
for her own sanity and well-being. "To keep things as they were
would have meant remaining small, scared, doubting myself and
needy for approval," she says now.

A few years later, her mother called out of the blue, wanting
to reconnect, and for a while they reestablished a relationship.
But it didn't last. Her aunt organized a family Christmas that
didn't include Kerry, which was hurtful. Then Kerry overheard
her mother on the phone with one of her brothers, laughing at
Kerry behind her back, calling her a nasty name. That was six
years ago, and since then Kerry hasn't seen or spoken to anyone on that side of the family, including her mother. "It was
never a healthy environment," she says now. "Whoever I am to
them, and how they respond to me, is never going to be helpful.
There's nothing there that's worth salvaging unless I'm willing
to go back to be that person they can beat up on, mentally and
emotionally. And I'm never going to be accepted in my own right
for who I am."

Kerry was lucky in one sense: she had a close relationship with her nan, her mother's mother, who loved and accepted her unconditionally. Just before she died ten years ago, Kerry's grandmother told her she could see, now, what her granddaughter had been saying all along, how she'd been treated by her mother and the rest of the family. That validation was the greatest gift Kerry had ever gotten. Someone she trusted and loved saw what she saw and named it. She wasn't the problem child the rest of the family thought she was. She still feels grief sometimes, but it's more of a theoretical sadness than a true mourning. "The sadness is for what never was," she says. "But regrets? No. My life and myself are better."

Mary, thirty-four, a graduate student in philosophy in Ohio, describes her family situation in similar terms. She's currently estranged from both parents, her four younger siblings, and most of her uncles and aunts. But the main estrangement is with her mother, a relationship that had always been complicated. As a child, Mary knew her mother wasn't like other mothers. "I just thought I was worse, and I thought she was really generous to put up with me," she says. She'd been diagnosed with bipolar disorder as a teen and put on a number of medications, including lithium. She became the family scapegoat, the crazy daughter whose parents were trying to help her. When her mother told her she was so fat they were going to have to make her clothes out of bedsheets, or that she was too insane to know if the house was burning down, Mary believed her. For anyone who's been lucky enough not to grow up with that kind of criticism, this kind of vulnerability may seem exaggerated. What child would doubt herself enough to think she might not know if the house was burning down? But children learn to see themselves through the eyes of their families. It takes maturity and a lot of hard emotional work to unlearn those early judgments and see your-self in a different light.

For a long time Mary thought she was the problem child, and the rest of the family agreed. Her parents insisted she live at home during college, so she was in her twenties before she was allowed to move out to go to a nearby university for gradu-ate school. Once she started making her own decisions, Mary realized that the lithium and other medications for bipolar disorder were actually part of the problem. "The further I got from my mother the less crazy I was," she says. She tried to set boundaries with her family, but when her mother threatened to call the police and tell them Mary was mentally ill and off her medication, she moved to a new apartment and didn't give her parents the address.

They tried to connect again a few years later. Mary had re-alized by then that she had OCD, not bipolar disorder, and she was learning to manage it. At one point she checked herself into a mental hospital a few hours away to deal with some medication issues. She asked her mother if she'd pick her up when she was discharged, and her mother agreed. But when Mary called to say she was ready to go home, her mother claimed both of the fam-ily's cars were broken and she couldn't come. Mary had to call a friend and ask to be picked up at the hospital, which was a big deal because it meant outing herself as mentally ill. When she got home her father told her that yeah, one car was broken but the other one was fine. Her mother could have picked her up; she just didn't choose to.

That was the last straw for Mary, the turning point, the mo-ment she realized she needed to walk away. She was twenty-four years old and she cried for days, grieving for the loss of her fam-ily. But in the midst of her sadness she also felt a new sense of freedom. She *wasn't* the problem child; she wasn't crazy or incompetent. Her mother's many betrayals hurt, but now that she understood them she was free to pursue her own life. Eight years later, she's happily married with a daughter. She'd like to have a relationship with her brothers, sister, and the rest of the extended family, but as far as she's concerned the estrangement with her mother will go on forever. "I've got to protect my daughter," she says, "so I'm going to be very, very cautious."

Taking a stand to protect a child is a common theme in estrangement stories. Behaviors that seem tolerable when directed at an adult can become unacceptable when aimed at a child—especially your child. That's what triggered the break for Andy, forty-one, an entrepreneur in southern Wisconsin, and his mother. For as long as he could remember his mother had been emotionally abusive, not just to him but to his father and the rest of the family as well. As a child he learned to predict her "explosions," where some little thing would trigger her and she'd lash out at whoever was close. These scenes occurred only with Andy, his sister, and his father, until the night his mother directed her rage at his five-year-old daughter.

He and his two children were eating dinner at his parents' house. His mother had served cooked carrots, and his daughter wasn't eating them. "My mom started asking her weird questions," he recalls. "Like, 'Didn't I cook the carrots right? Is something wrong with them?'" Andy's father said, *They're fine carrots,* and Andy told his mother they were delicious. But she kept making a big deal about the carrots, insisting something must be wrong with them since her granddaughter wasn't eating them.

Andy tried to defuse the situation. He reminded her that his daughter was only five, that she didn't like cooked carrots, and added, *And it's not her job to tell you how your food is.* Things escalated and his mother exploded in a rage. Andy glanced across the table at his nine-year-old son, who looked shocked, and something snapped. He got up from the table, collected his kids, and left. Later that night, when he called his father and said they had to do something about his mother's behavior, his father said, *I don't know what you mean. This is just how things are in the family.*

Which was true. The three of them were used to tiptoeing around Andy's mother, trying not to set her off, making sure she was happy at all times, placating her when she exploded. But when the familiar dynamic touched his kids, Andy had had enough. Sometime after the carrot incident he told his mother she had the power to heal the estrangement. *Just be polite,* he said. *Be polite to us like you would to the person checking out your groceries. Just treat us with respect and all your problems go away.* Despite an attempt at family counseling, though, nothing has changed. He told his kids, *Grandma's not nice to me and I don't want to be around her, so when the family gets together I'm not going to be there,* and they seem to understand, at least for now.

Andy still has contact with his father; they're business partners as well as family. His dad likes to pretend the estrangement doesn't exist. Andy blames him for letting it happen, for not standing up for himself, his kids, or his grandkids for so long. He used to look up to his father, but now, he says, he's lost a ton of respect for him. While the estrangement has definitely hurt their relationship, Andy knows it's both necessary and a relief. That doesn't make it easy, though. "I have dreams about it all the time," he says. "It's very stressful. All my mom wants to do is fight, and I don't want to fight. I'm not going to do it." In his most recent dream his mother had died and the last words she said to him were *Fuck off.*

Stella, a forty-five-year-old therapist in San Jose, California, clearly remembers the moment she knew her relationship with her father was over. They were close for a while when she was young, but when she was seven she found out he was having an affair. When she asked him about it he got cold and distant, and has pretty much stayed that way ever since. Stella went to college, then moved across the country; she came back to the Bay Area in her mid-thirties, ready to reconnect with family. She and her father disagreed about politics—she supported Obama, he watched Fox News—but otherwise got along. When Stella got married and had a baby she began to notice some disturbing patterns. Her father called her constantly, or just showed up demanding to see her daughter; he refused to accept any boundaries Stella tried to set. They had a conversation she describes as tense, and the relationship grew more and more strained.

Then her father had a series of heart attacks and strokes, spending most of a year in and out of hospitals. Every time Stella went to visit him she'd have a panic attack. Her anxiety got so bad she had to start taking medication for it. She realized she didn't like her father, that being around him made her feel sick, and she felt incredibly guilty about that. "My dad is sick, possibly dying, and I just realize I hate him," she says. Still, they kept in touch.

Stella got pregnant again and was planning to announce her pregnancy at a family picnic when she miscarried. She called her father to say she wouldn't be at the picnic, and to tell him why. He said he was sorry, in a tone that seemed insincere to Stella, and then said while he had her on the phone he wanted her to meet Stacy, a half-sister Stella hadn't known about. For Stella, that was the moment. The fact that her father couldn't focus on her for two seconds, could barely acknowledge her grief, hit her hard. Something inside her snapped—not the violent snapping of a rubber band but a connection disintegrating, like a really old cord that turned to dust. She thought, *I don't want to do this anymore.*

So she wrote him a letter saying she needed to take a break from the relationship, and blocked his number on her phone. The estrangement came as a huge relief. She could think again, feel again, as if parts of her brain that had been shut down by anxiety had now come back online. It's hard for her to articulate now how bad things were then, even to herself. She describes many interpersonal microaggressions, the kinds of small interactions that create an atmosphere of distance and mistrust. He would be dismissive of her, make her feel invisible, give her the silent treatment for little or no reason. He'd withhold affection. He had a way of making his feelings more important than anyone else's, certainly hers.

She still loved him. She was angry, but she didn't make the decision to walk away out of anger. She made it because for years she'd tried everything she could think of to make it better with him and none of it ever worked. They stayed estranged for the next few years, and then, at the end of his life, Stella decided to try to connect with him one more time. They exchanged texts and a few phone calls, and Stella even visited him. His last message to her, via text, was *I still love you.* "That was definitely very him," she says. "It's like he did love me but he wanted me to know there was an 'even though' in there. He wanted to leave me with self-doubt." He also wanted the last word: in his will he left her thirty silver dollars.

The last-straw incident isn't always clear to those on both sides of the estrangement. Marion, a forty-two-year-old writer in southern Wisconsin, hasn't spoken to one of her two younger brothers in several years. Actually, he stopped speaking to her. She describes a brother who always felt diminished and "less than" his two siblings, who framed every family interaction as something being done to him. She describes a child who struggled with learning disabilities and anger management, an adult with a longtime opioid addiction. He insists that Marion's never worked a day in her life while he's had to struggle for years, that their parents have given her everything and given him nothing; she says nothing could be further from the truth.

She told me there was no fight or event that triggered their estrangement. But she also told me this story: some years ago, her parents commissioned him to build another house on their property. He built a beautiful house, a structure his parents could be proud of. Then Marion found herself suddenly in the midst of a divorce, needing somewhere to live, and wound up moving into that beautiful house. "The fact that it was for me just did him in," she says now. He exploded, sending an email saying that he hated her, he'd always resented her relationship with their parents, he never wanted to speak to her again and didn't want her in his life on any level. For Marion's brother, the fact that she was now living in the house he built for their parents was the last straw. She doesn't see it that way because for her, moving into the house had nothing to do with him. "He's an unhappy guy and he has chosen me as the outlet for that, and it's surprisingly, remarkably painful for me," she says.

At first Marion felt calm about the estrangement; it was a relief to not have to listen to her brother's horrible comments and judgments all the time. But as time went on, the situation began to get to her. "He just hates me," she says. "It's hard and it's weird. It's embarrassing. You don't see this kind of thing on people's Instagrams."*

People who have cut themselves off from parents and other family members talk about the anxiety or depression or grief or anger or despair that drove them to take a step they and the rest of the culture see as desperate and extreme. "It's not because I don't want a family," says Kerry, the dietitian from Australia. "It's

---

* Though social media would be a very different place if you did. Imagine Dark Instagram—Dinstagram? Instadark?—full of stories about the less-than-pleasing side of life.

about the side effects of being around them. It's not because I'm a bitchy, horrible, nasty, uncaring person. It's actually because I *do* care."

People like Marion, though, who are on the receiving end of estrangements, express feelings of bewilderment, abandonment, defensiveness, and confusion. Sheri McGregor, author of *Done with the Crying*, a self-help book for mothers whose children have estranged themselves, describes herself as "a regular mom, a nice woman who is like so many I have come into contact with and interviewed for this book." Later she writes:

> Almost all of us remember things our own parents did that could be characterized as mistakes. But most of us wouldn't dream of severing the relationships. So, why today, do so many adult children cast off their parents, and even their entire families? And as many rejected parents ask: How can doing so seem so easy for them?

A few pages later she adds, "Even when a reason for [estrangement] is given it often makes no sense." Many parents apparently agree; 6 percent of the parents in the 2015 Texas Christian University study said they had no idea why their children cut them off. My mother would have been one of them. Over and over through the years of our chaotic back-and-forth she asked me why we couldn't have a closer relationship, why I was so upset, and no matter how I explained it, what I said or how I said it, she kept asking. I thought she was being willfully, stubbornly deaf, trying to punish me with her refusal to comprehend. I'm a reasonably articulate person; of *course* she understood the problems. I couldn't figure out why she acted like she didn't.

I understand now that she wanted me to name one interaction, one moment, one reason. If the cause of the rift is something you've said or done, or something that happened, maybe you can undo the damage, retract the comment, revisit the problem. But if the cause isn't a specific crisis but rather the way parents respond to the inevitable family crises, and to their children— well, that's much harder to articulate. When my mother asked me what she had done, how could I say it wasn't any one thing by itself but everything together? How could I tell her that while there were specific incidents that distressed me, it was more the way she looked at me, her tone of voice in talking to and about me, the disapproval and judgment she radiated in my direction? She wanted a description of something that had happened. All I had was a description of her. To really hear what I was trying to convey, she would have had to put aside the story she told herself not just about our interactions but about her own essential nature, and consider a different one.

That's a hugely threatening process, though some people do manage to pull it off. In her book *I Thought We'd Never Speak Again: The Road from Estrangement to Reconciliation*, Laura Davis tells a story about a woman named Miriam who went through a process of reconciliation with her children after alcoholism, sexual abuse, and rage caused a long estrangement. Miriam wrote her daughters letters expressing her regret about not protecting them from the sexual abuse and taking responsibility for her own frequent emotional outbursts. She went to therapy with one daughter and went through therapy on her own as well. With four of her five children things got much better, but one daughter remained angry and aloof. Miriam persisted, at one point going to her daughter's therapist and listening while her daughter read a four-page single-spaced list of grievances. "When she read the list," Miriam writes, "I listened and I wasn't defensive. Then I apologized for everything I might have done that hurt her."

The most poignant part of Miriam's story to me was this comment:

> The hardest part for me was hearing what [my children's] childhoods were like for them and knowing it is their truth. With each of my kids, I hoped that they would get to the point where they also wanted to hear from me. But in the meantime, I had to hear a lot of things I didn't want to know.[3]

I had to hear a lot of things I didn't want to know. I can imagine the truth of Miriam's words, can feel both intense empathy for her and something like awe at her ability to not just name this difficult act but follow it through. She was able to acknowledge the truth of her children's experiences *for them.* She didn't get bogged down in who did what or whether this or that actually happened. She accepted the wholeness of their experiences. She honored their feelings without passing judgment on whether they were valid. Maybe that's why she was able to reconcile with all of her children to some extent.

One way or another we've all confronted things we did not want to know, could not afford to let ourselves acknowledge. The act of burying them far from our consciousness shows that we already know. British sociologist Stanley Cohen, who grew up in South Africa and worked against apartheid, wrote about the emotional sleight of hand required to stay in a state of uncertainty. "Denial may be neither a matter of telling the truth nor intentionally telling a lie," he wrote. "There seem to be states of mind, or even whole cultures, in which we know and don't know at the same time."[4]

That feels exactly right. Years ago, when my fourteen-year-old daughter started behaving oddly—asking for a subscription to *Gourmet* magazine, freaking out about what we were going to have for dinner five days later—I called her pediatrician and got an appointment for three weeks later. I could have pushed for a quicker appointment; I could have said, "I think something's really wrong." I think I knew she had anorexia but didn't know, didn't want to know, because that would have been terrifying. It would also have meant that I had to do something, and I had no idea what to do.

According to Kristina Scharp, this was a natural response if not exactly an ideal one. In the process of studying estrangement, Scharp looked at what she calls "uncertainty management." She found that people have three options when faced with uncertainty: they can seek to reduce that uncertainty, maintain it, or increase it. The assumption is that people always want to reduce uncertainty, to gather as much information as possible. But that's not always true.

"In certain instances it behooves us, for our mental well-being, to not know," she explains. For example, if your family has a history of Alzheimer's disease, you might not want to get tested to see if you've got the APOE-4 allele, a genetic marker that's much more common in people who develop the disease than in those who don't. There's no cure and little effective treatment for Alzheimer's, so knowing you're at a higher risk won't improve your prognosis. And it might overwhelm you with such despair that you can't enjoy whatever time you have left.

In my case, I could have started educating myself about eating disorders (and I did that just a few weeks later, diving deeply into the literature). I could have asked for a quicker appointment and probably gotten one; but I didn't. That fact confused me for a long time, until I read Scharp's research on uncertainty. Then it made sense: I was hanging on to my uncertainty as long as possible because on some level it was easier than confronting reality.

"I wonder how many estranged parents are as confused as they articulate they are," says Scharp. It's not that she thinks they're lying, but they may be sabotaging their own understanding of the problem. Or they might know exactly why their child doesn't want to be with them, but not want to put that understanding into words. "To stick with 'I have no idea, I'm so confused' is a much better story to tell," says Scharp. Though not a particularly useful one.

For many people estrangement seems to come down to a sheer need for self-preservation. Stella, the therapist from San Jose, puts it starkly: "It was [my father] or me, and I chose me." If one of my children felt that way about our relationship, maybe I'd rather not know too.

Chapter Six

LOVE: THE UNRESOLVABLE DILEMMA

Mother love is a sacred concept in our culture, and like all things sacred it has a mythology of its own. . . . The myth of mother love pervades our thinking about family and other relationships in ways both simple and complex.

—**PEG STREEP**, *Mean Mothers*

After my mother died, when I crouched in the dirt of the Lahaina Pali Trail with emotion flooding my body, the word that came to me to describe it was *love*. It was brutal and powerful, unlike any love I'd ever felt before. It was not something I ever wanted to feel again. I have no concrete experience, now or ever, of loving my mother in the ordinary way: warm feelings, a longing to be physically close, a sense of fond tenderness. For a long time I thought I just didn't love her, which amplified my sense of inherent brokenness. So in some ways that terrible gush of feeling came as a relief. The fact that I could feel something for my mother beyond rage and fear felt like a gift. A scary, uncomfortable gift, but still.

When I began researching this book I wondered how other people felt about the families they were estranged from. Unsurprisingly, estranged parents aren't the only ones who grapple with uncertainty, especially around the question of love. Kristina Scharp's research also looked at the kinds of uncertainty adult children—who are often the ones doing the estranging—feel. Maybe the most resonant of those is what Scharp labeled "parental love uncertainty." In other words, children who have gone through years of back-and-forth with their parents and who have come to an estrangement wonder whether their parents love them or if those parents are even capable of love. As one of Scharp's subjects explained:

> It was very "I love you. I love you," but there was nothing behind it. You know, it was all words and no action . . . the intent wasn't really behind it. Um, so I think meaningful communication has, it's more than I love you. It's followed up with action. It's followed up with support. It's followed up with showing your love and not just saying it.[1]

The chasm between her father's words and his actions felt all too familiar to me. I wanted to believe my mother when she insisted she loved me but my body told me otherwise. I didn't *feel* loved by her. I wondered what was wrong with me that her words triggered a sense of dread and emptiness rather than warm fuzzy feelings of reciprocated love. I wondered what was wrong with me that I stuttered and fell silent when I tried to explain this to others. How can you question a parent's love when she talks about it all the time? How can you explain that despite the stream of words you feel pummeled rather than nurtured?

This sense of assault and confusion hit its peak with my mother's last email, sent when my daughter was having a serious relapse and she'd been offering to help. The gap between her words—*I love you so very much!*—and the substance of her message—*It's your fault your daughter is sick, and it's payback for what you did to me!*—sent a familiar queasiness ricocheting through my body. This was the cognitive dissonance I'd been trying to resolve my whole life. If my mother loved me, why would she want to hurt me? If she didn't love me, why not? And why would she keep saying she did?

Now I can see that I spent my childhood torn between two equally appalling possibilities. If my mother didn't love me, as I suspected, there must be something terribly wrong with me. The other explanation—that there was something terribly wrong with *her*—was simply unthinkable, an idea that threw my world as a child into disarray. So for a long time I didn't let myself know the truth as I experienced it: that my mother was unable to love me in any way I could recognize.

It takes a lot of mental and emotional energy to stay willfully blind on an issue so close to the heart. I wonder what I might have done with that energy if I hadn't needed to spend it in this way. I don't remember any moments of true closeness with my mother, but I must have experienced them. I must have gotten what I wanted from her at least once in a while as a child because for decades I went back to her again and again, Charlie Brown running at that football, foolishly hopeful that this time he would connect at last with the object of his desire. And like Charlie Brown I always found myself flat on my back, wondering what the hell had just happened.

The subject of love—what it is, what it means, what it looks like—comes up a lot when you talk to parents whose children have walked away from them. Sandy, a seventy-year-old retired pediatric nurse in Georgia, has been estranged from her only daughter (and therefore her two grandchildren) for nearly four years, though their difficulties aren't new. Sandy says her daughter first fell out with one of her brothers, and that upset Sandy. The mother, father, and daughter went into counseling together, but Sandy's daughter quickly stopped going. Soon afterward she told her parents she didn't consider them her parents anymore.

"I've tried everything I can think of, emails and cards and flowers, everything," says Sandy. "And all she does is email back a nastygram." She has lain awake many nights wondering what she did wrong when her children were growing up, what she would do differently. She wonders whether her daughter went through a traumatic experience as a child, something she never mentioned but blames Sandy for. One of the few specific accusations she remembers had to do with money: her daughter said Sandy didn't buy her new school clothes when she was thirteen. "And she was right," says Sandy. "I didn't. Because she was making quite a bit of money from babysitting, and she was always wanting, wanting, wanting more and more and more. She was never happy with what we gave her. And I just felt it was time to say no."

Sandy remembers that in part because she and her husband were financially generous with their children. They paid for college for all three of them; they gave their daughter a car when she learned to drive, bailed her out of credit card debt, paid for her wedding. They also supported their children's extracurricular activities, going on trips with their daughter's swim team, going to all the baseball and football games the boys played in. "So I don't get it," says Sandy sadly. "None of that must count toward anything in her mind."

I understand what Sandy means; she wants to believe her daughter values what Sandy has done and sacrificed for her daughter, what she's given her. But the idea of counting, of love as a tally sheet, is problematic. This kind of emotional reckoning leads only to resentment, never to affection. Certainly that was true for me. When my mother sobbed on my bed about why I didn't love her, why no one loved her, I felt guilt but very little else. If that was love, I wanted no part of it. Though I wanted to please my mother, needed to please her, I couldn't love her on command.

I thought I couldn't love her at all. So when I recently came across an entry in the journal I kept at age twenty-five it hit me like a gut punch. Six words, written in blue ink, in my own looping handwriting: *Of course I love my mother.* I don't remember being the person who wrote that. I don't remember feeling it. I certainly don't know what I meant. Maybe I was trying to convince myself: Of *course* I love my mother because that's what I'm supposed to do. Maybe I was making a point: Of course *I* love my mother; *she's* the one who doesn't love *me*. Or drawing a distinction: of course I *love* my mother—I just don't like her, respect her, admire her, ever want to see her again. I don't know and I can't know now, not really. This is something a lot of estranged children grapple with: What does it mean to love someone who treats you badly? What does love even mean in that context?

Diane, who works in nonprofits in Portland, says that for years she didn't question her feelings for her mother; she was supposed to love her and that was that. In adulthood, though, as other people started observing some of their dysfunctional family dynamics, she began seeing things differently. Friends would describe wanting to call their mothers to tell them some exciting news and Diane realized she'd never, ever wanted to do that. She loved her mother the way a loyal child loves a parent, out of custom and expectation and duty rather than real affection. It was a kind of love, but maybe not the kind most people experienced, the kind they're predisposed to feel through blood and hormones and proximity and lived experience.

Research on families suggests that the connection between mothers and daughters is especially strong, with the mother-daughter relationship described as "the closest, most enduring, and mutually supportive of all parent-child gender combinations."[2] Babies can identify their mothers' voices, and show a strong preference for them, within a few days of birth.[3] Preschoolers in a stressful situation who listen to recordings of their mothers feel better, even if those mothers are reading gibberish rather than saying something meaningful.[4] School-age girls under stress who hear their mothers' voices produce lower levels of cortisol, a stress hormone, and higher levels of oxytocin, the so-called love hormone.[5] Children love their parents no matter what those parents are like—wonderfully supportive, abusive, indifferent. Without them (or someone who fills their role) we can't survive long enough to reproduce. We're too helpless for too long. We're not just primed to love and need them; we're biologically required to, hardwired to look for comfort in their arms.

But that doesn't mean we'll find it. I can't remember a single time my mother's physical presence, real or imagined, made me feel safer. When I dreamed, as I often did, of picking up the phone and hearing her say my name, I woke in a cold sweat, my ears ringing. After one of the many times I cut off contact with her, I dreamed I was hooked up to a machine that controlled my heartbeat. My mother was torturing me by turning the dial, making my heart beat too fast, and then turning it all the way down so it didn't beat at all for nearly a minute. Just when I thought I would die she turned it up again and my heart began to pound. I knew this torture would end in my death and my mother would be the one to deliver it. And surely these dreams were yet more evidence in the case against me, the damning proof that I was pathologically cold and unloving. What kind of daughter imagines her mother a torturer? What kind of daughter feels fear rather than warmth at the sound of her mother's voice?

A bad daughter. A cold daughter. A shadow daughter unable to love. A daughter who was manipulative, deceitful, selfish. These were the words my mother used to describe me, the stories my mother told me about myself. And so much of parenting is storytelling, passing along to a child an idea of how she should see the world, shaping the way she feels about herself. Most of it is done without words, in the silences, in the binding narrative of a raised eyebrow, a shrug, a turning away. With her expressive blue eyes and eloquent hands my mother told me a story about myself that I live with to this day.

So maybe it's not surprising that estrangement, especially between parents and grown children, raises fundamental and even philosophical questions, not just for those directly involved but in the wider circles of family and community affected by the estrangement. I remember a moment when my mother was dying, when my father and sister and I sat in the family waiting room outside the ICU where she lay sedated, the ventilator pushing air in and out of her lungs. I rested my head on the wooden table for a minute and to everyone's surprise, especially mine, began to cry. "Now I'll never have the chance to have a relationship with her," I said through my tears.

My sister got up and put her arms around me. "She loves you, you know she does," she said, over and over. "She loves you." She meant her words to be comforting but they made me feel worse, not better. At the time I didn't know why. Talking to Kristina Scharp now, I begin to understand. According to Scharp, it can be intensely problematic when well-intentioned family members tell estranged children that their parents love them, for a variety of reasons. For one thing, it's as if that statement, true or not, should end all dissent or confusion or anger or grief. For another, it raises more questions than it answers. "If my parents love me, why are they abusing me?" she asks rhetorically. "If my parents don't love me, then who isn't loved by their parents?" Those questions cut both ways. "One of my participants said something I think about all the time," says Scharp. "She goes, 'What kind of person does not love their mother? Prisoners and rapists love their mothers. They probably have a tattoo that says I heart Mom.'"

When the story your mother or father tells you about yourself, with words or looks or silences, is that you are unkind, unloving, unworthy, you believe it. On some level you always believe it, even if you don't think it's true, even if your life is full of others who tell you otherwise. Those words and those beliefs become self-fulfilling prophecies as you learn self-doubt instead of confidence, mistrust instead of connection. Barbara, a fifty-three-year-old former advertising executive, learned those bitter associations early. "After my mother died my sister and I were both so relieved," she says. "You feel guilty that you're relieved that your own mother has died, but you just feel like, it's over, finally. She's not going to badmouth me anymore."

Barbara's estrangement from her mother was more emotional than physical. They never went through a long period without some kind of contact, but for years it was both sparse and superficial. Then about ten years ago Barbara was in a serious horseback-riding accident that put her into a coma for a month. When she woke up her father was leaning over her bed saying, "Barbara, welcome back, we love you." The first thing her mother said to her was "We were in Arizona visiting friends and you interrupted our visit with your accident. You made your father worry the whole plane ride. And the plane tickets were very expensive."

Barbara laughs now, a pained laugh. Before her accident, she once said to her father, "She's been bullying us and the family for years." Her father replied, "Well what did you want me to do about it?" After the accident, she began to understand that the more distance she could put between her mother and herself the better. She didn't want to give up the relationship with her father, though. Sometimes he'd call when her mother went out and say *OK, I can talk, she's left the house.*

Peg Streep, who's been writing about mothers like Barbara's for fifteen years, says this kind of compartmentalization is common. Her own parents behaved similarly, and while she thinks her father didn't know—or didn't let himself know—just how destructive her mother's actions were, it probably wouldn't have mattered if he had. "He would have bought in to whatever he had to buy into about me," she says. "My mother in his firmament was the way more important star."

Streep believes love is at the center of the issue for the children of such mothers. On the one hand, there's the hardwired and ongoing need for maternal love; on the other, there's the growing realization of how wounding a mother has been. The cognitive dissonance between them is unresolvable, an internal conflict that many people can manage only through estrangement, a coping tool but not a resolution. "I know women in their seventies still fighting it, and their mothers have been dead for thirty years," explains Streep.

She still feels that conflict herself, though she was estranged from her mother for many years before her death. "Why didn't my mother love me?" she wrote in *Mean Mothers*. "I know the answer now, and that knowledge absolutely coexists with a terrible longing for the mother love I never had and never will have."

Many of the people I interviewed talked about that longing, whether for mother love, father love, or the kind of encompassing love that comes from a close extended family. For Lee, who's estranged from her father and who's been in recovery from alcoholism and cocaine addiction for five years, that longing is front and center. Her best friend, who's also estranged from her father, has told Lee, "I don't care if my dad dies. I'd dance on his grave." But Lee doesn't feel that way. The problems with her father go way back, to long before the car accident and substance abuse that derailed her life. As a child and teenager she wondered why her father didn't seem to love her the way she loved him, why she couldn't be "Daddy's girl" as she wanted to be. Now that they've been estranged for years, those questions persist. "The part that I am bothered by a lot is the desire, that I still want his love," she says. "I still want it so bad. And why? I don't even want it from this person, but I do. You know?"

She's done a lot of therapy to come to terms with the situation, and says she knows intellectually that her father's decision to break off their relationship doesn't mean she's unlovable or horrible; he's got his issues too. He's only human. Still, she longs to reconnect with him, to have the relationship she's always wished for and may never have.

"I have a hole in my heart from never really having a father," says Cindy, a fifty-six-year-old photographer in Seattle. For most of her adult life she was out of touch with her father, who is now dead, after a chaotic childhood in which she and her sister were passed back and forth between their divorced parents like unwanted puppies and then more or less abandoned. Cindy put herself through college; when she graduated, her father sent her a pen. She invited him to her wedding, but he never responded. She thinks maybe he never got the invitation; maybe her stepmother threw it out. In twenty-five years she saw him exactly once, for dinner when he came through Seattle on a sales trip, and it didn't go well.

They reconnected electronically in the last two years of his life, when he was dying of cancer. She sent him some of her photographs, and they emailed back and forth. It was something. It wasn't enough. "I did always want a connection with family," she says now through tears. "I loved my dad."

There is alas no magic spell that can resolve this conflict between the real and the ideal, between the family we want and the family we have. We are born to be connected and can't just walk away from that instinct. Some people spend their lives longing for a connection they can't have or never had. Some bury it so deeply it never resurfaces. Some stay tangled in the anger that propelled them away from the dysfunctional relationship in the first place.

And some forge a path in a different direction. The estrangement between Janey, the Australian publishing executive, and her mother began in adolescence, when her parents divorced and each of them, for different reasons, essentially walked away from her. She and her sister lived with her mother at first, enduring both her mother's explosions and her tendency to disappear for days at a time. After Janey left home there were years when they rarely communicated. Her mother's deep betrayal during Janey's divorce, when she agreed to lie in court and say Janey was an unfit mother so her husband could get custody, didn't improve their relationship. Her mother agreed because, she told her daughter, he was paying attention to her and Janey wasn't. For a long while they had no contact at all, and then, years after Janey had remarried and had two children, her mother sent her flowers for her fortieth birthday. For a year or so they emailed back and forth, and then her mother asked if she could come see her. That meeting went reasonably well.

After Janey and her family moved overseas, she continued the email relationship. For the first time in her life she started to feel like she actually had a mother, that person in her corner no matter what. It was a lovely warm feeling. Then her mother emailed and said she'd bought a special calling card so she could call Janey once a week. Janey wrote back to say she was enjoying their emails but needed more time; she wasn't quite ready for a weekly call. She never heard from her mother again.

"That was the least surprising thing that went down," she says now. Her mother had a history of disappearing, so it was more or less in character. The fact that Janey had been confident enough to tell her mother what she needed in the relationship apparently wasn't OK with her mother. The whole thing was a turning point for Janey, who realized that the problems between them weren't caused by something she'd done or said or hadn't said. Her mother simply wasn't capable of sustaining a healthy relationship with her.

Janey looked at her own children and thought about how natural it was to love them. "It's the best job I have, watching them be them, allowing them to be them," she says. "There's nothing more satisfying and loving and joyful." She knows now that her mother didn't want to do that, probably couldn't do that. She feels sad for her mother. But the deep ache of longing has gone, releasing her into her life as it is rather than as she might wish it, a life filled with a loving husband and children, a career she enjoys, close friendships, travel.

When people ask about her family of origin she says simply that she doesn't have one. She lets them assume that either something catastrophic happened or that her parents aged and died in the usual way. She doesn't talk about it because she doesn't want that to become her narrative. She doesn't want the estrangement and everything that led up to it to be a negative thing, a drag.

For those who can pull it off, this seems like an ideal response to the dilemma. If, like Cindy, you mourn that missing connection, persist in looking for it, let yourself hope that your mother or father will one day become the mother or father you've always wanted, you're setting yourself up for disappointment and grief and a kind of obsession. If, however, you teach yourself to let go of the longing, accept your family for who they are, let go of the wish to have them in your life, you're faced with a host of consequences, most of which come from the deep stigmas we still attach to estrangement, stigmas so entrenched and so painful that most people stay in toxic family relationships to avoid them. Young adults are especially vulnerable to the fallout from family estrangement, which is one reason Becca Bland started her nonprofit, Stand Alone—to help them overcome some of the economic losses of a family split.

To sidestep the stigma, many people avoid telling others about their situation, especially if they're estranged from a parent or child. As one mother posted on a Facebook page for estranged parents, "It is very much like death, without the sympathy and the flowers and the casseroles from concerned friends and family. As painful as the estrangement is, the comments and the harsh judgment on the estrangement just add to the pain." Most of the adult children in Kristina Scharp's research say there's nothing in the world that could make them want to tell others about their estrangements from their parents.[6] They give a variety of reasons: They think others will react badly. They don't want to burden people. Or they literally don't know how to explain what went wrong.

And maybe they just don't want to hear what people say in response. The most common comment people get when they say they've chosen to be estranged from their parents is "Someday they're going to die and you'll regret your decision." This can feel more like a threat than a warning: you *should* regret your decision—now make a different one. It's part of the pressure society brings to bear on anyone who disrupts the blood-family bond. Ben, the social worker in Ohio, says when people say that to him his response is *I hope they get on with it.* "I really don't trust my parents," he says. "If they weren't around I wouldn't have to worry about them anymore. I mean, I wouldn't hurt them, but I'd just as soon they dropped dead."

His words are extreme, but the feelings behind them are surprisingly common. I've heard this idea expressed again and again from kind people, compassionate people, empathetic people who go out of their way to help others. One of Kristina Scharp's interview subjects was unusually frank about his feelings:

> This sounds really horrible to say, but, it would be a lot easier if they were just dead. Rather than try to explain, well, they're not good people. Because how do you explain that to an eight-year-old? That, well, your grandparents aren't good people, you know. Knowing that she is going to say, "But you are their son."[7]

There's shame in acknowledging that your family is so deeply broken, shame and guilt and the fear of being judged harshly. There's the impossibility of explaining the situation to anyone who hasn't gone through it and who's never been forced to choose between *them* and *me*. Between the well-being of a mother, father, siblings—and more, the well-being of a family, an entity that's bigger and more encompassing than the individuals who populate it—and your own well-being. I think of my own impossibly convoluted history with my mother, the fatigue and despair that sets in whenever I try to explain what went wrong between us. I think of the long and winding tales told by my interview subjects, many of whom sounded defensive, as if nothing could truly justify the choices they'd made. I think of this comment from one of the participants in the Stand Alone study:

> When people come from loving environments they really just don't have the capacity to understand why one would

ever have to make that choice. We are taught the impor-
tance of family from day one that no matter what those are
the people who love you and are there for you. People think
you're just upset, having a tantrum, because they just cannot understand how it could ever come to that.

The key words here are *why one would ever have to make that
choice*. Everyone I've talked to who has chosen to estrange from
family, especially from parents, has done it as a survival tactic.
They came to believe over a long period of time that they *had* to
make that choice or else pay with their lives—physically, emotionally, spiritually. Becca Bland says that the nine years since
estranging from her family have been the best years of her life.
"Much better than the preceding twenty-four in terms of the confusion and chaos that comes with not understanding why your
family's how it is, why they're treating you like that, and what you
can do about it and feeling helpless," she says. "Having agency
has really helped me to grow."

Much of the time estrangement is not about adjudicating
disputes or sorting out blame and responsibility. It's about the human instinct for self-preservation. As another Stand Alone study
participant said, "[Estrangement] saved my life. I was severely depressed and attempted suicide. Estrangement has been nothing but
a blessing for me. I will take the stigma any day over being dead."[8]

Those who push estranged families to reconcile either fail to
see this reality or fail to acknowledge it. Bill, the project manager
from Buffalo, thinks a lot of people who do this have a kind of
savior complex. "Everybody wants to be the person that gets me
back with my family, and I think that's an extraordinarily disrespectful position," he says. It's like when the main character in
a horror movie runs out of the house where the serial killer lies
in wait; you would never tell that character everything's OK, go

on back inside, there's no danger. But that's exactly what people are doing when they coax others to get back together with their families. They may do it with the best intentions, thinking they're being helpful, but they're actually behaving selfishly. They want the feeling of having saved the day and the emotional comfort of things returning to the norm.

Maybe that impulse to save, to meddle, to fix is helpful sometimes. I've never known it to do anything but create more bad feeling, but I'm willing to believe there are situations where it might make things better. In the case of, say, a relatively simple misunderstanding, or an event that needs clarification, having an outsider step in, smooth things out, keep either party from losing too much face—maybe that can get some strained relationships back on track. But when estrangement is a solution for an otherwise unresolvable problem, not a problem that needs resolving, this kind of intervention can't possibly help. When people choose the logistical and emotional pain of estrangement over the desperation they feel when they're connected with their families, it's disingenuous to think that if you throw enough hearts and flowers and confetti into the middle you can "fix" things.

Maggie, twenty-three, a TV production assistant in New York City, was in high school when her mother cut off her own mother. The estrangement made it harder for Maggie and her siblings to see their grandmother, and for a while Maggie was pissed about it. Then her mother explained that Maggie's grandmother had been an abusive parent and refused to acknowledge the past abuse or discuss it with her daughter. Now that Maggie understands where her mother's coming from, she's fine with the estrangement. She loves both her mother and her grandmother and has no intention of choosing one or the other. "I sort of applaud my mom for not just staying in a toxic relationship because there was a blood connection," she says. The worst part about the situation for Maggie is all the secrecy and shame. She thinks if people talked about estrangement as easily as they talk about divorce, it wouldn't be such a big deal. "I think it's a viable option so people don't have to suffer," she says.

Jennifer, the hospice-care physician in Pennsylvania, agrees. In her experience of estrangement no one talks about the issue, whatever it is; family members just sort of disappear, never to be discussed again. "I'm not at all sure that estrangement itself is all that damaging, if it could come without the secrecy," she says.

Penny, a forty-year-old therapist in Ohio, says she wouldn't be alive today if she hadn't estranged herself from her parents, sisters, and other relatives seven years ago. She has traumatic memories of being sexually abused by her father, but when she tried as an adult to talk to her parents about the abuse, her father denied it. Her mother's first response was to apologize over and over, but later she too claimed it had never happened. Penny was seriously ill with an eating disorder for years and says she couldn't have recovered if she'd stayed in touch with her family. She regrets that she needed to cut them off, but she doesn't regret her choice to do it. Her only worry now is what she'll tell her three young children when they're old enough to ask about their grandparents. "I'm kind of hoping my parents will die soon so I can just say they're dead and not have to deal with it," she says.

Ben, the social worker from Ohio, says he's gotten into arguments with family members and friends who have tried to guilt him back into touch with his parents. Most people find it unacceptable that he doesn't have a relationship with them. So he's learned not to talk about the estrangement much. He remembers one conversation in particular with someone who basically made the Elizabeth Vagnoni argument—that family problems are usually caused by children's lack of respect for and mistreatment of parents. He doesn't buy it. "I said, what about how the parents treat the children?" he asks. "The parents have no obligation? They can do unending shit and the children have an unending commitment to care for them?" He shakes his head. "I don't think that's right," he says.

For Mary, the graduate student in philosophy whose mother insisted she had bipolar disorder, the pressure to reconcile feels like a threat. The estrangement from her mother is relatively easy. It solves a lot of problems, and Mary's made her peace with it. Other people's comments, though, are a lot more challenging. When people in her faith community say they'll hope and pray for reconciliation between her and her mother, she hears *I will pray your mother comes back and puts you back on lithium.* Maybe they mean to be comforting or encouraging, but their words terrify Mary. They send her deep into the helplessness and despair of her childhood.

Pushing someone to reconcile with an estranged family member, especially a parent, is a lot like pushing someone to go on a diet: it's social pressure masquerading as helpful information. Those of us who have estranged ourselves are already painfully aware of the judgments of outsiders. We're not blind; we're surrounded by Hallmark images of happy families. We know perfectly well that everyone else would be a whole lot more comfortable if we sucked it up and "got along" again. So that insistence that we try again, give our family another chance, overlook the difficulties, is unhelpful. And it can backfire. Andi, the physical therapist from Queens, says pressure from other family members to reconcile with her parents has led to even more estrangements. "There's no one in my life who pressures me, because anyone who does that I do not talk to anymore," she says flatly.

Tracy, the teacher from Ann Arbor, says she got some family pressure to reconcile with her father, but it was relatively easy to deal with. What she struggled with more was the greater societal pressure she felt and internalized. "Estrangement is not the narrative we live with in our society, especially estrangement from parents," she says. "Our civilization is based on family. It's in the Bible. You're there for your parents. When you're estranged you're definitely flying in the face of your culture." Like virtually everyone I interviewed, she's clear that despite the pressures and guilt, estrangement was the best choice for her. For one thing, it preserved her own family. She thinks her marriage would have ended had she not cut off her father, because even the slightest contact with him derailed her for weeks. "That's how you know you really can't be in touch with that person," she says. "Nobody should require weeks of self-therapy or real therapy to get over a freaking conversation with somebody. Right?"

That all-encompassing cultural narrative of the happy intact family—or maybe the not-so-happy-but-still-stumbling-along intact family—produces a lot of the stigma around estrangement. And while that stigma can affect everyone in an estrangement, it tends to affect the lives of children who cut themselves off from their parents most deeply. Maybe that's why there are so many online forums for estranged parents but virtually none for children. We need to do our grieving alone because we feel a different kind of shame, one that grows out of the original power dynamic between parents and children. Admitting you're estranged from your parents is akin to admitting your parents didn't love you unconditionally, didn't take care of you, don't on some fundamental level accept you for who you are.

Bill, the project manager from Buffalo whose father tried to kill him, says his estrangement has been a social stumbling block, since the subject of family typically comes up early in the process of getting to know other people. When new acquaintances ask about his parents, he either has to lie or tell them the whole complicated and emotional story. And he really, *really* doesn't like to lie. Bill says he's lost both established and new friendships after explaining his situation. "It's like a very heavy stone," he says. "And that's not really a stone most people want to carry." He looks forward to the time when his parents aren't around anymore so he can say they're dead without having to spill the whole saga and endure the judgment of others.

That's understandable. Claire, who was estranged from her mother for four years, says she rarely told anyone what was going on. "It's very difficult when you're grieving for people who are alive," she explains. "Difficult for people to relate to, difficult to talk about. And a great source of shame as well." That shame can feel intensely personal. As one of the participants in the Stand Alone survey commented, "People think if your own kids hate you that much there must be something wrong with you. Before, if I said anything about my kids not talking to me or that I don't see my grandkids, it usually killed the conversation. Now if the question comes up I say, 'I have a son and a daughter and I don't see them nearly enough.' I try to avoid any more discussion."

Lisa, a fifty-seven-year-old fundraiser in the Chicago area, was estranged from both of her sons twenty years ago after a traumatic divorce. Her husband was an angry, volatile man who kept guns in the house, and while she didn't think he would hurt the boys, who were nine and fourteen, she was afraid he might actually kill her. So she was the one to leave. Her lawyer told her that because her husband had been a stay-at-home parent while she went out to work, he would get custody; maybe that was true and maybe it wasn't, but she believed it. Her ex-husband had the boys write vicious letters to her and to local news media during the divorce, letters that threatened her with violence and even murder. She doesn't blame them. "They were very young," she says. "They did whatever they had to do to survive with their father." But it meant that while she paid child support until her youngest son turned eighteen, she mostly stayed away.

Once the boys were out on their own, she tried to reconnect with them. They were still close with their father, though, and the relationships never quite took. It's been so long since they had any kind of closeness that she has to stop and do the math to remember how old they are. They've been estranged now for far longer than they ever were together.

Lisa has since remarried, and while she does talk to her second husband about the estrangement, he doesn't really get it. He doesn't understand why she holds herself aloof from many of his friends, why she avoids close relationships, why she never brings up the fact that she has two grown sons. She tells him it's because she never knows, when the subject does come up, how she will react. She might say, *Yes, I have two sons, they live in West Virginia, how about you?* She might burst into tears. She might feel like she's about to pass out, the way she often felt when it all began twenty years ago. Every conversation has the potential to lead her to a place where she must admit that she was a non-custodial mother, that her sons have turned against her, that she hasn't seen them in years. She really doesn't want to cry about it in front of other people, because that would be looking for sympathy she probably doesn't deserve.

So she keeps to herself, especially at work, where her co-workers are younger and female and someone's always having a baby. She doesn't volunteer advice or information or support to the other mothers. She doesn't offer anything. She's not close to anyone at the office and that's the way she wants it. That's the way she protects that tender part of herself. She has one or two good friends, but on the whole she tucks the grief and the shame and the longing away and tries to move forward with a life that in many ways feels like it never happened.

In my life the worst stigma and pressure to reconcile came from other family members. My decision to cut off the relationship with my mother seemed to threaten the whole family, though I lived thousands of miles from most of them and saw them maybe once a year. I used to dread seeing the 609 area code pop up on my phone because I knew it was one of a handful of family members calling to plead, intervene, cajole, or out-and-out threaten me.

My great-aunt, for instance, my grandmother's youngest sister, a former middle school principal, never in her life called me just to chat. When I heard her voice on the phone one night after work I knew what was coming. After asking about my daughters she posed the question at the heart of all of these conversations: *Why can't you just get along with your mother?*

The way the question is framed—the way it's *always* framed—is telling. It's *my* job as the child to get along with my mother. To respect my mother. From an anthropological standpoint this makes sense: the family is the building block of society, the zeroes and ones that shape the world. It cannot come apart. Not often, anyway. And so on top of the biological imperatives that hold parents and children together come layers of social ultimatums, starting with this one.

The thing is, I believed my great-aunt was right; it was my duty to do whatever it took to make the relationship work. To honor my mother and father, offer respect, defer to their opinions, their feelings, their wishes. I wished even then that I didn't believe this because my life would have been a lot simpler if I could just shut that door, wash my hands, be done with my parents once and for all.

But I also knew that when my great-aunt asked *Why can't you just get along with your mother?* she was really asking why I *wouldn't* get along with my mother. Why I wouldn't capitulate to whatever surely reasonable requests my mother made of me, why I wouldn't give her the respect she deserved. Really she wanted to know why she and the rest of the relatives still had to deal with the conflict between us. An estrangement between a parent and child, even a long-grown child, affects the whole family. It becomes a locus of infection, the spot where disease enters the body of the family and threatens its health and integrity. It threatens the *illusion* of family, the idea that the family—especially the link between parent and child—supersedes all other relationships.

This is, of course, exactly what the Fifth Commandment suggests. Honor thy father and mother. *Kavod et avicha v'et imecha.* The Fifth Commandment has no "but" attached. That respect is expected in every situation, every family. If you see the bond between a parent and child, especially a mother and child, as sacrosanct, a divine coupling that can't be undone, then the kind of alienation that's existed for years between my mother and me undermines the foundations of human life. And that's not an exaggeration. There's something so threatening, so dangerous about our estrangement that other members of the family can't bear it.

Then, too, there's the practical reason for her call, which neither of us will mention but which we're both well aware of. My mother has always been volatile. She's like a stick of dynamite with a lit but invisible fuse; you know it's going to explode but you don't know when, and you want to be as far away as possible when it does. My great-aunt's call is part of a years-long game of hot potato, where the rest of the family seems determined that I will be the one who gets burned.

"Why can't you get along with your mother?" my great-aunt asks again.

"What has she told you?" I say.

"That she doesn't understand why you're so cruel. That you've rejected her over and over. That . . ."

"That I'm cold-hearted and she loves me anyway," I finish for her. "That all she's ever wanted was for me to love her. That she has no idea why I'm so bitter, so angry, so hurtful."

She has the grace to go silent and I suppress the inappropriate urge to laugh. My great-aunt is one of the few people in the family who still talks to me. Who hasn't turned her back. I want her to keep talking to me. Her voice on the phone carries the same timbre and tone as my much-missed grandmother's. When I hear it I feel a wave of comfort.

I don't bother telling my great-aunt my side of things—the letters, the phone calls, the unpredictability and high drama of being my mother's daughter—because she's been in her own relationship with my mother for longer than I've been alive. She must know something of my mother's disordered responses. Though my mother's far less inhibited with me than with the rest of the family, and I doubt my great-aunt comes in for the same kind of emotional battering that I do.

Anyway, it doesn't matter. The child's job is to accommodate, shape herself to the parent's expectations. That's what the Fifth Commandment is all about—not honor in the sense of parades and confetti but honoring in the sense of self-sacrifice. I'd like to ask my great-aunt if there's an escape clause for this particular commandment. What, if any, extenuating circumstances let a child off the hook for this sort of honor? A long line of Talmudic scholars has commented on the Fifth Commandment, comparing the relationship between a parent and child to the relationship between a person and God. A number of them even came up with specific situations where the commandment still applies. For instance: "Even if he was wearing formal clothes and sitting at the head of an assembly, and his father and mother came and tore his clothes, beat him, and spit at him, he may not insult them but rather should remain quiet. Even if they took his wallet full of money and threw it into the sea, he should not insult them nor irritate them nor get angry at them."[9]

Fortunately, neither of these particular situations has come up in my dealings with my mother. And the scholars are pretty much mute on the question of whether a child needs to honor a parent who is emotionally abusive, who systematically destroys or tries to destroy that child's self-esteem, who sees the child only as a reflection of herself and fails to acknowledge the child's basic humanity.

I tell my great-aunt I'm sure she has everyone's best interests at heart but she really doesn't know the whole story. That she can't believe everything she hears from my mother without question. That I appreciate her call and am hanging up now. That night I cry for the thousandth time, for my mother, for myself, for this longing I can't satisfy and can't let go of. I know even as I cry that part of what I'm grieving for has nothing to do with my mother. Our estrangement has cost me the comforting fantasy that my family has my back. And it's lost me a connection with nearly everyone in the extended family, most of whom live within twenty miles of one another and share not just geography but values and a point of view. Most of them agree with my mother that I'm the one at fault. I'm the bad daughter, the ingrate. And while I know I was never going to be close to most of them, even the possibility is closed to me now.

Only four or five people out of the fifty or so relatives on this side of the family have tried to straddle the line between me and my mother: my grandparents, when they were alive. One aunt and uncle—my father's sister and her husband. My sister. That's pretty much it. A few cousins from my parents' generation have made it clear that they actively dislike me; most of the rest of the family is simply uninterested. This isn't all about my relationship with my mother, of course. Most of my extended family is firmly

entrenched in the busy materialism of suburban South Jersey;
I live in upstate New York with my non-Jewish husband. That
alone would set me apart. About my mother, I don't know what
any of them felt. They must have had more than an inkling of
her capacity for cruelty and narcissism. But as long as I was the
scapegoat, the decoy, the lightning rod who attracted my mother's
rage and grief, no one else had to deal with it quite as much.

And I get it. I really do. I also get how hard it's been on
the handful of relatives who didn't choose sides. My sister, for
instance, who's borne the emotional and financial brunt of decades of family celebrations that I refused to participate in. I
know she often felt unfairly caught between my mother and me.
When we were in our twenties our mother often begged her to
play the go-between. Back then my mother was always looking
for someone to "be the bridge" between us, though I'm not sure
how she imagined this would help. How could anything anyone
else said address the issues between us? All she had to do was
listen to my words and feelings, acknowledge them, hear them.
No one else could do that for her.

They tried, though. My *bubbe,* my mother's mother, calls
me for the first and last time in my life to push for reconciliation. Clearly she's uncomfortable in this peacemaker role. "I bet
you wish I wasn't butting in!" she chirps. My Aunt Selma, my
mother's sister, phones on a similar mission. "I know you'll think
I'm an interfering aunt," she begins. Yes I do. I'm not close with
either woman; we don't have the kind of relationship that includes
offering unsolicited advice. Still, the two phone calls produce so
much guilt that I call my mother for the first time in weeks and
we talk about nothing for a few minutes. At the end she starts
to cry. "I didn't know what to do!" she says, sobbing. I feel sad
and guilty and tell myself I will just suck it up, let her criticisms
blow by, stay calm in the face of her explosions. I don't live in my

mother's house anymore. I'm a grown woman with two daughters of my own. I don't have to react.

That night I dream I have been captured and held prisoner and I'm trying to escape. I wake panting, my back in a spasm of agony. I can't do this. Every phone call with my mother causes me pain, physical and otherwise. Every time our orbits overlap I go spinning into a dark place. Maybe if enough time went by without her tears or rages or accusations I could learn to trust her. It wouldn't take that long—six months? A year? But it's never going to happen.

I also know that even if my relatives were scrupulous about not taking sides (clearly they're not), the fallout from our conflict would affect everyone in the family. Eric, the CFO from Los Angeles, says his estrangement from his sister has meant he's basically an only child, with no sibling to share family holidays or brainstorm with. That's a bit of a burden at times, but it's nothing like what his parents are going through. "Their lives in this regard are damaged and broken," he says. He worries most about what will happen when one of his parents dies and the family has to come together for the one who's left. How will they manage that when they can't even exchange civil emails? Once both parents are gone, though, the problem is solved, at least for him. He will tell his sister to take whatever she wants and go on her way, and that will be the end of their relationship.

Bethany, a sixty-year-old professor of paleontology at a large Indiana university, felt devastated by the six-year estrangement between her oldest brother and their mother. The family had always been close, especially after Bethany's father died suddenly at age fifty-two, and they'd long been prominent in their small Texas community. The rift began when her brother's second marriage hit a rough patch and he began to be seen around town with another woman. Their mother, whom Bethany describes as a "steel magnolia," was furious with her son for what she saw as dishonorable behavior and felt humiliated by the inevitable small-town gossip about it. Her brother stopped showing up to family gatherings, stopped talking to his mother. When Bethany flew in to visit she had to make separate arrangements to see her brother and mother, who lived only two blocks apart. It was like stepping around the white chalk cutout at a crime scene, an absence that came to define the entire family. And it shook Bethany badly. "It made me feel as if my family wasn't there for me, in the sense that there wasn't a *there* there anymore," she says. "There were just individual relationships."

What she means is that the estrangement broke her trust in the family. If her brother and mother could stop speaking, stop interacting, maybe even stop loving each other, that could happen to her too. The thought chilled her to the core. She'd lived hundreds of miles away for many years but now she felt isolated in a new way, rootless and detached. She'd been orphaned, though she was still in touch with both her brother and her mother. The survival of the family was riding on their relationship, their estrangement. And that pissed her off. "It was as if each of these people, my mother and brother, was carrying a huge burden somehow, and they were doing it intentionally, and that burden had been brought to the others of us whose decision it hadn't been," she remembers. "I try not to be a judger, but I really do judge somebody who would be that willing to inflict pain on a family voluntarily."

From Bethany's perspective the estrangement was voluntary, deliberate, intentional. The family, on the other hand, was nonvoluntary—a given, a binding contract forged in chromosomes and reinforced by long habit and tradition. Years after the estrangement ended she still speaks of it with horror, wrapping her arms around her own body as if she can't get warm. It happened once; maybe it could happen again. She thinks one of the contributing factors in the reconciliation was that her mother developed a serious heart problem, and her brother, a health-care attorney, played a role in her care despite their ongoing estrangement.

That began a process Bethany describes in geological terms: a rift being annealed tectonically, the earth healing itself through small movements deep under the surface. Her brother showed up one year toward the end of Thanksgiving dinner, made an appearance at Christmas, brought his new wife to a family celebration, until his presence became less of a surprise than his absence. She's grateful for the rapprochement, for the fact that they can function as a family again. But it bothers her that as far as she knows neither her brother nor her mother apologized, that they never really talked through what happened. Which means it could happen again, over something as small as a missed date or as big as adultery. "I'm a paleontologist," she says. "My whole business is trying to understand the past. And I cannot pretend to understand this."

Holidays can be a huge trigger for estrangements, causing them, exacerbating the trauma, or, as for Bethany's family, playing a role in healing them. For Jo, the New York City writer who struggled with her family's annual dysfunctional Thanksgiving celebration, the pressure to pretend they were a happy family one day a year triggered an emotional funk that went on for weeks after the holiday. For Sandy, the retired nurse in Georgia, Christmas has become a painful day. The estrangement from her daughter means she and her husband aren't invited to celebrate the holiday with her or with their son, who lives in the same town. It hurts to see her friends post pictures on Facebook of their families smiling around a Christmas tree or raising a glass at the dinner table. "We can't do any of that," she says. "And that's what I had looked forward to at this age."

Kate, the artist in Philadelphia, has always hated Christmas, a holiday that brought out a lot of family drama. Now that she's chosen to cut herself off from both parents the day brings a different flavor of grief, reminding her that she's had to give up on the fantasy that her family will someday feel warm and close and loving. Victoria, the Tucson professor, used to hide the fact that she and her husband spend the holiday with friends by saying they were visiting "friends and family." She worried that people would judge her for not having relatives to visit on the most family-oriented day of the year.

My long estrangement with my mother left me with complicated feelings around holidays. My family didn't celebrate Christmas, and Hanukkah was never a big deal in our house, so for me the tricky holidays were Passover, Yom Kippur, and the ever-dreaded Mother's Day. I hated reading post after post on social media testifying to mother love. Some of the people posting, I knew, had had serious differences with their mothers. Some had cried to me over mean-spirited exchanges, vented irritations, complained at length. I wondered how they got from years of problems and distress to those public declarations of love and affection. It seemed they knew something I didn't about how to overlook the negative and celebrate the positive. Or maybe they were just better people than I was.

And then there were the practical dilemmas that came with the day. If my mother and I were speaking (or at least not actively *not* speaking) and I didn't get her a card, she'd be hurt and angry and we'd flip back into fighting for months. But I couldn't bring myself to buy a card announcing she was the best mother in the world or telling her how much I loved her or how glad I was to be her daughter because none of those things were true. To celebrate her mothering would have felt like celebrating a car accident where you walked away with *only* a broken arm. A few times I sent blank cards with abstract designs on the front and a bland message like "Thinking of you on Mother's Day!" Which was true enough, though I'm sure my thoughts would not have pleased her.

I'm not the only one who struggles with holidays, especially Mother's and Father's Day. "I don't even get on Facebook on those days," says Rachel, the journalist from Cincinnati. "It's twenty-four hours of 'I have such a great dad!'"

Tracy, the teacher from Ann Arbor, is all too aware of the censure and stigma that comes with estrangement, especially around holidays. "Nothing else I've done has made me feel more like an outlaw," she says. She describes this as Hallmark/social-media collusion, writing sarcastically:

> Have you heard? It's *Sister's Day*!!!!! Share this if your sister is the most loving, best friend you have ever had, the one person in whom you can confide everything!!!! Nine thousand six hundred and thirty-one people have shared this, including 35 of your friends.

◇◇◇◇◇

ONE COMMON STRATEGY for dealing with holidays among people who are estranged is to create other families for yourself, whether it's mother and father figures or simply other deeply connected groups of people—families of choice. Jenna, a forty-five-year-old educator from Ohio, has been estranged from her father for about ten years. Her parents divorced when she was five, and her father raised her and her brother with the help of his parents; her mother had moved in with another man and didn't want the children. Jenna's father was rarely affectionate, and she didn't feel close to him. As she became an adult, the differences in

their temperaments and values became more obvious: He's politically conservative and she's liberal. He had been something of a
hands-off, unemotional parent; she was a stay-at-home mom and
doula who was passionately attached to her daughter.

When her father remarried a woman who had children, Jenna
felt he fit better with those children than he had with her brother
and her. Still, they maintained a low-key relationship. They didn't
see each other often, and Jenna was aware of her father's unspoken criticisms of her own child-rearing. They muddled along
until Jenna's daughter turned thirteen and her father did nothing—no card, no gift, no phone call, no email. Jenna called him
and said she'd felt hurt that he let his granddaughter's teenage
birthday go by without acknowledgment. His response was that
he just figured he'd see them at Thanksgiving; then he added that
clearly they were different people and that he was fine seeing her
once or twice a year. He more or less acknowledged that he didn't
really like her. She remembers crying on the phone and saying
something like *I'm so glad we've had this conversation, it's very clarifying for me.* "While I was hurt, I was almost instantly relieved,"
she says. "A lot of people want it to be this other thing. It's like
they can't accept that they weren't loved well by their parents, so
they kind of just push on that bruise their whole life."

Like nearly everyone I talked to, Jenna rejects the idea that
blood is the only basis for family. She speaks blisteringly about
what she calls inauthentic family relationships, the kind of superficial connections that gloss over everything important, put people in roles and keep them there. Instead, she has created what
she calls a tribe, her family of choice. She takes her relationships
seriously. She shows up for other people. "I can love and be loved
successfully in spite of the fact that my formative primary relationships failed at that," she says.

As she keeps talking, her last comment echoes in my ears. It's impossible to overstate just how hard it is to come out of a family like hers intact. A wise therapist once told me that when your parents don't give you their blessing you must learn to bless yourself. The problem is that without their blessing you are dumb, stuck in the vocabulary of childhood: *I want. I need. I hurt.* You don't have, or don't believe you have, the ability to calm yourself, to release yourself into the world, into your life.

I ask Jenna how exactly she managed this. How has she been able to do what so many can't—let go of the impossible while building something new? How did she escape the trap so many estranged people find themselves in, longing for closeness with family even as they know it will never happen? To some degree, she says, her parents raised her to have zero expectations of a relationship with them, and that's what she's got. Then, too, her dad was pretty unemotional; actually, she uses the word *robotic*. When she would come home from school and start to tell him a story, he would ask if it was something he really needed to know. "I'm real clear, and I'm grateful for that," she says. "My parents showed me who they were. There wasn't really any emotional investment on their part. Why would I stamp my foot and fuss at that? I'm not important to them. And I don't take it personally."

My eyes fill with tears of grief and rage for Jenna, but she's calm, even matter-of-fact. "I do not pine for my parents in any way," she says. "I do not love my father." Her own parenting style has relied strongly on attachment: she had a home birth, nursed her daughter for years, was happy to be a stay-at-home mother. The contrast with the way she was parented herself is striking.

The notion of a family of choice is hugely liberating for many people. Rick, forty-one, a set dresser on TV shows in New York City, is estranged from his sister and two cousins. He says no one needs to be stuck in a relationship just because of genetics. He spends a fair amount of time with his mother and one aunt and uncle, and has had the same two close male friends for nearly twenty years. "I find a family of choice a lot more reliable and comforting," he says. "We spend as much time as we can together. We can bust each other's chops in a way that I think is deeper than brotherhood. Because it's a constant reaffirmation of our relationship as opposed to 'Oh, I'm just stuck with this person.'"

Andrea, the nurse from Madison, Wisconsin, who's estranged from her mother and sisters, started building her family of choice in her teens. She joined a women's climbing group where most of the women were ten to fifteen years older, and they've met up every few weeks for the last thirty years. Those women became her other mothers, her family.

Long-standing friendships make excellent families of choice. But sometimes newer relationships can stand in, too. Several years ago Sandy, the retired nurse in Georgia who's estranged from her daughter, started volunteering with a local pediatric hospice organization, in part to distract herself from missing her grandchildren. One of the first families she worked with had a three-year-old with a terminal brain tumor, as well as two older children. She and her husband quickly bonded with the whole family. They take the older children apple picking and have them for sleepovers, and they host the whole family at Christmas. "It's filled the void, but it's not the same," says Sandy. "There's still lurking in the back of my brain this rejection from my kids."

It's not the same, no. But it's still powerful. I don't know what would have happened to me without the four women I consider my other mothers: my grandmother, aunt, mother-in-law, and longtime therapist. Without them I might have drowned in the ocean of my own self-loathing. I might have parented the way my mother did, reflexively rather than reflectively, unable to see my daughters as they were, doomed to torment myself and everyone around me with my self-inflicted other-directed flailing. Without my mothers of choice, and my husband, and the wider circle of friends who have become my family, I might never have truly felt the deep connection with other people that makes us tender and alive and human.

Chapter Seven

THE HALF-LIFE OF GRIEF

I still have reconciliation dreams, which is how I can tell I'm still grieving. I have this long healing talk with one of my siblings and we embrace and get back in each other's lives and we're just so happy to be together again.

—LILY, sixty-five

One evening not long after my mother's death, while cooking dinner for my husband and daughters, I pull the apple cider vinegar out of the cabinet and nearly drop it in shock. Floating near the bottom of the glass bottle is a clotted mass. I shake the bottle but the clump remains, slimy and strangely menacing. A vinegar mother—that's what it's called. I've never seen one before. It's supposed to be good for you, this cloudy swirl of bacteria and proteins and sediment that blooms from unfermented sugar and alcohol and air. Too solid to be poured, too sturdy to dissolve, it bumps against the bottom of the bottle like something out of a horror movie, swaying slowly.

I shake the bottle again but the clot retains its shape. Some people prize these, ascribing semi-magical healing powers to them, and they do contain vitamins and iron and phytochemicals, compounds that are supposed to protect health and help ward off disease.

I peer through the glass and it feels like the vinegar mother peers back. It feels like a portent or maybe a message from beyond the grave, as if my mother's bitterness is reaching back for me, a bitterness that's supposed to be good for me. I don't know what to do with it. I'm not going to drink it. I can't dump it; the mother is too solid to drain out of the pouring spout. And I feel a superstitious dread about throwing it away. I screw the cap back on and leave the bottle beside the kitchen sink, where it sits for days, the mother revolving slowly in its acid bath. Then one morning the counter by the sink is empty; my husband has disposed of it. I don't ask him what he did with it. I'm just relieved it's gone. The metaphor was too damn obvious.

In the months since our mother has died, my sister has been grieving hard. She cries in the car on the way to work. She cries at home. She sees reminders of our mother everywhere and takes them as signs that our mother is watching over her, and she is comforted. Her voice breaks as she tells me this, over the phone from three thousand miles away, and I envy her clarity, her clean raw sorrow. There is nothing clear about what I'm feeling. My grief is dirty, contaminated with the rage I've felt toward my mother for so many years, with the cloudy residue of a thousand painful moments.

My sister has chosen to forget her worst moments with our mother: The time she stormed out of a restaurant in 100-degree desert heat and tried to walk home in a fury over not getting her way, forcing everyone else to abandon their meals and follow, pleading with her to get into the air-conditioned car. (She eventually did. Of course she did.) The garbage in the ice cream container. Leaving my infant daughter on the floor to teach her a lesson. My sister has forgotten that she more than once told me she thought our mother might be insane.

For my sister grief is a tidal wave sweeping everything out of its path, leaving behind an emptiness she can fill with sorrow and longing. For me it's a bruise I press on, watching the blood pool and move under my skin, the colors shifting from dark to light as it disappears. I've grieved the way my sister does for other losses: my grandmother, my grandfather, my mother-in-law. This feels different. I'm not sure that what I'm feeling even qualifies as grief, not the way I've known it before. After my grandmother died there were times when I felt sick with missing her. I used to dream about her physical presence, about wrapping my arms around her comforting body. I imagined her voice over and over in my mind, trying to imprint it into aural memory so I could hear it whenever I wanted.

When I think of my mother's voice I feel a familiar tinge of irritation, imagining her saying my name as she often did, rising through the scale on a single syllable—*Har?*—in a way that still makes me break out in a sweat. I wish I could forget it. I don't long for my mother's physical body or dream about her touch. In my dreams I am articulate and persuasive; I tell her exactly how I feel, and when she says something harsh—*You're manipulative! You're deceitful!*—I stare her silent. I never wish to feel her arm around me comfortingly. Actually, I can't remember ever wishing for that. If I did it's lost under a tide of fury and frustration.

Like most children, I once knew my mother's body well. But during the decades of our estrangement, when I saw my mother only once every few years, her physical presence grew foreign to me. I don't know when she started dyeing her hair blond rather than brown, when she got her first pair of reading glasses. I didn't see the hysterectomy scar from the year before she died. I never learned the folds and wrinkles of her seventy-five-year-old body the way I'd memorized, without meaning to, her shape at twenty-five and thirty and thirty-five. I couldn't have mapped her birth-marks and skin tags and moles. I didn't want to.

The details that stay with me all came from childhood, when I still lived within her insistent orbit: The specific click of her ankles as she bent over the laundry hamper outside my bedroom door. Her deep-set eyes, blue-gray under heavy lids. Her fingers flashing across the keyboard of a Selectric, her curved thumbs—hitchhiker's thumbs—drumming the space bar in a melody of speed. Much later, when I made beds or packed lunches or brushed hair for my two young daughters, I sometimes caught sight of my hands and felt surprise; their unbending thumbs and ragged nails looked nothing like a mother's hands to me.

Maybe I wore out my quota of grief for my mother long ago, mourning what passed between us and what did not and, later, our necessary estrangement. Long before she died I dreamed that she and I were leaning on opposite sides of a closed door. I was holding it shut with all my weight; she was trying to wrench it open. I was convinced that my life depended on keeping the door closed, and I did. The door stayed closed. And then, in the dream, a profound sense of desolation washed through me. I felt more sorrow and regret in that dream moment than I ever had awake.

Now, after her death, I find myself thinking about that dream and wondering why I felt desolate and bereft when I was the one holding the door closed. Why, in fact, I *still* feel desolate and bereft when I recall it. I knew, both in the dream and outside it, that I *had* to keep the door closed, that something terrible and unsurvivable would happen if it burst open. So why was I grieving it now? Or was this grief at all?

What I am experiencing, it turns out, is a complex and confusing phenomenon that psychotherapist Pauline Boss describes as ambiguous loss, a loss that lacks finality or a sense of resolution.[1] Closure, some people might call it. Ordinary loss and grief always contain elements of ambiguity, of course. A few months after my mother-in-law died, for instance, I had the insistent feeling that enough time had gone by, we'd suffered her absence long enough, and it was now time for her to reappear. I knew this was irrational; I understood intellectually that she wasn't coming back. But at the same time I felt she should, in a way that was different from hoping or wishing she hadn't died. On some level we are shielded from taking in the reality of death all at once, and it can take a long time to process it. For years after my grandmother died I would still reach for the phone to call her. Eventually my subconscious got the message and the impulse receded.

Ambiguous loss goes beyond ordinary levels of uncertainty. That person is both there and not there, physically missing but psychologically very much with you. Grieving for someone who's still alive but has Alzheimer's or another dementia is a classic example because the person is both present and absent, there in the flesh but gone in other ways. Grieving for someone whose physical fate is unclear—for instance, victims of the 9/11 attack whose bodies were never recovered—is another example. This kind of loss lives in the dissonance between the private and the public experience, between what you feel and what others expect you to feel.

Ambiguous loss is even more confusing in family estrangement, where it can raise logistical questions as well as emotional ones: Who takes care of aging parents when a grown child is estranged? Who gets called in times of emergency and who doesn't? Who is allowed information about family matters and who is shut out? Whose grief is supported publicly and who has to cry alone, in private?

When my mother died I felt I didn't deserve to mourn because what I was experiencing had little to do with the fact that she was no longer alive. It was a much older feeling, older and somehow more shameful. I grieved the loss that had been embedded in our relationship right from the start. The mirror I never had, the ear that never heard me. I cried not over her death but over the end of our story. Nothing between us would ever get better now.

That's the whole point of estrangement, after all. It's a giving up of hope, an acknowledgment that nothing more will change. It is itself a kind of ambiguous loss, an illicit and stigmatized grieving, even if—maybe especially if—you're the one holding the door closed. In one recent study, all of the estranged adult children said they felt grief, loss, and trauma despite the fact that they were the ones who started and/or kept up estrangements from one or both parents.[2] The symptoms they reported—sleeplessness, disbelief, shock, anxiety, anger—were identical to the kind of "ordinary" grief felt by close family members who were not estranged, but were further complicated by the stigma around estrangement. According to Kylie Agllias, an Australian social-work researcher who studies the issue, family estrangement brings a kind of disenfranchised grief and loss, one without rules or traditions or public recognition. There are no collective rituals around estrangement, no wakes or *shivas,* no sympathy cards or casseroles. Instead of love and companionship and support, estranged people often get disapproval, pressure to reconcile, even ostracism.

I think of Bill, the project manager from Buffalo, who found time after time that mentioning his estrangement from his family of origin made people so uncomfortable they would just drift away. Or Lisa, the Chicago fundraiser who avoids friendships so she doesn't have to explain why she hasn't talked to either of her grown sons in years. Or Victoria, the academic in Tucson, whose necessary estrangement from her family meant she had to distance herself from her tight group of childhood friends. Growing up, they looked up to her because she lived in a nice house and went to church regularly and had "good" parents, and now they don't understand why she of all people has made this decision. They say things like "I could see so-and-so, whose dad beat the kids and was an alcoholic, or so-and-so, who grew up so poor, but why Victoria?" She doesn't want to tell them about the sexual abuse and all the betrayals that followed it, maybe because most of those childhood friends still live in the same community as her parents. So that's another kind of grief for Victoria, loss upon loss, loss *creating* loss, yet another ripple from the original estrangement.

Jennifer, the hospice-care physician from Pennsylvania, says her family's multigenerational history of estrangement has left her with a more enduring sense of loss than any of her hospice experiences. "I have had a lot of disenfranchised losses in my life—not deaths which are recognized and ritualized and understood but deep losses for which there's no framework in ritual," she says thoughtfully. "There's a sort of deep well of grief that I'm really just beginning to understand at this stage in life. And I do grief for a living."

You're expected to grieve death and its losses. But you rarely get the chance to articulate the kind of grief that both leads to estrangements and accompanies them, especially if you're the one who's walked away. Rachel, the journalist from Cincinnati, describes it as grieving for something she's never had and always wanted. "I don't miss my brothers and my mom," she says. "I miss the *idea* of a family. I have a lot of times when I feel kind of like an orphan." That's a word that comes up again and again in talking about estrangement: the sense of being unparented, unanchored in the world, whether you're officially estranged from family or not. The need to hide this sense of being orphaned and alone, to avoid stigma and shame, amplifies that grief and becomes part of it. And keeping that secret costs us in so many ways. No wonder Kristina Scharp was inundated with responses when she put out a call for interview subjects. We don't just want to talk about this kind of grief—we need to.

A few years before my mother died, my father's sister, the one aunt I've been close to, came back from a visit to my mother and commented that my mother had no idea how critical and judgmental she was, that my mother didn't think of herself in that way. This was true; all her life my mother thought of herself as childlike in the best sense of the word: happy-go-lucky, fun-loving, spontaneous, warm. People who didn't know her well often thought of her this way at first. They loved the fact that she would dress up as the Pink Panther for Halloween, complete with a shiny pink wig and hand-drawn whiskers. They found her enthusiasm contagious. She had pep.

I thought of her as childlike, too, though in my case it wasn't a fond thought but an exhausting one. Spending time with my mother often felt like taking care of a barely socialized three-year-old. In her own mind she was the star of every story, in front of the footlights, and we were nothing but shadows on the back-drop, there to fill out the action and support her featured role. Of course we are all the protagonists of our own stories, though ideally we understand that other people have feelings too. I'm not sure if my mother got that. During my wedding, for example, she and my father walked me down the aisle, one on each side. When we got to the *chuppah* my father stepped away as we'd rehearsed but my mother held on, a bemused look on her face. I had to pry her fingers from my arm so I could step toward my groom. Her preoccupation had nothing to do with me; there was no shining-eyed look between us, no mother's embrace. I suspect she was thinking about her own wedding. I suspect she was barely aware I was there.

Then there was the time my younger daughter, then thirteen, decided she wanted to visit my parents in Florida. They were delighted; I was cautiously supportive. I told my mother several times beforehand that my daughter was introverted and shy and would need time to warm up. She would also need a fair amount of down time. *Take it slow,* I suggested. *She's excited to get to know you.* Within six hours of her arrival my daughter called me, crying hysterically, begging to come home. My mother got on the phone. "This is practically the first time I've heard her talk," she complained. "She's not talking to me. I told her if she wants a relationship she's got to meet me halfway. She's got to pull her weight!"

I reminded my mother that my daughter needed space. I reminded my daughter why she'd wanted to visit. But my mother wouldn't back off, and my daughter spent the rest of the trip hiding in her bedroom. Once she got home she never really spoke to my mother again, and I couldn't blame her. She'd gotten the message that she wasn't good enough for my mother the way she was, that she'd have to change herself to fit my mother's expectations if she wanted a relationship. At age thirteen she understood something it took me into my forties to get.

My aunt wondered out loud what it must have been like to grow up with a mother like that. For once I didn't carefully consider my response or censor myself. "I can tell you what it was like," I said. "It makes you into a person who never feels good enough, smart enough, kind enough, pretty enough. Who lies awake at 2 a.m. feeling ugly and worthless, then gets up in the morning and carries on."

Saying these words out loud for the first time to someone other than my husband, I felt suddenly light. Half the weight of this kind of grief comes from carrying it in secret, feeling that you and only you are that unlovable, that worthless, that damaged. The irony is that only by naming the grief do we ever find any sense of relief. Only by telling the story do we realize we're not alone.

Chapter Eight

ON FORGIVENESS

If I could just say sorry for something I've done—
believe me, it's liberating to say sorry. I'm not above
saying sorry. But I can't. It's not what it's about here.

—MARK, thirty-two, estranged from his parents,
sister, and grandmother

After our last terrible email exchange the rage I felt toward my mother intensified. It was an old friend, this anger. It had saved my life, kept me from sinking into worthlessness and emptiness and despair as a child and teen and young adult, during the years when I didn't have the understanding or maturity to survive them and so could not let myself feel them without some kind of buffer. In her book *Anger and Forgiveness: Resentment, Generosity, Justice,* the philosopher Martha C. Nussbaum argues that anger is a ritualistic emotion that keeps people from addressing the "real problem," whatever that is. She believes that "full-fledged anger is never appropriate," that anger "does nothing to solve . . . real problems, and it positively impedes progress."

Maybe that's true in the long run. But for me, struggling to get through, anger was a life preserver; its righteous buoyancy kept my head above water. Anger propelled me out of my parents' house at sixteen, and while I was in no way ready for the real world I knew, dimly, that if I stayed I would not have the life I wanted. Back then I couldn't have articulated exactly what life I wanted, only that it was different from the one I'd grown up in.

My mother's highest expectation for me was to become a secretary, as she was, to work in an office somewhere in South Jersey until, God willing, I married a nice Jewish boy (preferably a lawyer or doctor) and stayed home to raise my Jewish children. To have a life like hers. Not that there was anything wrong with that life—for her. But I knew if I didn't launch myself out of that house and away from the insular vessel of my family I would stay damaged and fearful. My mother's prophecies would come true. I would be unlovable and unloving, bored and boring and stupefied into a life I did not want.

Anger drove me out of my parents' house and kept me alive in those first years when I had no idea how to navigate the world and become the person I wanted to be. I went to a college that offered me generous scholarships because of the new federal requirements that it be coed. The school I chose was small and 80 percent male; a campus of two thousand students, most of whom were studying engineering, hosted twenty-two fraternities. I wanted to write but there were no writing classes offered, so I settled for taking every English class. Socially I floundered. I had no idea how to tell real friendships from fake ones. I smoked pot and did cocaine and crystal meth to escape my fear and grief. I used my body to bring men closer, to get them to take care of me, and when they didn't I suffered continuous panic attacks that made me needy and blind to other people. The few friends I did make were sarcastic and smart and angry just like me, and we clung to one another. It was easier for me to buoy up someone else than to learn to save myself.

Anger saved me until it didn't. The rage I felt toward my mother for years ate away at my sense of myself as a good person. I didn't want it to define me. And I didn't want it to contaminate other parts of my life. My deepest fear was that it would spill over onto my daughters. I had to do something different, find a way to shift my internal vision of and response to my parents, and I wondered if forgiveness might help me get unstuck. It is, after all, the first subject people mention when you bring up family estrangement. *It's your mother/father/sister/brother/child, can't you just forgive them?* We equate forgiveness with reconciliation, and we have a dozen platitudes that reflect this: Kiss and make up. Bury the hatchet. Wipe the slate clean. Forgive and forget. Let bygones be bygones.

Long favored by pretty much every faith tradition, forgiveness has become in the last several decades both a moral imperative and a medical one, though it means something different to everyone. Oprah Winfrey has been quoted as saying that the best definition she's ever heard is "letting go of the past we thought we wanted."[1] Mark Twain described forgiveness as the fragrance the violet leaves on the heel that has crushed it, an image that seems disturbingly masochistic. Christianity famously recommends turning the other cheek—equally masochistic—and offers vague concepts like "extending grace" and "pardoning." Polynesian cultures practice *ho'oponopono,* a healing process meant to correct "errors," which often involve anger.

Buddhism equates forgiveness with compassion and non-judgment, which also feature in the Jewish concept of *slicha,* the Hebrew word for "sorry." *Slicha* is more than simple apology, though; it grows out of empathy and compassion for the person who has hurt you. Offering someone *slicha* can take years or it might never happen. It's the product of grace, given freely and somewhat mysteriously if at all. Asking for forgiveness, on the other hand, is known as *tshuva,* or repentance, and requires a five-step process: recognizing one's offense, feeling remorse, stopping the offense, making amends, and confession to God. You can't be granted forgiveness if you don't go through all of these steps.

My mother never asked me to forgive her, never apologized for anything that passed between us, not even in the fake "I'm sorry you feel upset" kind of way. There were a few moments in our relationship when I thought she was edging closer to some kind of acknowledgment of what had passed between us. When she emailed me during my daughter's relapse, for instance, offering to help, insisting on it, reminding me over and over that I "have a family" that could support me. Inevitably, though, those have been the moments when rather than apologize or even offer generic regrets, she turned and attacked. She seemed to truly believe that she was always right and everyone else was wrong, that her feelings required sensitive consideration and everyone else's were just so much background noise.

I don't know how many times relatives asked me *Can't you just forgive your mother?* I don't know how many times I asked myself. It's a revealing question, one that told me that they knew, and I knew, that my mother was at least partially at fault. As Peg Streep wrote in a post on the *Psychology Today* website, "Forgiveness confirms the act or transgression as intentional since unintentional acts don't require forgiveness."[2] It was also a question that put me back into the universe of my childhood where it was my job to give my mother what she wanted and where my selfish coldness was responsible for her pain and her tears. Where she and I and the rest of our extended family all believed that if only

I did that—placated her, forgave her, put aside my anger—then everyone would have a quieter, happier, more convenient life.

I'm not sure what exactly I would have forgiven her for, even if I wanted to, even if I knew how. For the cruel remarks and cutting criticisms? For years of emotional manipulation? For being what Peg Streep calls a mean mother? Forgiving her for any of this would have been like saying *It's cool that you treated me like that, we're good, keep on doing what you've been doing.* Forgive and forget, except I can't. Or maybe I won't.

And anyway, I couldn't even think about forgiving my mother because forgiveness inevitably leads to reconciling, going back to our old relationship, and I wouldn't do that unless something changed between us. To me it seemed like an either/or: either I stayed estranged from my mother or I forgave her and we made up. I did expect to reconcile with her someday, in the distant future, when I'd somehow miraculously transformed into another person, someone more spiritually advanced who wasn't crushed by her words and presence. Until that miraculous metamorphosis, however, I worked to keep my distance. It took me so long to extricate myself (more or less) from the chaotic dissociation of our on-again off-again relationship; I wasn't going to blow it by diving back in. Not yet, anyway.

I wasn't alone in that dilemma. Kate, the Philadelphia artist, says a couple of her close friends have tried to talk her into forgiving her parents. She's not interested. For one thing, her parents have never even acknowledged Kate's distress, let alone apologized for any of their actions. For another, in the fundamentalist church where Kate was raised, forgiveness means moving forward as if the offense never happened—in other words, reconciliation. And that's unlikely. Her parents would need to be willing and able to have a different sort of conversation, and nothing she's seen makes her think that will ever happen.

Tracy, the teacher in Ann Arbor, couldn't imagine forgiving her father, either, for similar reasons. She had every reason to think he'd keep right on doing what he had always done: belittle and humiliate and manipulate her. Her estrangement from him was an ongoing act of self-defense in a conflict that never ended. The hurt wasn't in the past; it was still happening, if she'd let herself be close enough to him, and that was unacceptable. Forgiveness would make her too vulnerable. She had to keep protecting herself.

I've never been sure what forgiveness is, exactly, or how to go about it. For years I tried to forgive my father for not standing up to my mother, for not defending me, not protecting me from her anger and neediness. I tried to forgive my mother for specific incidents, like the graduation-dinner sex debacle, and for larger and more abstract offenses like her constant criticisms, her efforts to make me into someone different, her failure to love me as I was rather than who she needed me to be. "Trying" to forgive them mainly meant telling myself over and over that I should. That to be a good person, a moral person, a loving person I *needed* to forgive. But how? I wondered what precisely people meant when they said *I forgive you* and how specifically they did it. Was I missing some crucial knowledge that everyone else had? Or maybe, as in the story about the emperor's new clothes, no one actually knew what forgiveness meant or how to achieve it; they just pretended they did. Maybe people who said they had forgiven someone were just saying the words. Or maybe they were just much better, nicer people than me and forgiveness came naturally to them.

Over and over I tried to forgive my parents but it never stuck. Each time I thought I'd accomplished it our next bruising interaction would trigger the same queasy fury and hurt. For weeks afterward I'd be physically dizzy and nauseous; the old feelings of worthlessness and anxiety would rise through me again. I'd stop sleeping. I'd have twenty panic attacks a day. I was trapped in a

Möbius strip of emotions. To address my anger I tried to forgive; to deal with forgiveness I turned to anger. Rage was an anodyne to the helplessness and terror, a way to hang on to some sense of myself that went deeper than my mother's mean words and my father's silence.

The fact that I could not forgive my parents came to feel like one more way in which I was broken and inferior. I needed to forgive them because anger was taking over my life, but I couldn't forgive them because I couldn't stop being angry. And, truly, I didn't want to stop. I'd been angry for so long that I was afraid if I let go of it I would sink in the old familiar morass of anxiety and loss and terror. Without anger I didn't think I could survive it.

In the conversation around forgiveness anger is usually framed as an obstacle to be overcome, more for the sake of the forgiver than the person being forgiven. The capacity to forgive, known in the academic literature as forgivingness, has been linked to lower resting heart rates, lower blood pressure, lower levels of the stress hormone cortisol, and lower levels of inflammation—all significant health biomarkers. People who forgive sleep better, recover faster from stress, tend to be less anxious and angry and more resilient than those who don't. It's apparently good for your mental health, too. "As an adult, you probably can't be really successful until you have done that work," says Elizabeth Vagnoni. "Because it will always be in your head, that anger or that resentment. You can't live your life as a whole human being until you can find a way to let go of that, and you can't do it without forgiveness." Forgiveness is not just an optional religious virtue, then, something you might aspire to if you're observant; it's now best practice and required self-care as well.

Martha Nussbaum suggests that anger often stands in for emotions like grief that make people feel helpless and vulnerable, "promising agency and control when one's real situation does not offer control."[3] I understood that, at least vaguely, at the height of my anger. I knew that the rage I felt toward my mother, while justified in many ways, also covered up a lot of other feelings I didn't want to feel. I just didn't know what to do about it. In despair I began reading everything I could find on forgiveness, most of which comes from philosophers and social psychologists, who approach it from diametrically opposed angles.

Philosophers like Nussbaum argue over what constitutes forgiveness and what doesn't: Is saying the words *I forgive you* enough? Is some kind of action required? Must forgiveness mean reconciliation, or is it something that can be strictly internal? Are some acts simply unforgiveable, and, if so, which ones? Is it immoral to refuse to forgive? Or, alternatively, does forgiveness let the offender off the hook, and so are there situations where it shouldn't be offered?

The philosopher Kwame Anthony Appiah posed some of these same questions in his Ethicist column in the *New York Times Magazine*:

> What is it to forgive someone? It can't simply mean that you were angry at the person, for good reason, and no longer are. That could happen because you were conked on the head or simply forgot the offense, neither of which qualify as forgiveness. And it can't mean that you're now O.K. with the offense; then there would be nothing to forgive.

As an example, he described a hypothetical situation: What if someone sprayed graffiti on his house? He'd be mad. What if he then learned that the culprit had been forced at gunpoint to vandalize his house? His anger would diminish. That's not forgiveness, though, he argued; that's more reinterpreting the narrative in light of new information. Forgiveness would entail a different process, one that included feeling anger but then giving it up. Appiah quotes the American philosopher Jean Hampton, who argued that forgiving someone means separating them from the egregious action—in this case, the vandal from the vandalism.

In an essay published in 1988, Hampton suggested that forgiveness doesn't require turning the other cheek or sanctioning the wrongdoer's hurtful behaviors. Instead, she wrote,

> The forgiver never gives up her opposition to the wrongdoer's action, Nor does she even give up her opposition to the wrongdoer's bad character traits. Instead, she revises her judgment of the person himself—where that person is understood to be something other than or more than the character traits of which she does not approve. And she reaches the *honest* decision that this person does not merit her moral hatred, because he is still decent despite his action.[4]

In Hampton's perspective, behaviors and even personality traits are distinct from our fundamental essence—our souls, if you will. But if neither our actions nor our traits define us, what does? Hampton seems to be suggesting that our shared common humanity makes us worthy of forgiveness and love no matter what we do. I buy that in theory, but like most people I have a hard time getting behind it in practice. How do you separate the actions of a Hitler or a Pol Pot from their essential selves? Is everything forgivable, or are there people who can't and shouldn't be forgiven? Hampton doesn't take up this question.

I think of a story I heard from a woman named Deb, a businesswoman in Waltham, Massachusetts, who described her estranged mother as cold and narcissistic. Their estrangement isolated Deb from her sister and sister's family as well. When Deb finally left an abusive marriage of twenty years she reconnected with both her mother and sister, though by then her mother was showing signs of dementia. Deb doesn't use the word *forgiveness,* but the process she describes sounds familiar to me. She still mourns the mother-daughter connection she longed for but says she and her mother have a "lovely relationship," in part because she came to understand that her mother's coldness was her mother's issue and that she wasn't at fault.

Deb and her sister now coordinate their mother's care, each of them spending at least several nights a week with her. Their connection now, says Deb, is worlds away from what it once was. "She can't stop telling me she loves me and how glad she is that I'm back," she says. On the rare occasion that her mother says something critical or mean, Deb tells herself *It's not me, it's her* and changes the subject. For the most part, though, her mother has become more loving and grateful with dementia than she ever was without it.

I wonder if this is forgiveness or something else altogether. Not forgetting, exactly, but compartmentalizing. Maybe, as Hampton believed, that's what forgiveness is, separating past and present, someone's egregious words and actions from their loving ones. Maybe if my mother had developed dementia—the grateful kind, not the angry kind—I could have forgiven her too. I don't know.

Like nearly everyone who writes about such issues, Hampton still came down on the side of reconciliation, suggesting that eventually the forgiver would come to see the offender as "still *decent, not* rotten as a person, and someone with whom he may be able to renew a relationship."[5] The key word here is *may.* Forgiveness may lead to reconciliation or it may lead to a more peaceful estrangement. Either way it's got to be up to the person doing the forgiving.

In a short, provocative book called *The Sunflower,* Simon Wiesenthal, a Jewish architect from Eastern Europe who was captured by the Nazis and imprisoned during World War II, explored some of these questions in a different context. Wiesenthal, who spent his life after the war hunting down escaped German war criminals, described an experience he had as a prisoner in a death camp: a nurse plucked him out of the group of prisoners and brought him to a darkened room, where a young Nazi soldier with bandaged eyes lay dying. The Nazi wanted to tell his story to a Jew, any Jew, and so for several hours Wiesenthal sat by his bed and listened as the dying soldier described his childhood, his parents, how he joined the SS at age sixteen, and then, in excruciating detail, the many acts of violence and torture he'd committed against Jews. One offense in particular haunted the Nazi: he and his comrades had locked several hundred Jews into a house full of petrol and set it on fire. As parts of the house exploded, people jumped from windows and the soldiers shot them, including one man who covered his young son's eyes as he jumped with him.

At the end of the long afternoon, the Nazi begged Wiesenthal to forgive him so he could die in peace. He reached blindly for Wiesenthal's hand; he waited for words of forgiveness. After a long moment Wiesenthal stood up and left the room in silence, offering no words and no forgiveness.

But that wasn't the end of the encounter for Wiesenthal. He wondered whether he should have forgiven the dying Nazi, who made his confession with what seemed to be true repentance. Should he have comforted him on his deathbed? Maybe he should have said something, spoken up on behalf of the millions of people being tortured and imprisoned and killed, including his own family. He went around and around the questions and came to no conclusions. He was haunted by the confession and his natural response to it. Years later, he asked a number of prominent thinkers to explain what they thought he should have done and why, and published their answers along with his own narrative.

I'm not advocating for comparing family conflicts to genocide, of course. But *The Sunflower* explores questions about forgiveness that are relevant to any human interaction. For instance, many commenters wrote that Wiesenthal couldn't have done anything else because he could not in good conscience forgive something that hadn't been done to him. Several commenters suggested that there was no right or wrong choice because forgiveness is an individual decision, one that can't and shouldn't be judged by anyone outside the situation. Others made the distinction between forgiveness and justice. One interesting response came from Primo Levi, author of *The Periodic Table* and other books about the Holocaust. Levi, an Italian Jewish chemist who survived nearly a year in Auschwitz, wrote that to forgive the dying Nazi, Wiesenthal would have either had to lie or else do himself "a terrible moral violence." Levi reasoned that since Wiesenthal didn't actually believe that the Nazi was innocent, or that he'd been forced to commit the crimes he described, or that he didn't understand the significance of his actions, to say he forgave him would be a lie.

Levi didn't elaborate on the "terrible moral violence," on the idea that under certain circumstances the act of forgiving can hurt the person doing it rather than help. It feels right to me, though. In a culture that emphasizes forgiveness as an act of healing and self-care, this is a radical idea. It reminds me of something Ben, the social worker from Ohio, told me. He's worked with many patients who try to skip the anger stage and move right to forgiveness after someone hurts them. He remembers an incident when a local Amish child was killed and the parents and community elders publicly forgave the killer the very next day. "That's fucked up," he says. "This person just killed your child. You've got to be angry. You've got to be upset. You've got to be hurt."

Ben has forgiven his parents for the abuse they heaped on him as a child, though he's never actually told them so. He had to feel really, really angry for years before he could let most of his hurt and anger go. When people try to skip processing those deep feelings, he says, they wind up with a kind of fake forgiveness that doesn't last and certainly doesn't bring about true healing. In his view anger can be not just necessary but redemptive, because it's an integral part of the process of forgiveness. You can't forgive someone until you've let yourself really feel that anger and hurt. "We live in a Christian society where forgiveness is overvalued," he says. The price we pay for that devotion to forgiveness is the loss of authentic connections.

This is the same mechanism psychoanalyst Alice Miller describes in her book *The Drama of the Gifted Child*: When children show their parents only what those parents want to see, they bury not just their true feelings but also their ability to access those feelings. They lose touch with their essential selves, with their ability to experience true pain and joy and grief and excitement. The false faces they put on become their only faces. So yes, forgiveness can harm the forgiver, if it's done out of a need to conform, to appear virtuous, to please others, to win approval, rather than out of the slow and often agonizing processing of hurt and anger that leads to empathy. In her book *The Body Never Lies*, considering the way therapists often encourage grown children to forgive their parents, Alice Miller wrote simply, "Forgiveness has never had a healing effect."[6]

The writer Cynthia Ozick went a step further with this train of thought. In her commentary for Wiesenthal's book she quoted a Jewish proverb—"Whoever is merciful to the cruel will end by being indifferent to the innocent"—then wrote,

> Forgiveness can brutalize. . . . Forgiveness is pitiless. It forgets the victim. It negates the right of the victim to his own life. It blurs over suffering and death. It drowns the past. It

cultivates sensitiveness toward the murderer at the price of insensitiveness toward the victim.[7]

Forgiveness can desensitize us to cruelty, Ozick suggests, making a kind of false equivalence of offenses, implying that all actions are forgivable. In its rush to do the right thing it privileges the end over the means, and in the process can do even more damage to the person who was hurt. By focusing on the perpetrator's story rather than the victim's, it glosses over what happened to focus instead on what happens next.

This rings true to me. At one point, in a sort of last-ditch bid for "moving forward," my mother offered to take my sister and me to Israel to celebrate some milestone birthdays. "The one condition," she wrote in her invitation email, "is that we go in with 'no history'—just three bright, curious, vital women." On a practical level her offer shocked me: we couldn't get through a phone conversation without conflict, let alone being together 24/7 for three weeks. On a deeper level it enraged me. It wasn't the first time she'd suggested that we just start over, pretend our differences did not exist. No matter what I said she still seemed to believe our problems derived from childhood slights, that I was mired in the past and needed to turn my face toward the future. She could not seem to take in the fact that our problems came from the way we interacted now, not thirty years ago. That we had problems that needed to be addressed in the present, not buried. I think she wanted me to do what my father did: let her say and do whatever she wanted and suppress my own feelings, no matter what the cost. Only now I knew what that cost was, and I was no longer able to pay it. Even if I'd wanted to.

◇◇◇◇◇

As I WRESTLED with my anger, though, I kept thinking about forgiveness. Not for my mother's sake but for mine. Maybe there was a way forward that eased some of the anger and hurt but didn't lead to reconciliation. I put aside the philosophers and took a closer look at what social psychologists had to say about forgiveness. They didn't seem to worry as much about abstract classifications but were more interested in practical considerations, like how exactly to get from a state of anger to forgiveness. A number of them worked in countries like Rwanda and Northern Ireland, places that have been torn apart by generations of war and violence, and found that forgiveness can be helpful even in the wake of genocide.

More relevant to me was work done by Suzanne Freedman, a professor at the University of Northern Iowa, and Robert Enright, an educational psychologist at the University of Wisconsin–Madison and founder of the International Forgiveness Institute. Freedman created a forgiveness intervention with a group of incest survivors, women who arguably had the least incentive to forgive and the most right to anger. They met weekly, one-on-one, with a therapist and worked at their own pace through a curriculum comprising four phases of forgiveness: uncovering, decision, work, and discovery. The process took more than a year for most of the women, and at the end they all scored higher than before on measures of forgiveness, self-esteem, and hope, and lower on anxiety and depression. Nearly twenty years after the intervention, one of the women wrote,

> There is not a day that goes by where I don't think about how much my participation in your group changed my life and my attitude. Forgiveness is not just an act—it's a way of life. My strongest beliefs are not necessarily religious ones,

but ones rooted in Mother Theresa's idea that "we cannot hate someone whose story we know."[8]

Freedman and Enright went on to publish a number of studies on forgiveness among incest survivors, all with similar results. I read them with an increasing sense of both disbelief and hope. Incest, like genocide, is unjustifiable on any level. So if incest victims could learn to forgive their abusers, maybe I could find a way to forgive my parents. The real question was whether I wanted to.

Philosopher Martha Nussbaum suggests that as a culture we hold on to anger because we think it can be productive at times, and that makes us unwilling to pursue what she calls "non-anger," which includes the process of forgiveness. She has no patience for anger as a therapeutic tool, insisting that "anger does nothing to solve a person's real problems, and it positively impedes progress."[9] But anger is a normal human emotion. You have to feel anger just as much as you have to let yourself feel grief and joy. The alternative is to not feel it, to force it down below the surface of consciousness, pour concrete over it, and pretend it's not there. And much like a body buried under the garage floor, buried anger festers and stinks and eventually eats away at its container. The times in my life when I've tried to squash my anger it boiled up as deep anxiety, panic, and feelings of worthlessness that made it hard to function. The year I graduated from college was one of those times. I moved to New York City at age twenty, knowing only one person in the city (my college boyfriend), to start a job and a new life 100 miles away from my family. The day I left my father stood in the driveway to see me off. "You'll be back," he predicted, and I heard it as a threat: *You'll never make it. You'll fail. You'll have to come home.*

That year was one of the hardest of my life. I lived in a Salvation Army women's residence, a three-story brownstone in Greenwich Village, along with thirty other young women, most of them baby ballerinas at the nearby Joffrey Ballet. There was one telephone for everyone, and the great front doors were locked each night, ostensibly to keep us safe. The anxiety I'd dealt with since age ten flared into multiple panic attacks a day, a rash of new phobias (including elevators, not helpful when you work on the thirty-sixth floor), and persistent vertigo that made me reach for the wall when I walked down my office's hallways.

I told my parents none of this. Years earlier I'd tried to tell them about the nightly panic attacks that kept me wide-eyed and terrified in the dark, the feelings of claustrophobic doom I couldn't shake. My father shrugged. My mother said, "Your problem, my dear, is that you think too much." I got neither help nor sympathy from them. Instead I limped through my early twenties, learning to get through rather than live freely and fully. Now, looking back, I understand that I was furious with my parents for their lack of caring and support, for teaching me that love was a form of dependence and that the punishment for leaving home was to be even more completely abandoned than I had been. I couldn't afford to let myself feel that anger in such a vulnerable place, in my first steps toward true independence.

I'm not a terrified twenty-year-old anymore, of course. I've done years of counseling, some of it with an excellent therapist. I've descended through layer after layer of anger and hurt and made my slow way back again. I know I can survive any feelings that come up.

Interestingly, only a few of the people I interviewed for this book mentioned forgiving, or being forgiven by, estranged relatives, maybe because many of them are still angry. (Maybe those who *have* forgiven are less likely to need or want to talk about it.) Penny, the therapist from Ohio, was angry with her parents before estranging from them and continues to be angry now. There's anger at her father for sexually abusing her, anger at her mother for refusing to believe it, anger at both of them for responding to all of Penny's requests for help with glib offers to pray for her. "That's fine if you want to do that in addition to actual stuff, but that alone is not terribly effective," Penny says dryly.

She knows she is, in the words of Ann Landers, better off without her parents in her life. She can't let herself feel even the tiniest hint of affection or empathy for her father because that would open the door to a potential reconciliation. And that's never going to happen, especially now that she has children of her own, children she would shield from the kind of abuse that happened to her with her life if she had to. Penny needs her anger to protect herself and her children.

And I understand. For so many years of my adult life I lay down every night pulsing with rage at my mother. I carried it into every relationship and situation and interaction. Anger became my shield and my sword, the magical cloak that kept me hidden and safe. Sometimes I could feel it radiating from me like motion lines around a cartoon character. When my daughters were young I relied on that anger to protect them from my mother. And I used it to protect me from what lay underneath it, the terror and longing that erupted each time I got any closer.

But with my daughters half-grown into young adults, I decided it was time I learned to protect myself in other ways. I doubted forgiveness would be part of that process, but I could afford to explore it and see what else might shift. I'd grown weary of being angry. It wasn't the person I aspired to be.

So one summer I made my way to New York City for a weekend workshop with Dr. Frederic Luskin, co-founder and director of the Stanford Forgiveness Project at Stanford University, whose course description promised to help me let go of hurt, helplessness, and anger while increasing confidence, hope, and happiness. Luskin is tall and rangy, with a beaky nose that gives him the look of an intelligent raptor. He slouched at the head of a conference-room table at the Ackerman Family Institute wearing sneakers, a long-sleeved plaid shirt tied around his waist, looking ready to sail down the Hudson, not lead a workshop on forgiveness. He carried no laptop, no briefcase, no handouts or notes of any kind, not even a copy of his book, *Forgive for Good*. He simply sat down and started to talk in a low, patient voice, his hands smoothing and re-smoothing his bushy hair, his gaze falling on each of the dozen or so of us around the table in turn.

His appearance and demeanor, it turned out, were perfectly suited to the message he was delivering. Luskin, who has a Ph.D. in counseling and health psychology from Stanford University, is all about the *how*, not the *what* or the *why*. He'd come not to discuss forgiveness but to show this roomful of hopeful students how to practice it.

Freedman, Enright, and others in the field talk about multistage forgiveness "journeys" that progress through steps and layers. Luskin believes there are only two steps to forgiving: grieving and letting go. Grieving means letting yourself relive the original anger, hurt, and betrayal, really feeling it, and he told us that two years was plenty of time to work through those feelings. When we hang on to hurt and resentment for longer than that, when we get stuck in rage and helplessness, he suggested, we're having a kind of cosmic tantrum, throwing a hissy fit about not getting something we want. "We think the world owes us," he said. "The guy who loses a parking space to a more aggressive driver thinks, 'I want that parking space.' A mother whose child has been murdered thinks, 'I want my child to be alive.'" He smiled disarmingly. "Either way, that's just not how it works."

A ripple of shock ran around the table. One woman timidly murmured something about the tragedy of losing a child to

murder. Luskin's angular face softened. Though he didn't mention it in class, he'd had plenty of practice in forgiving the world's
injustices. Several years before the workshop, his twenty-year-
old daughter had been killed in a car accident. "It's better not
to get caught up in content," he said. By *content* he meant each
person's story of woundedness and resentment, the event that
inspired our hurt, our moral outrage, our sense of how unfair
things are. Forgiveness, he said, is about the gap between what
we want and think we're entitled to and what is. There is no
such thing as *fair,* and the sooner we're clear about that the better. Forgiveness is one way—the best way—to respond to a world
that owes us nothing.

This attitude reminded me of an analogy Robert Enright
made in one of our interviews: If you're running and you tear your
meniscus, causing a lot of knee pain, you have two choices—go
through the pain of surgery and rehab or learn to live with the
degenerating knee. "We all want that third alternative," Enright
told me. "'I don't want my knee to be broken!' But it is."

My relationship with my mother had been broken for a long
time and I could never seem to find a way to live with the pain of
it. I imagined what Luskin might say: *Boo-hoo, the world doesn't
give us what we need or want.* I couldn't argue with that. But how
exactly did I make the necessary leap from grief to forgiveness?

The second half of the workshop took a more concrete approach. We learned abdominal breathing. We visualized someone
we cared about and were encouraged to feel our hearts open and
fill with love. I pictured my mother-in-law, who had died several
years earlier and who was one of my "other mothers," and was
surprised to feel my eyes fill with tears. This was all a lot more
woo-woo than I expected after the morning session, but Luskin
framed it in biological terms. "When you think about a wrong
someone did to you, your fight-or-flight system is aroused," he

said. "Your heart beats faster, your blood pressure goes up, you feel hurt and mad and upset. When you could be sitting here feeling how good it is to be alive on such a beautiful day. You won't always be alive, you know. So doesn't it make more sense to appreciate this moment, this now?"

Yes but seemed to be the response around the table. *Yes but* I don't know how to do that. *Yes but* I'm stuck in all these feelings. *Yes but* that person really, really hurt me.

Luskin held up his hands. Most of us, he said, respond on one end of the emotional spectrum, where we feel rage, anger, and hatred. "But there's this whole other part of the spectrum where we feel love, gratitude, and pleasure," he said. Forgiveness is very simple, he went on. Not easy, but simple. It's a choice in each moment, a choice in how you react. It's about practicing responding out of kindness rather than anger.

After the workshop I sat down to talk one-on-one with Luskin and came away with the beginning of a glimmer of what he was talking about. Forgiveness, for him, is active and intentional, a practice, like meditation or endurance training. He suggested I ask myself this question: if I could use the part of me that's peaceful and kind to think about my mother, what would it say? He told me that when I feel myself getting angry or anxious I should remind myself that I have no control over the fact that I have a difficult mother; I do have control, though, over what I say to myself about her and about the rest of my life. He suggested I learn to tell "the compassionate story" about my mother, and actually tell it—to myself, to my husband, to friends and family— because language can change our perceptions. Saying the words out loud can help shift how we feel.

At the end he asked how I would go forward with my mother. "I'm going to stay away from her," I said. "Nothing has changed there. That's the only way I can feel safe."

He nodded, acknowledging that this was after all my choice, my past, my life. He leaned forward, turning his intense gaze on mine. "Now, can you stay away with an open heart?" he said. "Because *that's* the forgiveness piece."

It was the first time I'd heard anyone talk about forgiveness *without* reconciliation, and the thought was somehow exhilarating. Forgiveness, Luskin was saying, means finding compassion for the person who has hurt you, but it's not prescriptive. It doesn't tell you what you should do next. It doesn't judge you for whatever you choose to do. It crowns no winner or loser. It's more, as the subject in Suzanne Freedman's study put it, a way of life. I still wasn't sure whether it was a way of life I wanted to try out. I still wasn't sure I was capable of forgiveness, frankly. Maybe I was broken in some fundamental way that prevented me from opening my heart, as Luskin put it. That was OK for now, I thought. It was enough to catch a glimpse of another way of being, even if I wasn't ready to go there.

Andrea, the nurse from Madison, also struggled to separate forgiveness from reconciliation. When she would tell people that she wasn't in touch with her mother and explain why, they often said something along the lines of *Well things must have been hard for her too.* And it was true, she knew. Her mother's life was no Hollywood fantasy; she'd raised six children while married to an abusive alcoholic who wound up in prison. So why, Andrea wondered, couldn't she cut her mother a break, give her the benefit of the doubt? How could she be so hard-hearted about her own mother? What was wrong with her?

Eventually Andrea realized that her inability to forgive came from her need to protect herself from the florid dysfunction of her family. Her five brothers and sisters all led chaotic lives full of substance abuse, alcoholism, and problematic relationships with their partners and children, and Andrea didn't want to live like that. It took her a long time to figure out that forgiveness didn't have to be a one-way ticket back into her mother's life, that she could feel compassion for her mother and at the same time keep her distance. "It's OK for me to realize that her life was probably really hard *and* I needed to extract in order to survive," she says now. Once she got that, a lot of her anxieties subsided. She hasn't had a nightmare about her mother in more than ten years. She feels at peace with her life, her children, and her choice to put her own well-being ahead of her mother's needs.

It's ironic, really, that the kind of boundaries that estrangements require can actually facilitate forgiveness. Andrea, for instance, wouldn't have been able to forgive her mother if they were still in touch. Estrangement kept her out of immediate danger. It made her feel safe enough to experience and process her feelings of anger and grief, then find her way to compassion and even empathy for her mother. It was necessary, part of the solution for her rather than the problem. Similarly, Mary, the graduate student who's estranged from her mother, says she absolutely forgives her. It's just that she's not going to let her mother abuse her again. "I'm not holding a grudge," she says. "I'm being matter-of-fact. You don't let her bite you twice."

Sharon, the therapist in Columbus, Ohio, says she's been forgiving her mother for her whole life. "I *have* forgiven her," she adds. "I just don't want to be around her." She no longer thinks of her mother as a kind of evil monster; instead she sees her as somehow broken, someone who hates herself so much that she can't help lashing out at others. Many of the women Sharon sees in her practice remind her of her mother. They come to her office and talk, however ineffectively, trying a lot harder than many other parents manage to. Which means they're trying a lot harder than her own mother does. Because they are her clients, because her job is to be on their side, she has nothing but empathy for them, though she knows they are almost certainly doing emotional damage to their children. Working with them gives her the chance to practice forgiving her own mother again and again.

And there's no question that for some people, forgiving—no matter how egregious and devastating the offense—is a better option than not. For Meret, a forty-five-year-old radio DJ in Sweden, forgiveness helps with the depression and other mental-health issues that have plagued her since childhood. Her parents divorced before she was born, and she lived with her alcoholic mother, who was both physically and emotionally abusive. As a child, Meret was often afraid for her life. She never knew what a day might bring: Would she find her mother unconscious or sober and mean? Would there be yelling? Beatings? Would she ridicule Meret, throw food at her, starve her? Would she accuse Meret of driving her to drink? Would she pass out while smoking and set the bedroom on fire, then blame her daughter for saving her?

When Meret was fourteen her mother died of cirrhosis, and her father, who'd kept his distance throughout her childhood, reluctantly took her in. Life with him was better in many ways than it had been with her mother. He didn't drink or start fires or throw things at her; he rarely hit her. In fact she saw very little of him, and when he did come home she wasn't allowed to eat his food or watch his TV. She was always aware that she was a guest in his house, and not a welcome one. At sixteen, Meret moved out on her own; the world, which had always felt to her like a dangerous place, couldn't possibly be worse than her father's house. By now she hated him for his coldness, for not caring enough to save her from her mother's abuse, for being indifferent and unloving. She wanted nothing to do with him.

For the next twenty years she lived in a state of painful ambivalence, cycling between overachieving and rage, trying to make her father love her and then swearing she'd dance on his grave when he died. She found success as a national radio host even as she struggled with depression and an eating disorder. It took a long time and a lot of distance to understand that her anger and resentment weren't hurting *him,* only herself. They were covering up the pain she'd carried since childhood, the terror of a child who felt unsafe, unworthy, unloved and unlovable. A child who would do anything in the world to make her father care. The fact that he didn't, that he couldn't, had nothing to do with her.

Slowly, Meret realized she didn't need or want to be totally estranged from her father. It's not that he's changed; he's still the same cold and indifferent and limited man who is unable to build a stable connection with anyone. But she's changed. She understands that the love she wanted from him is impossible, that he can't offer it. More important, she no longer needs it to survive. She can afford to feel compassion along with the anger, and the anger is fading. Every few months now she calls her father for a friendly chat or puts a card in his mailbox, something to remind him that he's not alone in the world and that she cares. Once or twice recently they've met for coffee, something that would have been unthinkable even a few years ago.

"I accept the distance between us now because I know it has nothing to do with me," she says. "And when he starts acting mean, I am able to set up boundaries and speak up in a respectful way." It works for both of them.

I think of a quote that the late Fred Rogers supposedly carried everywhere he went, a quote attributed to a Benedictine nun and writer named Mary Lou Kownacki: "There isn't anyone you couldn't love once you've heard their story." Hmmm. Elizabeth Vagnoni told me she forgave her mother by understanding her story, by realizing that she really couldn't help herself, that she wasn't rubbing her hands together and thinking *How can I make Elizabeth miserable?* For her that understanding was enough to facilitate forgiveness and to make her end their estrangement. It isn't always, though. In one Australian study, estranged adult children empathized with their parents' histories, which included migration, war, child abuse, poverty, and other damaging early life experiences.[10] Their empathy and understanding didn't excuse their parents' bad behavior, though, or change their stance on estrangement. The study doesn't say whether they felt they loved their parents, or whether they forgave them. But they certainly didn't want them in their lives.

◇◇◇◇◇

SOMETIMES FORGIVENESS SEEMS to come about organically, without a lot of planning or agonizing. That's what happened for Alyssa, the content marketer in Princeton, New Jersey, whose relationship with her father was strained after her parents divorced when she was seven. Alyssa's memories of the obligatory visits with her dad were uncomfortable at best, unpleasant at worst. Every couple of weeks they'd have dinner at his apartment, get chocolate fudge nut ice cream, and then she'd sit on the couch while he spent time online until he took her home. He had no idea what to do with her. After a while Alyssa stopped visiting; she couldn't seem to develop any emotional rapport with him, and it just got too frustrating. Their phone conversations dwindled and fell away.

Alyssa made a few other attempts to connect with her father. In her freshman year of college she traveled a thousand miles to his third wedding, thinking it was a chance to show him who she was and forge a connection at last, but things didn't go well. Six years later when Alyssa got married she didn't even tell her father. She didn't want him to show up and put a damper on the day for her mother, who had raised her single-handedly. For years there was no contact between them at all, until Alyssa learned through one of her half-sisters that her father's wife had died and he was in treatment for leukemia. "I had this moment of wanting to tell him how I felt," she says. She wrote him a long email with the subject line "Things I Need to Say," not attacking him in any way, just being matter-of-fact about how distant and disconnected she felt from him. She spent the next few days obsessively checking her inbox. She'd never been this honest with him before.

When he finally did respond, it was as if he'd turned into a different person. He told her he was still in rehab but was hoping to come home soon. He said he wished he'd been a better father, and that he was sorry. Her father's email shocked Alyssa so much that she handed the phone to her husband and walked away, tears in her eyes. It took her a day or so to calm down enough to write him back, thank him for his honesty, and begin a sporadic email relationship. And even though his subsequent emails haven't shown the same level of vulnerability and reflectiveness, Alyssa is OK with it. She'd convinced herself that he wasn't capable of loving people because he had a rough childhood. His email was exactly what she'd always wanted to hear from him, and it let her get to some level of forgiveness. "Before, I felt I wanted the best for him but in a way that had absolutely nothing to do with my life," she says. "Now I want the best for him and I'd also like to have an email conversation every once in a while."

One of the most moving forgiveness stories I've heard comes from a woman I'll call Hannah, forty-eight, a poet and fiction writer who teaches at a community college in Kentucky. She describes it as a story about generational violence, one that begins with her mother and two aunts. "They were raised in horror," says Hannah. "There's no other way to talk about it." Their mother struggled with severe postpartum depression and turned violent toward her daughters. She beat them with wire hangers and burned them with cigarettes. Once, she lined them up outside, took a shotgun, and prepared to kill them; the only reason she didn't is that her husband came home unexpectedly and rammed her with his pickup truck.

Hannah's mother married a man who was also violent; one of Hannah's earliest memories is her father throwing a claw hammer at her mother. The kitchen linoleum was dented for years where the hammer landed. Eventually he left the family and Hannah's mother took up with a series of boyfriends, often leaving her daughter for periods of time with her own sister. Her sister's husband was a sex offender who preferred young girls, a fact that was well known but unspoken in their small community. He started grooming Hannah when she was five or six, asking her to sit on his back and give him a back rub, finding excuses to be alone with her. One night when Hannah was sixteen he climbed into the shower with her and tried to rape her. She fought him off. But her aunt refused to believe what he'd done.

"We had this terrible, terrible fight," Hannah says now. "I said, I am not staying with you anymore. I would rather live on the streets. You are a child molester. I've told my high school guidance counselor and he tells me what you really are." Her aunt and her grandmother forced her to go to church. She sat in a pew, her life in turmoil, and all they could offer was *God loves you.* When they got home she locked herself in the car with a pair of scissors and threatened to kill herself, until her mother's youngest sister came and got her, took her back to her mother's house, and left her there alone. Which was fine with Hannah.

The attempted rape, and Hannah's refusal to keep it quiet, broke the family apart. That's how Hannah describes it now. Over the next few years she stayed away. In her thirties, Hannah had twelve miscarriages in a row. She and her husband accumulated half a million dollars in debt on the farm they were trying to run. Hannah imagined herself coping by going down any

number of self-destructive paths—overwork, substance abuse—
but instead she turned to Buddhism. Having to live each day in
the present, facing the mistakes she'd made and the losses she'd
suffered, shifted something inside her. Her spiritual teacher, a
woman who would sit and meditate for four hours at a time, told
her *We can love people and not love their actions. We can separate
those two things.*

"And that just got inside of me," says Hannah. "What are
those worms that get into your muscles when you eat pork? Trichinosis. I got trichinosis of the soul. Because I can love my aunt
and find a kind of forgiveness for her without loving what she did,
which is allowing this to happen." Her uncle is a different story,
one she's still working on. She doesn't trust him. She sure as hell
wouldn't let her son be alone with him.

For Hannah, forgiving her aunt was something she did for
her own psychic survival, a way to make peace with some of the
worst things that had happened to her. Things she carried with
her. Things that made her suffer all the time, that could derail
her life and change her as a person. She didn't want to be that
person. So she forgave her aunt, and then, separately, was given
the chance to reconcile when she and her husband volunteered
to pick up her mother from her aunt's house. Hannah knew
she'd come face-to-face with her aunt. She didn't know what
she would do until the moment arrived.

When they pulled up her aunt was standing outside, waiting for them. She said *Welcome to the farm.* She looked like she
was going to throw up. Hannah had planned on being polite, but
when she saw how fear ran through her aunt's body she felt a
great surge of love, the love she had once felt for her. It hadn't
gone away; it had simply changed because of what happened.
"I don't understand why she didn't protect me," says Hannah
through tears. "But I understand now that she couldn't."

She got out of the car and hugged her aunt. They hadn't touched in twenty years and now her aunt felt frail in her arms. Buddhism teaches you to stay in the moment, and in that moment, in that embrace, she saw her aunt walking toward death, walking toward the light, and she thought, *I don't understand why you wouldn't protect me.* She thought, *My son is the most precious thing in the world and I would let someone cut up my body while I was still alive if it meant he didn't die.* She thought, *I don't understand it, but I don't hate you anymore.* Her aunt took them on a tour of the house, and then they all sat on the porch and talked. Nothing serious, just chitchat, but for Hannah there was grace and light in that moment, and she felt a weight lift off her body.

They said goodbye, and Hannah and her husband and son and mother left for a day out. That night they took her aunt and uncle out for dinner. Afterward her aunt said to her sister, *I couldn't believe they bought me dinner. Why did they buy me dinner?* She wrote Hannah a note saying *Thank you so much for dinner, thank you so much for letting me meet your son, thank you thank you thank you times a thousand.*

These days they exchange holiday greetings and talk easily when they meet. "Am I going to have them come stay with me? Probably not," says Hannah. "But I feel better knowing that some part of me could soften, could let go. At some point you have to just say it's not going to eat me alive anymore."

Hannah's experience illustrates what experts like Robert Enright mean when they talk about the empowering nature of forgiveness. "It's like a time machine," Enright told me. "You can go back in time and do something about what happened to you thirty years ago. You can actually heal from the effects of something that happened to you years ago." I remember raising a metaphorical eyebrow (at least I hope it was metaphorical) and thinking *Really?* How could any process I went through now, no matter how empowering and liberating, change the past? And of course it can't. What it changes, for some people in some situations, is the simple present, which therefore changes everything that's yet to come as well.

◇◇◇◇◇

A FEW WEEKS after the forgiveness workshop, I call my father on his cell phone to wish him a happy Father's Day. It's the first time I've talked to either of my parents in more than a year. My father has never been an especially talkative man; in fact, I was once asked by a concerned restaurant hostess whether he was mute. We got a good laugh out of that. So our phone call lasts maybe two minutes, and that's fine. It's a normal conversation for us. It's the best conversation we've had in ages. Afterward I call my sister, who tells me she had a big fight with our mother the day before and isn't speaking to her right now. While we're on the phone I hear the beep that signals an incoming call and see it's from my father's cell phone. Later, when I pick up the voicemail, I hear my mother's voice saying *We're sorry to hear your daughter is still not doing well. She and you are in our prayers.*

My first thought is how typical of my mother to call from my father's phone so I would think it was him and pick up the call. Then I consider how lonely and sad she must feel. We haven't talked since that terrible email exchange, and now she's on the outs with my sister, which means neither of her daughters is in touch at the moment. That's got to hurt, even if she bears most of the responsibility for those silences. I think about how awful I would feel if neither of my daughters was speaking to me. The spark of meanness that flared up when I heard her voice dies away and for just a moment I get a wave of compassion for my mother. It's not a kind or cozy feeling; it has sharp edges. It's raw and dark and deep. If you dropped a stone into it you would never hear it land. For a second I feel something of what I imagine it might be like to be my mother.

Another thought pops into my head: *My mother's in pain. She called me. If I don't call her back I'll cause her more pain.* My heart starts to pound and skip, the way it does whenever I contemplate interacting with my mother. I'm sweating and clammy, a sure sign of a panic attack about to hit. Then, as if in a dream, I hear a voice say *Keep yourself safe.* Not a literal hallucinatory voice-of-God kind of voice—just a sentence fully formed, ringing in my consciousness.

I understand all at once what Fred Luskin was talking about when he asked *Can you stay away with an open heart?* I have the sense that I'm keeping hold of two contradictory thoughts at once, like a pair of perfectly balanced old-fashioned scales. I can feel compassion for my mother but still also protect myself. I can feel something of her pain and also choose to not call her back. I can stay away with an open heart.

I wonder if this is forgiveness. It doesn't feel the way I imagined, which involved tears and a Hollywood soundtrack. I'm completely dry-eyed. In fact I'm still pissed at my mother, but now along with the hot sluice of anger I also feel a trickle of empathy, the reluctant seep of it cooling my rage. It's as if I can see out of my eyes and her eyes at the same time, and this double vision is eerily uncomfortable. I'm so used to thinking of my mother one-dimensionally that this sudden shift to a deeper perspective disorients me, makes me want to shake my head to clear it.

I think back to a dream I had more than ten years earlier, when my youngest daughter was two and I realized I would never have another child. In the dream my mother told me she was pregnant and I was shocked, trying to figure out how old she was and how she could possibly be pregnant. Then the baby was born and was crying and crying. My mother wouldn't nurse it so

I reached for the baby to feed it, but she wouldn't let me nurse it either, or pick it up and comfort it. I felt frantic, wanting to feed and hug the baby, trapped into inaction just because my mother said so. I woke up enraged at my mother's familiar manipulations, but as I lay in bed my rage turned to sadness—for her, for myself, for the baby in the dream who I saw was both my mother and myself, whose hunger and loneliness and despair would never be assuaged.

◇◇◇◇◇

As a child and teenager I fantasized about my mother's death. Or maybe just her disappearance—I didn't wish her dead; I just wanted to spend time with my father and grandparents without her dramatic eruptions and power plays. Now that she's dead I hope to rebuild a relationship with my father, a quiet man with an aversion to conflict who was married for fifty-seven years to a woman who thrived on battle. Somewhere in my forties I confronted him about it, on one of the rare occasions I saw him. In the tiny living room of my great-aunt's apartment, when my mother had drifted away to talk to someone else, I said, "You know we could still be in touch even though Mom forbids it."

He looked at me without saying a word. I went on: "You could drop me a note now and then. I could call on your cell phone. I don't want to talk about her. I just want to talk to you."

My father stared down at the tasteful gray carpet. His arms hung relaxed at his sides. He looked up at me and said, "If I were a different kind of person I could do that. But I'm not that kind of person."

I stared into his dark eyes. In his twenties he could have passed for Franz Kafka's twin. At the time of this conversation he was a handsome man in his sixties. People loved him for his gentle humor, the fact that he made no waves. They didn't really know him, though. I didn't really know him. I'd never been more aware of this in my life. I felt the tears rise and pushed them back down.

"What kind of person are you, Dad?" I said. "Are you the kind of person who throws his daughter away to make his own life easier? Or are you the kind of person who never really loved me at all?"

He shrugged but stayed silent and I walked away. I saw him face-to-face only two or three times over the next eight years; we spoke only once or twice, and only when I called him. Yet I still need to believe that he cares about me. I know he can't show that he loves me and also stay married to my mother. To challenge her authority would be to make his own life hellish, and while he might be a weak man he's not a mean one. In the right circumstances he would stand up for me, I know he would. I'm just not sure what those circumstances would be. I don't let myself wonder what my mother would have to say or do to make him take my side because, of course, I already know. I know but I can't know that he will never stand up for me, never defend me to my mother. He won't challenge her opinions about the weather, never mind anything that actually matters.

Once I know this I can never go back to the fantasy that has sustained me all these years, the one where my father loves me enough to protect me. Once I know this I will be orphaned all over again. Like the parents in Kristina Scharp's study who maintained their uncertainty about the causes of their estrangement when they might easily have let themselves know the truth, I'm not ready to know, to understand, to face a reality that might destroy me. So I don't.

Which is why, about ten days after my mother dies, the email from my father comes as such a shock. He used to write short notes when he sent me checks in college, one or two lines on his office letterhead. I've never gotten an actual email from him. My mother sent all the emails, typing "and Dad" at the end, though I doubt he even read them.

The email makes me sit down hard on the kitchen floor. My father writes that he's going to see a therapist to deal with the grief of losing my mother. He writes that I've "inflicted years of carnage" on my mother, which spilled over onto him, and that he needs "a very long time" to figure out how he feels about me. He's not sure whether he wants a relationship with me or what it might look like; he'll be in touch when he figures it out.

The room tilts and I can't catch my breath. The old feelings wash over me: I'm a monster with a stone instead of a heart, incapable of love. I'm the cold fish, the problem child, the bad seed that has infected the whole family. He writes, *Your mother always had to be right, and you couldn't accept that,* and I flush at this evidence of my own petty priggishness. He writes, *You can't just wave your hand and forget twenty-five years of things that happened.* Is that really what I was doing?

I've been fooling myself. I thought whatever choices my father made he still understood my feelings. On the rare occasions when we met we slid into easy conversation. He seemed interested in my life. The story I told myself is that he loved my mother and wanted to stay married so he went along with her need to be right, to be in charge, with her wrath and her judgment. But underneath that, I believed, he saw that she was harsh toward me, that she wasn't always right. I thought he wished to know me even though he chose not to.

I thought he loved me.

Grief beats in my body. I am helpless and afraid, abandoned and alone in a darkness that will never end. It is an old darkness and a fear that goes back to a time before words, a terror that consumed my childhood and young adulthood. My father's words ignite that fear again, the biggest fear of my life, and it pulses through me with each thump of my heart. This is the thing I did not want to know, this absolute betrayal, this double orphaning. When I was younger it could have destroyed me; now I can endure it. Just.

Maybe I should walk away from my father now, reject him as he's rejecting me, excuse myself from the whole miserable web of connections that passes for my family of origin. Just be done with the whole thing. Except one thing I know by now is that it wouldn't be done. Walking away from my mother was both the best decision I ever made and the hardest. But it didn't get her out of my life. As Elizabeth Vagnoni told me, no matter how hard you try to make your parents go away, they live on in your head.

And I find I don't want to walk away from my father. I'm hurt, and after a few hours I'm angry, too, but at some point I'll be able to talk to him about my feelings. I think. So I let things sit; I let the feelings swell and recede. I don't miss my mother but I'm in mourning for the loss of the possibility of being mothered. At least I think that's what makes me burst into tears in the middle of a bike ride, before sleep, at the dinner table. I don't miss my mother but now things between us can never change, and that thought is both terribly sad and oddly exhilarating. The image of her lying in the ICU, her eyes closed, liquid seeping out of her pores, her lungs mechanically inflating and deflating haunts me, pops into my mind whenever it's idle, appears as I'm falling asleep. I wonder why, and then realize it was one of the very few times—maybe the only time—I can ever remember when my mother wasn't telling me what to do and how to feel. I don't know if that makes it a good memory or a troublingly anomalous one.

Much of the time I feel slow and dopey and forgetful, as if someone has removed a crucial chunk of my brain. One night I dream that an old friend appears for a visit carrying a tall silver pole with many odd attachments, like an enormous Swiss Army knife. I try to get him to leave it behind when we go out but he insists on carrying it with him everywhere. I tell another friend about the dream, and she laughs and says, "Well, that's obvious."

"What?" I say.

"It's about not being able to leave some things behind," she explains patiently. "It's about having to drag them around with you all the time."

"Oh," I say, and this makes immediate sense on many levels. Only now, I think, I *will* leave my mother behind. The more time goes by the further she will recede into the past—a potent past, to be sure, but one that will get smaller and smaller, like the view of where you were from a train window, becoming two-dimensional, dwindling to a speck on the horizon. The story is over now, at least the part that involved the two of us. The thought makes me both terribly sad and grateful.

My older daughter, who's twenty, comes home from visiting her boyfriend and waxes enthusiastic about how much she liked his mother. I'm reminded of my own first visits to my mother-in-law, how she welcomed me into the family. Having birthed two sons she was glad to have a daughter-in-law, and I needed her mothering. My mother was always jealous of my relationship with her, as she was jealous of my relationships with my grandmother and my aunt, recognizing them as qualitatively different from hers with me. My mother saw herself as a good mother, maybe even a brilliant one, and I wonder for the thousandth time whose perspective was more accurate. I wonder how I came to be who I am and how I can make my way out of the darkness that still has hold of me. And isn't that what we all want? Isn't that the question that all literature and music and art seeks to help us answer?

One afternoon a few weeks after my mother's death I go for a walk with my husband. After a warm fall it's finally turned cold, with a dusting of frozen snow. Our boots crunch over mud and barely frozen dirt. I tell him I feel a rather astonishing sense of liberation now that my mother is dead, despite the fact that I've spent more time thinking about her since she died than in the ten years previous. I'm free to explore our relationship in ways I never could before because, I tell him, "She can't hurt me anymore."

"And that tells you something," he says.

"What?"

"That you did what you had to do, all those years," he says. "That you had to protect yourself, and you did it as best you could by being estranged. That yeah, maybe someone else could have let her abuse roll by, let it go, and could have changed the course of the relationship that way. You did what you could. What you had to."

I did what I could. I did what I had to do.

Chapter Nine

OUT OF THE SHADOW

My mother's death ended any chance of our reconciliation. Really that chance had vanished years earlier, in the anger and hurt that crackled between us like heat lightning. Still, death marks the end of possibility, the loss of some hazy ill-defined future, however unlikely. But my mother's death did highlight a tiny door in the wall between my father and me. Like Alice in Wonderland I need to figure out how to find the key and fit myself through that unexpected opening. I feel guilty for even thinking it, but in some ways it's lucky for me that my mother died when she did, that she didn't live on into her nineties as *her* mother did. I feel guilty but it's still true.

In the months after my mother's death, I email my father once a week, checking in on him, and he always emails back immediately, saying he's glad to hear from me. My sister is flying to Florida to visit him, a trip that had been planned before our mother's death, so in my next email I suggest that I come down on another weekend, and get no reply. I call my sister to talk to her before she leaves and ask her what she thinks of my going down to see him. She says, carefully, "I think he has a lot of feelings."

"So do I," I say. I press her until she tells me again that what I did caused both our father and her a lot of harm, and they are both wrestling with it.

"Well it caused me harm too," I say, "and it wasn't what *I* did—it's what *happened*." I change the subject. But the next day I wake up remembering how angry my sister sounded, how quick she was to repeat my father's accusation. I understand that she and my father are in the process of deciding whether they will let me back into the family orbit or keep me circling at a distance, Pluto to their Earth. The gravity of our fractured connection is still exerting its pull, still determining the shape of my life. Although my mother has died, our estrangement is far from over.

I don't expect my father and sister to adopt my point of view, but I'd hoped they would at least empathize. All my life I've stood outside the circle looking in because of who I am, because of the way I see things, because I was unwilling or unable to go along. Because my mother and I brought out the worst in each other. Whatever my sister and father think, this is who I am. This is exactly what my mother has been trying to eradicate for so long, the qualities and perspective and character that make me the person I am in the world.

Maybe I'm better off outside the family orbit after all. As I think these words a lump rises in my throat and my eyes fill. That's not what I want, not after all this time. But maybe that's what's going to happen. As Fred Luskin would say, *Boo-hoo.*

For months things go on as they are. My father and I exchange brief but pleasant emails. My sister visits him and they arrange that they will meet up in Las Vegas later this year to celebrate his eightieth birthday. I'm not invited. Or rather, I'm not specifically disinvited; I'm just not part of the conversation. The day I learn this I cry for a long time. I tell my husband I don't even know anymore what story to tell myself about my relationship with my family.

"The story is simple," he says with an uncharacteristic edge. "Your mother was mean to you and your father abandoned you a long time ago." He's not mad at me but at them. I cry some more because he's right.

That night I slam my hand in the bathroom door. It hurts a little but mostly it's a shock. The fingers splay out stiffly, red and puffed up. It occurs to me that this is a metaphor for how I'm feeling: frozen, paralyzed, numb with an underlayer of pain. And I realize this is a familiar feeling, this jarred paralysis. My body remembers it before my mind does. It's the feeling I got sitting on the bed in my room as my mother raged and sobbed and threw her arms around me. For the first time I understand that my silence and unresponsiveness back then reflected not cold detachment or a stony heart but shock, the psychic equivalent of what's happened to my hand. A shock that lasted through my childhood and well into adulthood. A shock I took for an essential aspect of myself rather than an understandable reaction to trauma.

Somehow that helps. In the months that follow, as my father responds to emails but takes no initiative, as my sister calls him every night and visits often, I go about my business. I teach my classes, I write, I parent my daughters, I lie down with my husband. I try to observe the current of grief that runs underneath everything rather than analyze it. I try to live my life.

On the first Mother's Day after our mother's death I call my sister. I know it will be a hard day for her. She says she has to tell me that our father says this is the easiest Mother's Day he's had in years. I ask why, though I suspect I know the answer.

"Because it was a really bad day for Mom, a really bad day," she says. "And this year he feels relief."

"Are you saying it was a bad day because of me?"

"No matter what I did—send flowers, send three cards, call, it was never good enough," she says.

"Wait a minute," I say. "I sent cards and flowers and called, most of the time, up until the last three years. What are you talking about?"

"I'm just telling you how it is," says my sister. Neither of us wants a fight, so we move on to other subjects.

I'm still gnawing on this conversation a few weeks later when my father calls and asks if I want to fly down so we can "reconnect," as he puts it. Our visit goes better than I expect. He meets me in the airport and tells me right away that he's glad I've come down because things are hitting him differently now, six months after my mother's death. His apartment—their apartment—is full of photographs of my sister and her partner, my grandparents, various aunts and uncles and cousins, but there's only one photo of my daughters and not a single picture of me or my husband. My husband and daughters and I have been thoroughly erased. I tell myself this is understandable; my mother didn't want to be reminded every day of our lost relationship. And my father clearly isn't ready either. I get it, but I'm surprised at how much it hurts.

For the next three days we inch our way around some of the silences between us. He tells me about his routine now, how he plays bridge and goes to a grief group and overall leads a life that's about a thousand times more social than he did when my mother was alive. He explains that for many years he wished the four of us felt more like a family, that my difficult relationship with my mother got in the way. That our problems made his life hard. I tell him I'm glad he's building a life for himself that feels meaningful, and it's true, I am glad. I always wondered what his life might be like without the drama that ruled our house. I tell him the trouble with my mother wasn't all my fault, that her behavior was unacceptable, that it caused me a lot of pain over the years. I say I feel abandoned and betrayed by him, that I still don't understand why he didn't protect me from my mother, why he didn't believe me, why he didn't care enough to keep up some sort of connection. He listens, says nothing. I tell myself it's enough that he's listening, for now, that we'll have plenty of time to explore those feelings.

One night, waking in the Murphy bed in the den, I open my eyes and see my mother's face shining in the darkness, and for a second I lie rigid with terror, sure she's come back to haunt me. Then I realize the computer across from the bed has popped on and I'm looking at a larger-than-life-size screensaver of my mother. It's like her ghost is looking down at me and does not approve. Which she wouldn't, come to think of it; she wouldn't be at all happy at my re-entering the circle of the family. Especially in her absence. I can't get the computer to shut down, no matter what I try, and in the end I unplug the monitor and the screen finally, blessedly goes dark.

I go with my father to the clubhouse one night and watch the group of seventy- and eighty-somethings shoot pool and kibbitz. One of the guys is ninety-nine years old and still shoots well, though he's a bit tottery. I'm pleased by my father's camaraderie with this group of men his age. Afterward, as we walk to the car, he tells me about each of them—widowers who have remarried, men who have never married, wealthy guys and a few just scraping by. We are easy together in the moment, though it remains to be seen how we will connect over time.

I think of Claire, the stay-at-home mom in England who was totally estranged from her mother for four years and who says it was lonelier than she'd imagined it could be. She described the process of reconnecting with her mother the way you might describe defusing a bomb, using words like *tricky* and *delicate* and *complicated.* There was no pivotal conversation, no declaration of forgiveness, just the shifting of some of the foundations of their relationship. Her mother got older and a little less independent; Claire went through therapy. She also moved to a small village in Yorkshire, England, about seven hours away from her mother. *That* helped.

These days they see each other for visits once or twice a year, which Claire manages with carefully constructed boundaries. She stays in an Airbnb rather than her mother's house; she arranges visits for weekends when her partner will be around to help buffer. On one recent visit, when her mother criticized her for continuing to breastfeed her toddler, Claire nearly packed the car and left; only the thought of the long dark seven-hour drive home kept her from leaving. If they lived closer, ironically, they might still be fully estranged. Their connection now is based in part on Claire's understanding and accepting that her mother will never be deeply concerned about her well-being. She feels this kind of attenuated relationship is better than a big dramatic break, but still. "It's a painfully sad state of affairs," she says.

It's different with my father and me, of course. Our estrangement has mostly been more de facto than de jure, secondary to the drama between my mother and me rather than its own conflict. My mother's death has made it possible for us to begin to reconnect, and I'm grateful for that. It's also altered things with others in the family. My aunt and uncle, for instance. We've always had a pretty good relationship, but one night in the car, driving home after a meal with them, I comment to my husband that things feel better between us. *I don't know what changed, but I like it,* I say. He looks at me, one eyebrow raised, across the darkened seat. "Your mother died," he says. Oh yeah. The tension of trying to stay in touch with my mother and with me is gone. They're "allowed" to care now without feeling disloyal. And so am I.

I see my father three more times in the next year, a 300 percent increase in the number of our annual encounters. On one
of those visits I ask him what my mother believed about our estrangement. What story did she tell him, and maybe herself? "She
decided you didn't want a relationship with your parents because
you just wanted to focus on your husband and daughters," he says.
I stare at him; can he actually believe this? He looks down and
adds, "But really she thought you didn't like her and didn't want to
have a relationship with her." Which at that point was true.

My father tells me that in the last few years of my mother's
life, the years when I stopped talking to her altogether, she spent
a lot of time alone. Most people liked her when they met her,
found her charming and high-spirited and funny. But her charm
wore off quickly. When they'd go out to dinner, say, with another
couple, my mother would often get into an argument with the
other husband, insisting she was right about whatever they were
discussing—politics, religion, news—whether she knew anything
about it or not. She would not, or could not, compromise or listen
or diplomatically change the subject. She would argue until the
other husband got annoyed or angry. And that would be the end
of that friendship. In the last few years of her life she spent hours
sitting on the screened lanai attached to their condo, beading
the earrings and necklaces that she sold on Etsy and at small
craft fairs. I feel sad hearing this, picturing my mother stringing
gaudy bits of colored glass and stones onto wires, singing along to
a Debbie Friedman album. I don't know if she felt lonely or sad
or happy enough with her beads and music. I can wonder about
these things now because there's no chance of my walking out
onto that lanai with her or picking up the phone and hearing her
voice. Because I am finally safe, I can let myself feel something
beyond the rage and anxiety that propelled me out of my mother's
house and into the world.

During my last visit my father introduces me to his new "friend," a woman just a few years older than me. *Oh, Dad,* I think, but really, why shouldn't he spend time with whomever he wants to? He and I visit the mausoleum where my mother is—buried? shelved? I don't know the right word. It's cool and dark inside after the heat of the Florida summer. Standing beside my father, I take a few photos of the front of the drawer that houses her remains, engraved with her name and dates. When we walk back outside my eyes water and spill over, and I can't tell if they're reacting to the sudden blazing light or if I'm crying. At the end of my visit, when he drops me off at the airport, I ask how he's feeling about our relationship. He's silent for a moment, then says, "After today I think we're back to normal." Whatever normal is for us.

In the two years since my mother died my father and I have made a start on a different kind of connection, something my mother and I were never able to do. My father and I are intentionally walking a different road, getting to know each other again in the here and now. It doesn't change the past. It doesn't change my *feelings* about the past. We're getting to know each other as adults now without the ongoing complications my mother brought to the relationship. I'm getting used to having a father again. I think we will find ways to keep talking about the past even as we connect in the present.

◇◇◇◇◇

I'M WRONG, AS it turns out, but not for any reason I could have predicted. One night as he's getting ready for bed my father falls to the floor, where he lies, unable to move, all night. The next morning his girlfriend, worried at not being able to reach him, finds him there and calls an ambulance. By the time my sister and I converge on the Fort Lauderdale airport we know that our father has suffered a left-side stroke, which leaves him unable to swallow, speak, or read, though his mind seems otherwise intact. For the rest of that summer we spend long days with him and each other in the hospital, in the rehab facility, and then at his apartment, where we've arranged for around-the-clock caregivers.

This is the most time I've spent with my family of origin since I left my parents' house at sixteen. It seems like a milestone in an otherwise murky landscape, marking a journey to a place I never wanted to go, that none of us want to go. There are hours at my father's bedside with my sister and his girlfriend, more hours scouring big-box stores, assembling the accoutrements he needs now. It's as if he has entered a strange afterlife, one that requires a blender for pureeing food, a thickener for liquids, a walker, commode, raised toilet seat, shower chair, cane. A handicapped tag for the car he will never drive again. We accompany him through grueling hours of occupational therapy, physical therapy, speech therapy. The muscles of his throat and mouth are too weak to form most consonants, so his speech is mainly vowel sounds. He understands language, but reading is difficult. I watch him struggle to make sense of a sentence of four words and feel pity like a bruise rise in my chest, turn my face away so he doesn't see the quick tears.

Along with pity, though, I feel a growing admiration for my father's quiet good humor and perseverance. Jokes become our new language, though I can't tell whether he understands them or just laughs along with us, sharing a moment of pleasure in the difficult world he now inhabits. The nurses and therapists and aides adore him and tell my sister and me often how lucky we are, how frustrated and angry some people with aphasia become. We say we love him too.

And I do love my father, though I don't like what he did or respect his past expediency, his willingness to sacrifice me for his own comfort. Our history and estrangement make this sudden new intimacy confusing as well as complicated. I feel tender toward him as I cook his dinner, tie the bib around his neck, wipe his mouth. In the morning I dress him: Apply deodorant to one armpit, then the other, trying not to press too hard into the withered alcoves of his flesh. Maneuver his right arm, which is still weak and paralyzed, into one sleeve, then the good arm and his head. Pull down his pajama bottoms, averting my eyes from his sex. Slide one leg into his pants, then the other, then slip on his socks and shoes, laced with elastics that need no tying.

He's slowly acquiring more use of his right arm, but he's had to learn to do most things left-handed: lift a spoon to his mouth, laboriously form letters on a white board, type letter by letter in an email program. Writing becomes his lifeline, his way to communicate with us beyond gesture and pantomime, which he's surprisingly good at, miming fairly complex thoughts with a roll of his eyes, a sweep of his good hand. After one of my trips down to see him he sends me an email that I know took long minutes to compose and send. *The picture of my daughter is missing from this house,* he writes. *Please bring one when you come.*

I'm absurdly touched by his oddly elegant phrasing, his formal redrawing of the circle of our family to include me. I ask myself whether I forgive him and I don't even know what that means. Am I still angry and hurt about his past betrayals? Do I wish he'd been a better father? Yes, of course. And not all of those betrayals are old ones. On one visit he shows me the folder containing his will. I assume he wants me to read it, so I do, that night after he's gone to bed. I'm not surprised that he's left me nothing, but two clauses come as a shock. One reads "For personal reasons known to me I leave nothing to my daughter Harriet Brown." I know this is legalese, designed to ward off any potential challenges. I know without having to ask that this was my mother's idea, and that the same clause appeared in her will.

The other clause lays out a list of people with power of attorney, should he become incapacitated. My sister comes first, which I'd expect. The list includes a cousin who's never been close to my parents. My name appears nowhere. I understand all this, but still. This isn't an old will; he and my mother signed new documents a few months before she died. Over the two and a half years between her death and his stroke he had plenty of time to change it. But he didn't.

The next morning I tell him that I read it and I'm upset. He writes a note: *Mom's will.* I say, *Yes, I know this was in her will, but I'm talking about what's in your will now.* He turns up his palms, a look of distress on his face. I want to say never mind, it doesn't matter, but it does. It's not the money; I doubt there will be any money left after he dies. My parents weren't wealthy, and my father retired early. I've literally been written out of the family, I tell him, the family as it is now. That's what hurts. I thought we were reconnecting. I thought we were building something new, that's all. I tell him and then we move on because there's nothing to be gained by upsetting him right now.

But the clause in the will reminds me that estrangement takes on a life of its own. As Natalie said about her brother, *He left us first but then we decided to leave him too.* I left my mother and then my father decided to leave me too. And now we are somewhere on the continuum and I don't know, truly, where we're heading. I imagine Fred Luskin asking *Can you care for your father with an open heart?* Not so much after reading his will. Even less when his girlfriend says to me *Since your father's stroke you've become a much nicer person.* She intends this as a compliment, though she met me only once before the stroke. And I know what she means. My father must have told her that I was selfish and cold and unloving, a longtime problem child. A disappointment. This new reminder that he bought into everything my mother said about me still hurts. Bought into it, believed it, embraced it, and, obviously, told his girlfriend about it. Maybe he thinks I'm nicer now because I'm helping take care of him. Maybe he didn't think I was capable of extending myself. This is love at its most conditional, and I want to say *No thanks, I'm leaving.*

Instead, I find myself getting ready to move my father to an assisted-living facility. A year after his stroke it becomes clear to all of us that living in his apartment with full-time caregivers is both awkward and frustrating for him and a lot for us to manage long distance. He'd have more autonomy and a better life in a good assisted-living facility. He wants to leave Florida and I don't blame him. My sister has already looked at places and found a couple of possibilities within half an hour of her house. It would be a relief for me; she could take charge of his care on a day-to-day basis, and I could fly in for visits once or twice a year.

My father and I haven't lived in the same town since I was sixteen. We've spent more time together in the last year than in the previous thirty. In some ways it makes more sense for him to go to my sister. They know each other far better; they've traveled together, eaten together, played cards and talked together. For months after our mother died she called our father every night, checking in for both their sakes. They've shared both grief over her death and the beginnings of recovery from that grief.

But if my father moves across the country I'll never get to know him any better than I do now. All of our interactions will be mediated on some level through my sister. And while I love her dearly I want the chance she's had, to connect with our father one-on-one. There's something else, too: I'll never get the chance to show my father, my sister, my aunt and uncle that I can be kind and nurturing and responsible. They've known me largely through my mother's eyes for the last few decades. I want them to see there's more to me. I want my father to move close to me.

For weeks my sister and father and I discuss the question of where he will go. My father seems keen to come to my town, in part because my aunt and uncle live there four months a year too, giving him another set of connections. I watch my sister struggle with this paradigm shift, so different from what we've all assumed would happen. She too would love to integrate our father into her daily life, take care of him and on some level be cared for by him. She and I talk gingerly around the issue. Our new relationship is built on mutual respect and affection, and neither of us wants to blow it.

In the end we agree: our father will move to my town. In a month he will come to live in one sunny, newly carpeted, newly painted room with a view of the grassy grounds outside, with a shower and folding seat, two closets, a tiny fridge, and microwave. His life will contract like the pupil in an eye exposed to too much light. I think that shrinking will comfort him; his apartment in Florida, the car he can no longer drive, the friends he can no longer speak to, are all too much. They weigh on his mind. Here in this one room he will be able to see everything in his kingdom. He will not be haunted by his own past. He will feel secure.

And so here I am at Target, poring over a display of end tables as if they might tip some invisible balance between us, prove to my father that I am after all a decent human being, a lovable person, a mensch. What I'm really looking for, here among the pillows and bathmats and picture frames, is nothing less than redemption. My father and sister see me through my mother's eyes and know me through her stories. I want to ditch my role as the bad daughter, the unloving sister. I shouldn't care. But oh, I do.

I never imagined that I'd become my father's primary care-giver, that I'd take him out to eat and to doctors' appointments and clothes shopping and to the movies. That he would sit at my table for Thanksgiving dinner and at Hanukkah and for birthdays, get to know my friends and my daughters. That we would sit to-gether beside a lake, talking about baseball. (That I would even be *aware* of baseball.) That he would hold on to my cart at the grocery store, wait without complaint as I measure out Assam tea and weigh cauliflower. What would he say if he could speak? *Oh look, bananas are on sale.* Or *Who are you voting for this Novem-ber?* Or *I missed you all those years?*

If you'd told me, back when I was sixteen, that my father and I would be companionably shuffling around Wegmans on a Sat-urday night I would have fallen on the floor laughing.

When the silence between us gets too loud I revert to a kind of running monologue and find all kinds of things coming out of my mouth. On the anniversary of my mother's death, I sit with my father as he plugs in an electric *yahrzeit* candle, right next to a larger-than-life-size photo of my mother that my sister made for her memorial service. In the photo my mother's dyed blond hair swoops over one eye. Her chin is propped in her hands, her fingers festooned with huge rings. She's wearing her favorite col-ors—red, white, and blue—and the look on her face, delighted and childlike, is a look I never saw in real life. "I don't think Mom would be very happy about this," I say, meaning my presence not just here in the room but in my father's life. She'd be furious at me for giving my father what *she* wanted all her life. But imme-diately I want to take back the words. What's the point of saying this, especially today?

I know why, of course. I want him to say that *he's* happy I'm here, never mind what my mother would think. I want him to regret the way he thought of me and treated me when my mother was alive. *Boo-hoo, the world isn't fair.* It's unfair to prompt him in this way, to ask him to betray sixty years of marriage to my mother to please me. Anyway, it's not going to happen. Even when my father *could* speak I never heard him express regret about anything.

I think about Jill, the retired schoolteacher who kept up a relationship with her mother because she didn't want to lose her adored father. She prayed for her mother to die first, and bitterly resented the time she lost with her father. I think about Tracy, the Michigan teacher, who spent her adolescence wishing her mother and father would divorce so she could be with her beloved mother. Or, if not divorce, something more permanent. "Remember in *The Godfather* the exploding car?" she told me with a wry laugh. "Key in the ignition and kaboom!"

I had both of those fantasies over the years. This time with my father is a gift, one I longed for but never expected. I fought to keep my mother at a distance but yearned for connection with my father. The men I chose as romantic partners resembled him emotionally if not physically: smart, funny, shut down. Now that I've worked through that longing, now that being close to him has lost its urgency, I've got all the time in the world with my father. How ironic.

One night about two years after my father moved here, as my husband and I drive over to pick him up for dinner, I realize with a jolt that I've forgiven him, without planning or even knowing it had happened. I say this out loud to my husband, and he says, "You've forgiven the present him." That's exactly right. My anger and hurt over the past have been detached from my feelings about him now. I enjoy his company, most of the time. We laugh at the same jokes. I feel tender toward him, admire his resilience in the face of loss.

I find I'm thinking about some of our past interactions in a new light, too. Like the day he stood in the driveway as I left for

New York City, saying *You'll be back.* I heard it then as a threat: *You'll be back because you'll never make it there.* Now I hear it as a talisman, a reassurance to himself: *You'll be back, right? This isn't goodbye forever?* I have no idea which interpretation is right. Maybe both. Maybe neither.

Of course, it helps that I'm an adult now and I don't need his love and approval, though I still want it. Irony upon irony. For a long time I couldn't experience anything but hurt toward my father and rage at my mother. Now that I've learned to feel how pissed I am at my father's betrayals, I can feel love for him as well. This is a lesson I seem to need to keep repeating, that suppressing one feeling means suppressing most of them. That the only way to be wholly alive is to let the rage and hurt and sorrow and excitement have their way with you, tear through your body like labor pangs until eventually you give birth to something else altogether.

Maybe I could never forgive my mother because there was no present her to detach from the past her, nothing besides the hurt and rage. We never got beyond the same hamster wheel of emotional call and response, action and reaction. I'm still struggling to understand what it would mean to forgive her.

I try to conjure specific memories of my mother that weren't hurtful or scary or upsetting and come up with a few. There was the day I came home from seventh grade and wondered out loud what a Tampax was, and she sat me down and matter-of-factly explained menstruation. *Her* mother had never explained it to her, and she wanted me to know the facts. She believed in "straight talk," and, this time at least, I appreciated it.

I remember the rainy summer vacation in Margate, New Jersey, when my mother bought my sister and me an elaborate cardboard castle and we spent hours setting it up in our motel room. We played mini-golf and Skee-Ball, strolled the boardwalk, stopped for frozen custard. These pleasant family memories are less about what my mother did than what she didn't do—throw a fit, make a scene, ruin the day. In later years my mother often insisted that we'd had plenty of good times that I wasn't "counting," as if feelings were a function that could be calculated: bad times divided by good times squared.

The philosopher Jean Hampton wrote that a necessary step toward forgiveness entails "regaining one's confidence in one's own worth despite the immoral action challenging it." So forgiving my mother would mean rejecting her view of me as cold, unloving, and unlovable and deciding for myself that I'm a good person, a worthy person. It would mean that *I* get to tell my own story, not my mother.

So then: It's true that my long and fractured relationship with my mother shaped me in many ways. I'm prone to social insecurity, quick to think others don't like me and to feel left out. I too often take things personally, though I know the world doesn't revolve around me and that other people are absorbed in their own lives, as they should be. I can be prickly and outspoken, though I see that as both an asset and a liability. The tattoo on my left arm, which reads *Your job is to tell the story,* reminds me that it's not just OK for me to speak out—it's imperative.

But other realities have shaped me too. I'm loyal and tenacious (my mother would have said *formidable*), and I care about doing the right thing even if I don't always manage it. I've spent a lot of my career advocating for women and children. Most important, I can love other people—my daughters, my husband, my sister and my friends—and some of them love me too.

Hampton's concept of forgiveness fits better when it comes to my father. I still resent his abandonment and betrayal, mourn his failure to protect me or even just acknowledge the reality of my situation. I see him as a weak person, one who has often taken the path of least resistance. But I also believe he is, as Hampton puts it, a decent person, maybe because I've had a chance to witness that part of him over the last few years.

◇◇◇◇◇

ESTRANGEMENT SAVED MY life. If I hadn't made a space between my mother and me I would have been lost in her bitterness and need, grown needy and bitter myself in the parching vinegar of what passed for love in our house. In the choice between myself and her I chose myself and I'm not sorry. I stepped away from my family out of self-preservation, against the biological and social forces meant to prevent that dissolution, and the price I paid was simply the cost of being born into a family that could not or would not nurture me.

Part of that cost has been a lingering sense of loneliness, an existential angst that no longer surprises me. Our early experiences are written into our cells, a lasting time signature, a pulse that beats in us for the rest of our lives. I always thought the deep sense of emptiness and grief that has plagued me for as long as I can remember reflected my own brokenness and inadequacy. Only recently have I come to understand that it grew from the experience of not being mothered, not being seen or heard or cared for. My husband once told me, in a rare burst of anger, "That's what your mother did to you. I'm sorry she died but what she did was not nice and it was not OK. She made you feel like there was something wrong with you for just being you."

One of the lessons of estrangement for me has been to learn to embrace that emptiness rather than try to cover it up. It is, after all, part of me now. It makes me who I am, for better and for worse.

Being separate has been my greatest fear, the source of my deepest anxieties. It has also been my emancipation. And not just mine. I've heard some version of this from nearly everyone I've talked to. In interview after interview people like Bill and Sarah and Ben and Kerry and Rachel have told me that being estranged from their mother or father or siblings or whole family has changed their lives for the better, has freed them in some essential way, made it possible for them to love other people and be loved.

This doesn't mean estrangement is a benign outcome. Its consequences can ripple through families and generations, calling into question the most primal of connections. The people who struggle most with it are the ones who haven't chosen it themselves, who have had it imposed on them. People like Sandy, whose daughter has walked away; Lee, whose father cut her off when she struggled with substance abuse; Marion, whose brother blames and refuses to see her. People like my mother. Their pain is real, and their narratives can be poignant. Lily, a sixty-five-year-old academic in Florida who has been estranged from all three of her siblings for years, still has reconciliation dreams where they talk and hug and re-enter one another's lives. "The nature of people is to be connected," she tells me, beginning to cry. "The lack of that connection makes me sometimes feel scared and adrift and not anchored in the way I would like to be."

I feel for Lily and Sandy and Lee and Marion. And my mother. But that doesn't change the fact that for some of us estrangement is necessary. Even though it violates cultural taboos. Even if it causes pain. Kristina Scharp, who has been studying family estrangement systematically, says this is the most important thing she wants people to take away from her research. "Stop trying to reconcile these people," she says. "Imagine for a moment that these people have good reasons. Telling them to get back together is not helping them."

Sometimes the hole in the circle of the family isn't an empty space but the start of a new shape.

◇◇◇◇◇

ON A RECENT evening, when the violet spring sky is mottled with clouds, I park the car in front of my father's assisted-living facility. We've been shopping for soap and toothpaste and other necessities, and then we ate an early dinner at one of his favorite restaurants. He unclicks the seat belt and opens the door and I come around to help him out; he walks pretty well on his own but sometimes needs a little balance check or help with a curb. Together we proceed up the front walkway, where I slide my key fob over the electronic pad, pull open the door, and walk my father inside the double doors. His wavy white hair, still thick, shines under the entrance light. He likes to saunter into the facility on his own, swaggering a little as he makes his way past the front desk, waving to the aides and other residents parked in wheelchairs, so we say goodbye here. As usual I put my arms around him, kiss his stubbled cheek, say *Love you, Dad*. Usually he pats my back and walks away, eager to get back to his room. But tonight, for whatever reason, he puts his good arm around me and leans his head into my neck for a moment. *Ai uh oo oo,* he says.

We leave it at that.

ACKNOWLEDGMENTS

Writing is a solitary occupation; publishing a book is not. My deepest thanks go to all who supported me and this work through the process. My agent, Miriam Altshuler, is as always part cheerleader and part insightful critic. She's also my first, best, and most devoted reader, and I would not have been able to write this book without her. Renee Sedliar is without question one of the best editors in the biz, and I am lucky, lucky, lucky to have had the benefit of both her big heart and eagle eye on this most challenging of projects. Joan Fischer, Jennifer Masters, Ellen Murland, and Pamela Reilly read the manuscript at various stages and gave me invaluable feedback. My husband, Jamie Young, is my rock and my joy. He's been listening to me talk, cry, and angst about my family for the last thirty years, and for that (and many other things) he deserves a medal. Since I don't have a medal, my love and gratitude will have to do.

NOTES

Prologue: First and Last

1. Jonathan Gottschall, *The Storytelling Animal: How Stories Make Us Human* (Boston: Houghton Mifflin, 2012).

Chapter One: Thicker Than Water

1. This concept comes in part from a quote taken from J.H. Harvey, A.L. Weber, K.L. Yarkin, and B.E. Stewart, "An attributional approach to relationship breakdown and dissolution," in *Personal Relationships. 4: Dissolving Personal Relationships,* edited by S. Duck (London: Academic Press, 1982), 107–126.

2. K. Agllias, "Family Estrangement: Aberration or Common Occurrence?" blog post, *Psychology Today,* 2015.

3. Marc Szydlik, "Intergenerational Solidarity and Conflict," *Journal of Comparative Family Studies* 39, no. 1 (2008): 97–114.

4. Kee Jeong Kim, "Parent-Adolescent Conflict, Negative Emotion, and Estrangement from the Family of Origin," *Research in Human Development* 3, no. 1 (2006): 45–58.

5. http://disinherited.com/family-estrangement-a-silent-epidemic/; http://www.nextavenue.org/estranged-parents-and-adult-children-silent-epidemic/.

6. Megan Gilligan, et al., "Estrangement Between Mothers and Adult Children: The Role of Norms and Values," *Journal of Marriage and Family* 77, no. 4 (August 2015); Marc Szydlik, "Intergenerational Solidarity and Conflict."

7. M. Silverstein and V.L. Bengston, "Intergenerational solidarity and the structure of adult child–parent relationships in American families," *American Journal of Sociology* 103, no. 2 (1997): 429–460.

8. Lucy Blake and Becca Bland, "Hidden Voices: Family Estrangement in Adulthood," University of Cambridge Centre for Family Research, 2015.

9. Kee Jeong Kim, "Parent-Adolescent Conflict."

10. Kristina Scharp, Lindsey J. Thomas, and Christina G. Paxman, "'It Was the Straw that Broke the Camel's Back': Exploring the Distancing Processes Communicatively Constructed in Parent-Child Estrangement Backstories," *Journal of Family Communication* 15, no. 4 (2015): 330–348.

11. Kylie Agllias, "Family Estrangement," in *Encyclopedia of Social Work,* edited by C. Franklin (Washington, DC: National Association of Social Workers Press and Oxford University Press, 2013).

12. Michael T. McGuire and Michael J. Raleigh, "Animal Analogues of Ostracism: Biological Mechanisms and Social Consequences," *Ethology and Sociobiology* 7, nos. 3–4 (1986): 201–214.

13. Anthony J. Wilgus, "Lone Wolves and Rogue Elephants: Emotional Cutoff Among Animals," in *Emotional Cutoff: Bowen Family Systems Theory Perspectives,* edited by Peter Titelman (New York: Haworth Clinical Practice Press, 2003).

14. K. Lee Raby, et al., "The Enduring Predictive Significance of Early Maternal Sensitivity: Social and Academic Competence Through Age 32 Years," *Child Development* 86, no. 3 (2015): 695–708.

15. National Scientific Council on the Developing Child, *Excessive Stress Disrupts the Architecture of the Developing Brain: Working Paper #3.* Available at: https://developingchild.harvard.edu/resources/reports_and_working_papers/.

16. Jack P. Shonkoff, et al., "The Lifelong Effects of Early Childhood Adversity and Toxic Stress," *Pediatrics* 129, no.1 (2012): e232–246.

17. N. Tottenham, et al., "Prolonged institutional rearing is associated with atypically large amygdala volume and difficulties in emotion regulation," *Developing Science* 13, no. 1 (2010): 46–61.

18. Divya Mehta, et al., "Childhood maltreatment is associated with distinct genomic and epigenetic profiles in posttraumatic stress disorder," *Proceedings of the National Academy of Sciences of the United States of America* 110, no. 20 (May 14, 2013): 8302–8307.

19. For complete survey results see http://standalone.org.uk/wp-content/uploads/2015/12/HiddenVoices.FinalReport.pdf.

Chapter Two: The Roots of Estrangement

1. Kylie Agllias, "Difference, Choice, and Punishment: Parental Beliefs and Understandings About Adult Child Estrangement," *Australian Social Work* 68, no. 1 (2015): 115–129; Kylie Agllias, "Disconnection and Decision-making: Adult Children Explain Their Reasons for Estranging from Parents," *Australian Social Work* 69, no. 1 (2015): 92–104; Kristen Carr, et al., "Giving Voice to the Silence of Family Estrangement: Comparing Reasons of Estranged Parents and Adult Children in a Nonmatched Sample," *Journal of Family Communication* 15, no. 2 (2015): 130–140.

2. Carr, et al., "Giving Voice," 135.

3. Agllias, "Difference," 120.

4. Carr, et al., "Giving Voice," 134.

5. Sheri McGregor, *Done with the Crying: Help and Healing for Mothers of Estranged Adult Children* (San Marcos, CA: Sowing Creek Press, 2016), 75.

6. Joshua Coleman, *When Parents Hurt: Compassionate Strategies When You and Your Grown Child Don't Get Along* (New York: HarperCollins, 2008), 227.

7. Ibid., 232.

8. Researchers didn't match up parent-child pairs, so there was no way to compare answers within families. The comments in these studies are essentially self-reported.

9. Carr, et al., "Giving Voice," 135.

10. Ibid., 136.

11. Kylie Agllias, "Missing Family: The Adult Child's Experience of Parental Estrangement," *Journal of Social Work Practice* 32, no. 1 (2018): 59–72.

12. Carr, et al., "Giving Voice," 130.

13. Agllias, "Difference."

14. Carr, et al., "Giving Voice," 130.

Chapter Three: Mean Mothers (and Fathers)

1. Rebecca Webber, "Meet the Real Narcissists. (They're Not What You Think.)" *Psychology Today,* September 2016.

2. Karen L. Fingerman, Elizabeth L. Hay, and Kira S. Birditt, "The Best of Ties, the Worst of Ties: Close, Problematic, and Ambivalent Social Relationships," *Journal of Marriage and Family* 66 (August 2004): 792–808.

Chapter Four: The Myth of the Worst-Case Scenario

1. U.S. Department of Health & Human Services, Child Maltreatment 2013, (2015), available at http://www.acf.hhs.gov/programs/cb/resource/child -maltreatment-2013.

2. Emmy E. Werner, "Risk, resilience, and recovery: Perspectives from the Kauai Longitudinal Study," *Development and Psychopathology* 5 (1993): 503–515.

3. Sara Santarelli, et al., "An adverse early life environment can enhance stress resilience in adulthood," *Psychoneuroendocrinology* (April 2017): 213–221.

4. R. Kumsta, et al., "5HTT genotype moderates the influence of early institutional deprivation on emotional problems in adolescence: evidence from the English and Romanian Adoptee (ERA) study," *Journal of Child Psychology and Psychiatry* 51 (2010): 755–762.

5. "Adult Survivors Continuing Relationships with Abusive Family," Pandora's Project, 2010, http://www.pandys.org/articles/continuingrelationshipswith abusivefamily.html.

6. Harry F. Harlow, "The Nature of Love," an address given at the 66th Annual Convention of the American Psychological Association, August 31, 1958, Washington, DC.

7. Alice Miller, *The Drama of the Gifted Child: The Search for the True Self* (New York: Basic Books, 2007), 27.

8. Mario Beauregard, Jérôme Courtemanche, Vincent Paquette, and Évelyne Landry-St Pierre, "The Neural Basis of Unconditional Love," *Psychiatry Research: Neuroimaging,* 172, no. 2 (2008): 93–98.

9. This idea evolved from a personal conversation with Ellyn Satter.

10. Alfie Kohn, *Unconditional Parenting: Moving from Rewards and Punishments to Love and Reason* (New York: Atria, 2006), 17.

11. Ibid., 10–11.

12. Miller, *The Drama of the Gifted Child,* 30. The book was originally published in German as *Das Drama des begabten Kindes* in 1979. By "gifted" Miller meant not intellectually or artistically talented but rather children who had adapted to abusive or neglectful childhoods by repressing their feelings, by cutting off their own authentic feelings and opinions and taking on those of their parents.

Chapter Five: The Last Straw

1. Kristina Scharp, Lindsey J. Thomas, and Christina G. Paxman, "'It Was the Straw that Broke the Camel's Back': Exploring the Distancing Processes Communicatively Constructed in Parent-Child Estrangement Backstories," *Journal of Family Communication* 15, no. 4 (2015): 330–348.

2. Ibid.

3. Laura Davis, *I Thought We'd Never Speak Again: The Road from Estrangement to Reconciliation* (New York: HarperCollins, 2002).

4. Stanley Cohen, *States of Denial: Knowing About Atrocities and Suffering* (Hoboken, NJ: Wiley-Blackwell, 2000), 4–5.

Chapter Six: Love: The Unresolvable Dilemma

1. Kristina M. Scharp and Rachel M. McLaren, "Uncertainty Issues and Management in Adult Children's Stories of Their Estrangement With Their Parents," *Journal of Social and Personal Relationships*, 2017. Available at: http://journals.sagepub.com/doi/abs/10.1177/0265407517699097.

2. Megan Gilligan, J. Jill Suitor, Karl Pillemer, "Estrangement Between Mothers and Adult Children: The Role of Norms and Values," *Journal of Marriage and Family*, 77, no. 4 (2015): 908–920.

3. A.J. DeCasper and W.P. Fifer, "Of human bonding: newborns prefer their mothers' voices," *Science* 208, no. 4448 (June 1980): 1174–1176.

4. Roderick E. Adams and Richard H. Passman, "Effects of visual and auditory aspects of mothers and strangers on the play and exploration of children," *Developmental Psychology* 15, no. 3 (May 1979): 269–274.

5. Leslie J. Seltzer, Ashley R. Prososki, Toni E. Ziegler, and Seth D. Pollak, "Instant messages vs. speech: hormones and why we still need to hear each other," *Evolution and Human Behavior* 33, no. 1 (2012): 42–45.

6. Kristina Scharp, "Parent-Child Estrangement: Conditions for Disclosure and Perceived Social Network Member Reactions," *Family Relations* 65, no. 5 (December 2016): 688–700.

7. Scharp, "Parent-Child Estrangement."

8. Lucy Blake and Becca Bland, "Hidden Voices: Family Estrangement in Adulthood," University of Cambridge Centre for Family Research, 2015.

9. From the Shulchan Aruch, as cited at https://www.ou.org/torah/machshava/jewish-ethicist/taking-fifth-commandment.

Chapter Seven: The Half-Life of Grief

1. Pauline Boss, *Ambiguous Loss: Learning to Live with Unresolved Grief* (Cambridge, MA: Harvard University Press, 1999).

2. Kylie Agllias, "Missing Family: The Adult Child's Experience of Parental Estrangement," *Journal of Social Work Practice*, 32, no. 1 (2018): 59–72.

Chapter Eight: On Forgiveness

1. "Oprah on Forgiveness: This Definition Was 'Bigger Than an Aha Moment,'" *Huffington Post*, 3/7/13, available at: https://www.huffingtonpost.com/2013/03/07/oprah-on-forgiveness-how-to-forgive_n_2821736.html.

2. Peg Streep, "Should You Forgive Your Unloving Mother?" *www.psychologytoday.com,* December 16, 2016.

3. Martha C. Nussbaum, *Anger and Forgiveness: Resentment, Generosity, Justice* (New York: Oxford University Press, 2016), 95.

4. Jean Hampton, "Forgiveness, Resentment, and Hatred," in *Forgiveness and Mercy,* edited by Jeffrie G. Murphy and Jean Hampton (Cambridge, UK: Cambridge University Press, 1988), 35–87.

5. Ibid., 83.

6. Alice Miller, *The Body Never Lies: The Lingering Effects of Hurtful Parenting* (New York: W.W. Norton & Co., 2006), 25.

7. Simon Wiesenthal, *The Sunflower* (New York: Schocken Books, 1976), 186–187.

8. Suzanne Freedman and Robert D. Enright, "Forgiveness as an intervention goal with incest survivors," *Journal of Consulting and Clinical Psychology*, 64, no. 5 (1996): 983–992.

9. Nussbaum, *Anger and Forgiveness*, 125.

10. Kylie Agllias, "Disconnection and Decision-Making: Adult Children Explain Their Reasons for Estranging from Parents," *Australian Journal of Social Work,* 69, no. 1 (2015): 92–104.

INDEX